Norfolk Record Society
Volume LXXIII for 2009

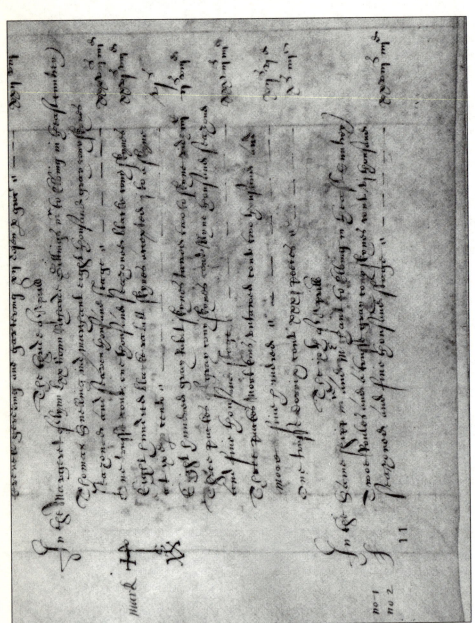

Entry number 343, from TNA PRO E190/433/12, showing merchant's mark of Thomas Snelling 1612

THE KING'S LYNN PORT BOOKS

1610–1614

Edited by

G. ALAN METTERS

Norfolk Record Society
Volume LXXIII for 2009

© The Norfolk Record Society, 2009

First Published in 2009
by the Norfolk Record Society

ISBN 978 0 9556357 2 4

Produced by John Saunders Design & Production
Printed by Athenæum Press Limited, Gateshead

To A. Hassell Smith

Contents

Illustrations, tables and maps

ILLUSTRATIONS

Frontispiece   Entry number 343, from TNA PRO E190/433/12, showing merchant's mark of Thomas Snelling 1612

Following page xvi

TABLES

MAPS

Rules of transcription and editorial conventions

Original spelling has been retained, with the modern usage of i, j, u and v.

Capitalisation has been modernised. Initial 'ff' has been transcribed as 'F' and in the middle of words other than names as 'f'. Initial 'tt' as in 'ttonn[s]' has been transcribed as 't', but the repeated 'n' at the end has been retained.

Punctuation has been added or deleted in order to make the sense of the text clear.

Foreign words have not been translated but have been shown in *italics*, and abbreviated forms expanded as far as possible. Where an ending is unclear or disputable a final apostrophe has been used (e.g. 'ind' has been transcribed as *ind'*, and 'prd' as *predict'*).

Forenames have been expanded and modernised when rendered in the documents in an abbreviated form (e.g. 'Jnᵒ' and 'Jon:' have been transcribed as 'John', 'Robt' as 'Robert', 'Wm' and 'Willm' as 'William'). Where only odd single letters have been missing from recognisable names, these have been supplied in italics and within square brackets (e.g. 'Jarvic[*e*]').

Surnames have mostly been transcribed exactly as they appear in the documents, except where an obvious abbreviation has been used, in which case the contraction has been expanded (e.g. 'Jon:sone' has been transcribed as 'Johnsone', 'Willmson' as 'Williamson').

Place names have normally been transcribed as they appear in the documents, except for certain abbreviated names which have usually been expanded using italics and square brackets (e.g. 'ffl'' has been transcribed as 'Fl[*ushing*]', 'Hambro:' as 'Hambro[*ugh*]'). 'Amster' and 'Amstr'' have been transcribed as 'Amsterdam' and 'Amstredam' when it is clear that they refer to the major Dutch port and not to Anstruther in Scotland. 'Noʳ' has been transcribed as 'Norway', 'Scoᵗ' and 'Scotᵖ' as 'Scotland' when they clearly refer to the countries.

Arabic numerals have been used in all cases and roman numerals translated, with two exceptions: 'C' for hundred has been retained as *C* (*italicised*), since there remains some uncertainty about whether the metric hundred of 100 or the long hundred of 120 (or 112) was intended; similarly 'M' for thousand has been retained as *M*. Ambiguous or contentious cases have been highlighted in notes to the text. In dates the superscript 'th' and 'o' have been omitted.

Suspensions and contractions have normally been expanded and modernised without further comment (e.g. 'mr' and 'mʳ' have been transcribed as 'master', 'Ingl' as 'Inglish', 'Spa:' as 'Spanish', 'cust' as 'custom', 'viz' as '*videlicet*'). 'Scot' and 'Scott' in relation to merchants' nationalities have been left as written in the documents because it is not clear whether 'Scot[t]ch' or 'Scottish' was intended. Standard abbreviations for units of weight and measurement have been routinely expanded (e.g. 'cha:' has been transcribed 'chalder[s]', 'hhd' has been transcribed 'hogshead[s]'), as have the abbreviations for 'containing' and 'valued'. The superior letters denoting amounts of money have been transcribed £ s d and placed on the line; *ob'* has been transcribed ½ d, *qu'* as ¼ d and *ob'qu'* as ¾ d.

Symbols

* *	words which have been inserted
< >	words or letters which have been deleted
f.1r, f.1v	folio numbers in the documents
/*italics*/	marginal entry or annotation
[*italics*]	editorial remarks within the text
[*123*]	port book entry numbers as supplied by the editor
[*illegible*]	word(s) which cannot be read
[?]blue	doubt about the transcription of a word
[twoe], pre[wn]es	words or letters missing through damage to the manuscript which have been supplied
[?members]	as above but there is doubt about the word
[? of all goods]	as above but there is doubt about the whole phrase
[*of*] coppi[*e*] paper	words and letters omitted in the manuscript which have been supplied

Abbreviations

Bacon Papers	*The Papers of Nathaniel Bacon of Stiffkey: vol. 2, 1578–1585*, ed. A. Hassell Smith and G. M. Baker (Norfolk Record Society, vol. XLIX, 1982 & 1983); *vol. 3, 1586-1595*, ed. A. Hassell Smith and G. M. Baker (Norfolk Record Society, vol. LIII, 1987 & 1988); *vol. 4, 1596–1602*, ed. V. Morgan, J. Key and B. Taylor (Norfolk Record Society, vol. LXIV, 2000)
CSPD	*Calendar of State Papers, Domestic*
CUL	Cambridge University Library
f.	*Folio*
Groth, 'Trade and Merchants in the Baltic Ports'	A. Groth, 'Trade and Merchants from Lynn in the Baltic Ports at the End of the 16th Century and in the First Half of the 17th Century', in K. Friedland and P. Richards, eds, *Essays in Hanseatic History: the King's Lynn Symposium 1998* (Larks Press, 2005), pp. 51–63
Hinton, *Boston*	R. W. K. Hinton, ed., *The Port Books of Boston 1601–1640* (Lincoln Record Society, vol. 50, 1956)
Hovell	E. M. W. Hovell, *Complete List of the Inscriptions on the Tablets, Slabs and Monuments in the Chapel of St Nicholas, King's Lynn, Existing in the Year 1937* (King's Lynn, 1937)
Mackerell	B. Mackerell, *History of King's Lynn* (1738)
Metters, 'Rulers'	G. A. Metters, 'The Rulers and Merchants of King's Lynn in the Early Seventeenth Century', University of East Anglia PhD thesis, 2 vols. (1982)
NRO	Norfolk Record Office
PCC	Prerogative Court of Canterbury
PRO	Public Record Office
r.	*Recto*
TNA	The National Archives
v.	*Verso*
Williams, *Maritime Trade*	N. J. Williams, *The Maritime Trade of the East Anglian Ports 1550–1590* (Oxford, 1988)

Acknowledgements

The text of the King's Lynn port books and the facsimile of part of one of the folios are published by permission of the Keeper of the Public Records at The National Archives. The civic portraits of William Atkin and Thomas Snelling are reproduced by permission of the Borough of King's Lynn and West Norfolk, and the Society is also grateful to the Norfolk Heritage Centre, at the Forum, Norwich, for permission to use part of the image of Henry Bell's West Prospect of King's Lynn for the dustjacket. Thanks are due to the Trustees of the Lady Neville Charity of the London Skinners' Company for a grant towards the cost of the colour plates. Phillip Judge has drawn the maps from the editor's originals.

The editor wishes to thank a number of other people and organisations for their assistance and support: the King's Lynn Museum; the National Archives of Scotland for help in identifying some of the Scottish ports; the Norfolk Record Office and especially Susan Maddock, who has answered many queries with her accustomed efficiency and good humour; the library of the Maritime Museum at Belem, Lisbon, for help in trying to resolve the location of 'Sanct Ovis'; my former colleague Tom Carslaw for helpful initial discussions about obscure Scottish ports; Philip Marriage for the photographs of the memorials in St Nicholas Chapel, the reproduction of the Bell engraving and for other photographic help and advice; Mrs Janet Hammond for information about the early history of Thomas Snelling; Christopher Kemp for allowing access to his ongoing 'Selective Glossary' of legal, trade and other unusual terms; David Higgins for information on Henry Bell's engravings and other possible illustrations; Hassell Smith, who first got me working on King's Lynn many years ago and to whom I dedicate the volume with gratitude and affection; Paul Rutledge, the general editor, for his friendly but always perceptive advice; and my wife, Sue, for reading the introduction, providing much constructive comment, and also for putting up with all my distractions and preoccupations while working on port books (both very early in our marriage and again more recently).

G. Alan Metters
Norwich

Plate 1. Civic portrait of William Atkin (King's Lynn Town Hall)

Plate 2. Civic portrait of Thomas Snelling (King's Lynn Town Hall)

Plate 3. Memorial to Thomas Snelling in St Nicholas Chapel, King's Lynn

Plate 4. Memorial to Richard and Matthew Clarke in St Nicholas Chapel,
King's Lynn.
*Matthew Clarke and his second wife to the right, his deceased first wife below, and his
parents opposite, to the left.*

INTRODUCTION

The port books published here document much of the legal overseas trade (but not the coastal trade) of King's Lynn in the second decade of the seventeenth century. Port books are customs records; and strictly speaking they are accounts, compiled for a financial, rather than a commercial, purpose. The E190 series, more formally known as Exchequer King's or Queen's Remembrancer Port Books,[1] was inaugurated in 1565 in a concerted effort to impose a much greater degree of central control over customs administration throughout England and Wales. As a major part of this new initiative, blank parchment books were sent out to all customs officials and these had to be returned to the exchequer duly completed at the end of each accounting year, giving details of all customable items of trade passing through each port, whether they were bound for or coming from 'beyond the seas' or 'by way of merchandise' (overseas trade) or simply passing 'from port to port' (coastal trade). The entire coastline had been divided up into administrative units clustered around principal, or head, ports, where the customs officers were to be based. These crown appointees also had supervision of all the minor harbours, called creeks and members, in the immediate vicinity of each headport, where they might or might not employ deputies. They each compiled their own port books, according to the different responsibilities that they had.

The principal officer in each provincial headport[2] was the **customer** (also sometimes called the collector) who was primarily responsible for recording the duties payable on imported and exported goods and, initially, for collecting the money from the merchants who owned the cargoes, or from their factors or representatives.[3] The **controller** kept a duplicate book, as a check on what the customer was doing, while the **searcher** filled in a slightly different kind of book, abbreviating cargo details and not bothering with duty amounts because his job was to maintain an oversight of the landing and

---

[1] See TNA PRO, *Descriptive List of Exchequer, Queen's Remembrancer Port Books, Part 1, 1565–1700* (1960), with a useful short introduction; D. M. Woodward, 'Short Guides to Records: Port Books', *History*, 55 (June 1970), pp. 207–210; and R. W. K. Hinton, ed., *The Port Books of Boston 1601–1640* (Lincoln Record Society, vol. 50, 1956), pp. xiii–xliii, for a very full discussion of the inauguration of the series, how the books were compiled, and many of their strengths and weaknesses.

[2] The arrangement for the port of London, by far the largest and most important in the kingdom, was more complex, with a far greater number of officials involved – B. Dietz, ed., *The Port and Trade of Elizabethan London* (London Record Society, vol. 8, 1972); N. J. Williams, 'The London Port Books', *Transactions of the London and Middlesex Archaeological Society*, 18, pt. 1 (1955), pp. 13–26.

[3] After the inauguration of the great farm of the customs in 1605 the money was handled by the farmers' deputies – F. C. Dietz, *English Public Finance, vol. 2, 1558–1641* (2nd ed. 1964), p. 338; and see below.

loading of cargo, against the warrants and cockets, or authorisation slips, which were issued in the custom house once duties had been paid or goods had been otherwise cleared for unloading or shipping. By the early-seventeenth century the searcher also usually entered details of both overseas and coastal shipments, so his books made up in other ways for the lack of precision about quantities and duties. Occasionally additional officials crop up, the **surveyor** for example who, by the time the documents in this volume were produced, seemed to fulfil a similar function to the controller, and after 1608 the **collector of the new impositions**, whose job was fairly self-explanatory. This series of records continued, even during periods when the customs were farmed, until it was terminated by a Treasury Order of 14 March 1799 and the books were then left in sacks, in increasing states of decay, subject to the depredations of damp, mould and vermin.

As a result of both this neglect and more wanton destruction, at times when the books were considered to be of no practical use whatsoever, relatively few now survive and those that do can sometimes be in a lamentable condition. A good many of the London port books, particularly those for the late-seventeenth and eighteenth centuries and covering the greater part of England's recorded trade at that time, have gone completely, a major loss to historians. For the port of King's Lynn, and concentrating on only the three major officials (customer, controller and searcher), we can estimate that between the accession of James I in 1603 and the calling of the Long Parliament in 1640, there should be at least 114 overseas port books, but in fact we now only have twenty. For coastal trade in the same period the situation is even worse. The customer and controller kept joint books here (no money was involved, because coastal shipments were duty free, although they still had to be recorded and the coastal certificates either issued, for exports, or verified, in the case of goods coming in), and so the minimum number which we should have is seventy six; and yet only nine have survived. Fortunately for Lynn the extant records are not too badly scattered and it has been possible for this edition to focus attention on a period of four consecutive years for which we have 100 per cent coverage of the recorded overseas trade. *Table 1* shows the full extent of the surviving Lynn port books for the period 1603–1640, with the years covered by this volume highlighted. It is very unusual to find, for a major English port, continuous coverage for any kind of extended period, however short, and it does enable us to reconcile all the information recorded for one brief block of time, rather than having to rely on the kind of enforced random sampling that has characterised many studies of commercial activity.[4]

---

[4] See, for example, W. B. Stephens, *Seventeenth Century Exeter 1625–1688* (Exeter, 1958), pp. 167–179, or D. M. Woodward, *The Trade of Elizabethan Chester* (Hull, 1970), pp. 130–137, both of which are still excellent and most valuable studies.

TABLE 1 *The King's Lynn Port Books 1603-1640 (E190 series)*

| Year | OVERSEAS | | | | | COASTAL | |
	Customer	Controller	Searcher	Surveyor	Collector of New Impositions	Customer and Controller	Searcher
1604	433/6						
1604-5				433/5			
1605-6	433/7						
1607-8	433/8		433/9				433/9
1608-9			433/10		433/11		433/10
1610-11	*433/13*						
1611-12	*433/12*						
1612-13	*434/1*				*434/2*		
1613-14		*434/3*			*434/4*		
1615-16						434/5	
1618-19	434/6						
1619-20	434/8				434/7		
1620-21						434/9	
1621-22	434/10						
1623-24	343/11						
1625					434/12		
1627-28					434/13		
1628-29		434/14					
1630-31					434/16	434/15	
1631-32		435/1	435/2				
1633					603/13		
1633-34						435/3	
1634-35			435/4				435/4
1635					435/5		
1637-38	435/6						
1638-39			435/7				435/7
1639-40			435/8				435/8

The late-Tudor and Jacobean customs system[5]

The evolution of the English and Welsh customs under Queen Elizabeth and her immediate successor is largely a story of increasing unification and centralisation, resulting in the creation of what amounted, in effect, to a genuinely national administrative system, with so much to commend it that the revolutionary governments of the 1640s could take it over almost as a complete package. The process had begun in the reign of Queen Mary (with, among other things, a new and much revised book of rates in 1558) and it continued apace in the early years of Elizabeth with the reforming policies of Lord Treasurer Winchester, in a frantic effort to increase royal revenues. Winchester was responsible for the compilation of a lengthy book of orders, promulgated by the exchequer in November 1564, which laid down an elaborate new procedure for taking goods through the customs. If followed to the letter, this would have generated an enormous amount of extra local documentation, and taken a very long time to complete, but it would appear that practical considerations fairly quickly led to some relaxation, and there is little evidence that much, if any, of the new documentation survived. What have survived, albeit patchily as we have seen, were the port books, called initially 'the queen's original books', which were to be completed from Easter 1565 onwards. They constituted a fairly new kind of record, blank parchment books with a specified number of pages determined by the presumed size and importance of each port, sent out to the customs officers in sealed boxes, with strict instructions that, when completed, they were to be returned to the exchequer at the end of each accounting year. There would then follow an exhaustive process whereby the records were checked against the moneys the customer had received, set against the various claims for expenses and allowances, and only when the exchequer officials were satisfied would the customs officers be discharged and the accounts closed.

The details to be entered into the new port books covered all goods liable for customs duties. Certain items were exempted altogether, the so-called 'free list', so these would not be recorded at all. They included things like ships' stores, goods which owners could claim were for their own personal use (largely various kinds of household items), anything that constituted the crown's trade goods, together with bullion, whether exported under licence or imported (which was always to be preferred). After that there were certain specific duties, on imported wines (tunnage) at various rates according to

[5] This section is largely based on the following sources: N. J. Williams, *The Maritime Trade of the East Anglian Ports 1550–1590* (Oxford, 1988), pp. 10–49; N. S. B. Gras, *The Early English Customs System* (Cambridge, Mass., 1918); F. C. Dietz, *English Public Finance, vol. 2, 1558–1641* (2nd ed., 1964), pp. 305–379; T. S. Willan, ed., *A Tudor Book of Rates* (Manchester, 1962), pp. xi–xlviii; and Hinton, *Boston*, as cited in note 1 above.

type (Rhenish wine, French wine, sweet wines, and so on), the very heavy duties on exported wool, and the increasingly important duties on woollen cloth, which were largely based on the amount of wool that had been used in manufacture and thereby varied according to the different kinds of cloth. Everything else, unless explicitly excluded, carried an *ad valorem* duty, which had initially been based on a rate of one shilling in the pound, or in other words 5 per cent. Aliens had to pay an extra *3d* (or 25 per cent) on top of that. The lists of goods liable for these duties, with their values, were what constituted the 'books of rates', although these perhaps ought more properly to be understood as valuation books (as the rates actually stayed the same), and they were periodically reissued with revisions, as perceived values changed and the crown's financial demands inexorably increased. The new 'book of rates' introduced in 1604 was the first comprehensive reissue since the last year of Mary's reign and the first of Elizabeth's, and it was considerably more detailed. Whereas the 1558 book had comprised twenty six leaves the new edition stretched to thirty seven, and although many items, such as glass, lead and prunes, remained unchanged, most were subject to increases of between 25 per cent and 50 per cent. A few items had their duties doubled, but rather unexpectedly the specific duties on cloth were kept at the 1558 level. Even so, this was not enough to relieve the crown's financial problems and further measures would be needed sooner rather than later.

A significant innovation was introduced when the customs were farmed at various times, or in other words leased out to private contractors who paid an initially agreed rent and then proceeded to recoup their outlay through the collection of duties on the items specified in each lease . This began seriously in the reign of Queen Elizabeth, with various wine farms from 1568, then the lease of some of the London customs to Thomas Smythe between 1572 and 1588, and Sir Francis Walsingham's farm of the customs in fourteen of the outports (including Lynn). Walsingham's farm began in 1585 and was intended to last for six years, but following his death in 1590 the lease was surrendered, and for most of the rest of that decade there was more direct government management of what was still rapidly becoming a considerably more centralised and unified customs system. Farming re-emerged after the death of Lord Burghley in 1598, when Lord Buckhurst and Robert Cecil (later Lord Salisbury) showed a renewed interest in the benefits of having a more knowable income, secured against the possibly volatile funds to be derived from duties on trade. There was, as yet, no general scheme of farming however; it was more a question of individual cases coming up as opportunities presented themselves and being dealt with on an *ad hoc* basis. The end of the reign also saw the first appearance of additional customs duties in the form of impositions, something that was to become a major feature of the succeeding regime.

The first years of King James saw a major review of the situation, particularly in the light of the fact that overall revenues had been falling steadily for ten years or more, while the transition from a parsimonious, if not downright mean, ruler to one whose extravagance knew few, if any, bounds did little to help the general situation. The desperate need for a secure income stream once more saw customs farming emerge as a very desirable option, particularly after the conclusion of peace with Spain in 1604 opened up the possibility of a very profitable increase in commercial activity. This would surely make the London merchants, in particular, much more amenable to invitations from the crown's ministers to enter into new financial agreements on reasonably negotiated terms. Consequently there was a spate of new leases on a variety of goods: wines; coal exports; currants; silks, lawns and cambrics; tobacco; and gold and silver thread. All this was a build-up to the consolidation of all of the remaining customs duties into a single 'great farm'[6] and an essential part of this preparation had been the issuing of the new book of rates in 1604. The merchants likely to bid for the proposed great farm would need firm reassurance about the values on which their anticipated income would be based, just as the crown would need to be clear about the 'medium' on which its own officials would base the calculation of the annual rent. The new lease was finally sealed on 6 February 1605 in favour of a syndicate headed by the London merchants Francis Jones and Nicholas Salter, after Robert Cecil, who had been involved at an earlier stage, had pulled out of the deal, having made a tidy profit of his own in what looks suspiciously like a piece of cynical manipulation.[7] The lease was to run for seven years from Christmas 1604, but it was altered in 1607, with a recalculation of the agreed rent, and then when it expired in 1611 was extended by another three years. However the arrangement clearly worked so well that it was next formally reissued in 1621 and actually continued down to 1641. Its scope covered all of the customs and subsidies of poundage in force from the time of the sealing of the first lease, upon all goods imported and exported, with the following exceptions: tunnage and prisage of wines, together with butlerage and other duties on wine; silk, lawns and cambrics; Venice gold and silver (thread); impositions on seacoals, iron ordnance, tin, pewter or any other goods except cloth; currants, tobacco and (in an odd grouping) various kinds of horses; gold bullion; calfskins exported from Chester, with certain other duties on leather; customs collected at Carlisle; imposts on beer; and all forfeitures. The beer licence was farmed separately between 1607 and 1611, and then included in the great farm.

    [6] See also A. P. Newton, 'The Establishment of the Great Farm of the English Customs', *Transactions of the Royal Historical Society*, 4th series, I (1918), pp. 129–156.

    [7] In 1610 Cecil, as Lord Salisbury, did get his hands on the lease for the customs and subsidies on velvet, satin, taffeta, silks, cambric and lawns, but this was reassigned after his death in 1612 and ultimately surrendered back to the crown – see NRO NRS 12386, a copy of the surrender document enrolled in the chancery in December 1619. I am grateful to Paul Rutledge for drawing my attention to this reference.

These new arrangements had important implications for customs officers and for the records which they kept, and some of the effects can be discerned in the King's Lynn port books that comprise this volume. All customs officers were to complete their books, as before, but their accounting year would now run from Christmas to Christmas and not according to the exchequer year beginning at Michaelmas. They were then to deposit their books with two 'general surveyors', rather than with the exchequer, although the records were still to be made available to the lord treasurer and his staff to assist him in determining the 'medium' for new leases. The annual accounting ritual with the judges of the exchequer also now ceased, and so, more significantly, did the enrolment of the totals collected by each customer in the general accounts of the exchequer (now the series known as TNA PRO E356), which makes the surviving port books all the more valuable to historians. From 1606–7 the farmers were also to deposit in the exchequer 'fair and true books' in parchment of all ships, goods, and duties collected, within six months of the end of each year, but it is not clear whether or how these differed from the official port books, nor what happened to them. It was further laid down that customers were still to issue official warrants for entries and clearances of goods but only when authorised to do so by the farmers' deputies, who were now to make all the arrangements with merchants for the collection of money (see entries *339, 470* and *916* for specific references to this). More alarming still for the regular officers were the new arrangements for their remuneration. They were be paid their usual salaries, but were now to be deprived of the lucrative additional fees that they had hitherto received from the merchants for the issuing of warrants and other documents for the passage of goods through the system; these were now to go to the farmers.[8] There seems to have been something of a commotion over this, and years later a compromise was finally agreed whereby the officers, though still denied their fees, were to receive increased allowances.

From 1608 further additional duties, or 'new impositions', were introduced on a variety of goods, particularly on certain imports, as Lord Treasurer Salisbury resorted to a more systematic way of raising extra revenue, for this was the sole purpose behind the new measures; there was not even a pretence of protecting English trade or manufactures. Impositions had been experimented with earlier in the reign of Elizabeth, with new duties on sweet wines, and later on beer exports and on coal, among other items, but James I's reign saw the biggest extension of this practice, which for a time aroused

---

[8] A rather unusual document in the Norfolk Record Office (NRO NRS 8028), dating from the post-Restoration period and signed by a number of corporation members from that time, enumerates the fees payable to customs officers in the reign of James I (February 1605). It begins with an initial fee payable by all English merchant for their overseas ventures (5s to the customer; 3s 4d to the controller; and 3s 4d to the searcher) and then details a whole range of further fees to cover both other merchants and a variety of other occasions. The loss of such fees would amount to a not inconsiderable sum per year.

furious political opposition. The most notorious incident had been the well-known Bate's case of 1606, when a Levant merchant challenged the new king's right to levy additional impositions on imported currants, even though the practice had actually started in the previous reign.[9] The crown won that particular round, and no doubt encouraged by its success proceeded to impose new additional duties on a whole range of other commodities. The list was so complicated that a special schedule had to be produced to accompany the book of rates. Various items were exempted: victuals, with the exception of salmon and sturgeon; naval stores, munitions and horses; raw materials, such as hides; certain luxury items, including silks; items already being charged, such as French and sweet wines; and staple exports and re-exports. All other dutiable goods were to pay the same amount as for the subsidy of poundage, as can be seen in the documents comprising this edition. There was some revision of the impositions after 1610, when the debates over the so-called 'Great Contract' re-awakened the furore, and a number of items were freed from the new duties, including deals and clapboards, iron, and grain exports. However this still left a significant list of items that remained chargeable: cloth of gold and silver; silks, cambrics and lawns; linen and hemp; spices, almonds, currants, and sugar; skins and hides; millstones; and many foreign manufactured goods. Other taxable items can be identified in the two King's Lynn collectors' books for 1613 and 1614, by which time Lionel Cranfield had extended the scheme with a further levy of 3d in the pound on aliens. Further changes in 1615 and 1618 appear to have been introduced without excessive political opposition and in general, purely as a revenue-increasing measure, the impositions can be considered to have been something of a success. Interestingly, too, the administration of the new duties was placed in the hands of the, by now possibly somewhat under-employed, crown officials in the ports. They were not farmed separately, even though in due course the farmers were apparently able to procure some kind of share of the proceeds; and Francis Jones, a member of the great farm syndicate, did become king's collector for the 'northern' ports, which included King's Lynn. There was little comfort here, perhaps, for the hard-pressed and probably increasingly frustrated outport customs officers who would still have to content themselves with crumbs from the tables of the more privileged, while remaining more directly answerable to the exchequer.

The Lynn port books for 1610–14

What, then, do the Lynn port books actually contain? We must establish at the outset that, just as the surviving documents are in a very variable condition, they are not all the same in format or organisation, as was suggested in

[9] J. P. Kenyon, *The Stuart Constitution* (Cambridge, 1969), pp. 53–57, 62–76.

the opening paragraphs of this introduction. *Table 2* summarises the contents of those that comprise the current volume, and includes on the right hand side the individual entry numbers that have been supplied by the editor to make the use of this edition a little easier.

The 'Port of King's Lynn' included the headport of Lynn itself, along with the principal creeks of Wells and Burnham, and some of the other minor harbours along the coast which are never explicitly named (Dersingham-with-Snettisham and Heacham were the most important), and extended as far as Wisbech.[10] The area of coastline from just beyond Wisbech came under the headport of Boston, while that from Blakeney all the way round to Woodbridge in Suffolk was the responsibility of the officers at Great Yarmouth. From 1611–12 the extant overseas books for King's Lynn contain separate sections for Wells and Burnham, but it is clear from detailed analysis (by looking, for example, at the activities of individual merchants, such as Henry Congham, across a more extended period and using earlier material)[11] that at other times trade through the creeks was simply subsumed under 'Lynn'. However, overseas trade through the creeks never seems to have amounted to much in comparison with the headport, although that, in turn, might simply be a reflection of much more lax administration in the minor harbours. Even later some books included separate sections for Wisbech,[12] which suggests that in the short period covered by this volume there may well be hidden entries relating to Lynn's other major creek, although it is unlikely that there would have been very many, this being perhaps of more significance for the coastal port books which are not part of the current volume. Some others also include additional separate sections, for shipments from Iceland, for instance, or in one case for all entries relating to trade with Scotland.[13] How the information was recorded would depend very much on the preoccupations of, or the pressures put upon, the officials and their clerks.

The first book in this edition (full reference TNA PRO E190/433/13), covering the accounting year Christmas 1610 to Christmas 1611, is in a generally good condition, very clean and legible, although with a few unusual features. The second section, recording shipments inwards, commences at the back of the book, with the document turned upside down so that the foliation can follow in the conventional way. It is odd in another way, too, which may suggest that it is some kind of summary copy of an original now lost (or it might even be a farmers' deputy's book rather than a true exchequer port book). It is the only one in the series of principal officers' books that contains heavily abbreviated entries. Various details, notably the tonnages of ships, the names of shipmasters and (most annoyingly) the identification of

10 Williams, *Maritime Trade*, p.5.
11 Metters, 'Rulers', vol 2, appendices D.1, E.1, F.1, G.1.
12 From E190/435/7, the searcher's book for 1638–9.
13 E190/433/7 for a separate Scottish section, E190/433/10 for imports from Iceland.

TABLE 2 *Arrangement of the contents of the King's Lynn port books 1610-1614*

MS ref. (E190)	Official and year (normally Xmas - Xmas)	Named Port or Creek	Section of manuscript	Time frame for section	Entry nos. (as supplied)
433/13	Customer 1610-1611	Lynn (with Wells & Burnham)	Outwards	Whole year	1-94
		Lynn (with Wells & Burnham)	Inwards	Whole year	95-207
433/12 [sic]	Customer 1611-1612	Lynn	Inwards	Whole year	208-317
		Wells & Burnham	Inwards	Whole year	318-334
		Lynn	Outwards	Whole year	335-382
		Wells & Burnham	Outwards	Whole year	383-385
		Lynn	French & Rhenish wine imports	Mich 1611- Mich 1612	386-397
		Wells & Burnham	French & Rhenish wine imports	Mich 1611- Mich 1612	398-403
		Lynn	Spanish wine imports	Mich 1611- Mich 1612	404-405
		Wells & Burnham	Spanish wine imports	Mich 1611- Mich 1612	406-407
434/1	Customer 1612-1613	Lynn	Inwards	First quarter	408-449
		Lynn	Outwards	First quarter	450-470
		Wells & Burnham	Inwards	First quarter	471-475
		Wells & Burnham	Outwards	First quarter	476-477
		Lynn	Inwards	Second quarter	478-502
		Lynn	Outwards	Second quarter	503-521
		Wells & Burnham	Inwards	Second quarter	522-526
		Wells & Burnham	Outwards	Second quarter	527-530
		Lynn	Inwards	Third quarter	531-562
		Lynn	Outwards	Third quarter	563-591

Ref	Place		Period	
	Wells & Burnham	Inwards	Third quarter	592-598
	Wells & Burnham	Outwards	Third quarter	599-600
	Lynn	Inwards	Fourth quarter	601-634
	Lynn	Outwards	Fourth quarter	635-651
	Wells & Burnham	Inwards	Fourth quarter	652
	Wells & Burnham	Outwards	Fourth quarter	653-655
	Lynn	French & Rhenish wine imports	Mich 1612 – Xmas 1613	656-664
	Wells & Burnham	French & Rhenish wine imports	Mich 1612 – Xmas 1613	665-677
	Lynn	Spanish wine imports	Mich 1612 – Xmas 1613	678-681
	Wells & Burnham	Spanish wine imports	Mich 1612 – Xmas 1613	682-684
434/2	C.N.I.* 1613 (Eas – Mich) (Lynn)	(Inwards)	Half year	685-692
	Burnham [sic]	(Inwards)	Half year	693-695
434/3	Controller 1613-1614 Lynn	Inwards	Whole year	696-889
	Lynn	Outwards	Whole year	890-962
	Lynn with Wells & Burnham	Spanish, French & Rhenish wine imports	Whole year	963-979
	Wells & Burnham	Inwards	Whole year	980-985
	Wells & Burnham	Outwards	Whole year	986
434/4	C.N.I.* 1614 (Eas – Mich) (Lynn)	Inwards	Half year	987-1001
	Wells & Burnham	Inwards	Half year	1002

* Collector of New Impositions

the trade ports for virtually all of the entries are missing, invariably replaced by the use of the term *predict'* even though no previous references had been made. Only the first 'Inward' entry (no. *95*) unaccountably gives the names of both the shipmaster and the trade port, but even here the ship's tonnage is missing. Cargo items, although fully described, have been generally lumped together and given a final consolidated duty amount rather than the individualised treatment that is more common elsewhere. The handwriting also changes significantly about half way through, with the same change of hand apparent in both of the sections, so it looks as though the book was made up at roughly six-monthly intervals.

All of the remaining main books are written in consistent hands throughout, and each one is likely to have been compiled in this generally neat and formal manner at the end of the year – none of them has the appearance of a rough working document compiled in a busy customs house during normal business hours. The second book (reference E190/433/12 – *sic*) for the following year, 1611–12, used to be in very poor condition but has recently been cleaned and repaired, with fresh numbers newly inserted on the *verso* side of each folio. The text of this edition was originally produced from microfilm copies of the dirty and damaged originals, and in the case of the book for 1611–12 the conservation work has both helped and hindered. A few uncertain readings have now been clarified but equally some details have also become rather harder to decipher. It is the first book to have separate sections for the creeks of Wells and Burnham, and also separate sections for wine entries which, being subject to different farms from the rest of the book, observed the more traditional accounting year, extending from Michaelmas to Michaelmas. Fortunately, since we do have the books for the preceding and succeeding years, relevant entries can be reconciled and the integrity of the records verified, or queried in the (relatively few) cases where there is conflicting information.[14] The customer's book for 1612–13 (ref. E190/434/1) is in a poor condition, with the front cover crumpled and wholly illegible and many of the folios either very thin or otherwise hard to read. It is the only one for these years to be arranged quarterly, with further subdivisions for the two creeks of Wells and Burnham and also for the wine imports. In the latter case the accounting year has been extended and runs from Michaelmas 1612 to Christmas 1613, bringing the wine entries thereafter into conformity with the more general sections. The controller's book for 1613–14 (ref. E190/434/3) is in a dreadful state, by far the worst of the whole set, and at some time it was labelled 'unfit for production'. Fortunately it has been possible to microfilm it and the original can also now be consulted. It remains particularly fragile, with holes in it (whether from general decay or the activities of rodents is not altogether clear) and much consequent illegibility. The various sections are annual rather than quarterly, with

---

[14] Cross-references to all such 'related' entries have been provided in the notes to the text.

separate general entries for Wells and Burnham, but the wine entries relate both to the headport of Lynn and also to the creeks.

There are two books compiled by the collectors of the new impositions (E190/434/2 and E190/434/4), the first for the half-year Easter to Michaelmas 1613 and the second for the same half-year in 1614. Both are in reasonable condition and are very short, their entries largely repeating information already recorded in the more 'general' books, although, like the customer's book for 1610–11 they invariably abbreviate the entries, omitting details such as the names of shipmasters and, for the 1613 book, the trade ports as well. There are a few other discrepancies in the information recorded, as identified in the notes to the text of this edition, but for the most part the reconciliation can be judged to be generally good. They are the only books to bear the annotation *Ex'* (for *Examinatur*) to indicate the exchequer acquittance of the officers, who still had to present these documents to the court rather than to the farmers' representatives.[15]

The individual port book entry

'The 26 daye of December 1611
'In the Fortune of Amsterdam 60 tonn, John Johnson master,
from Flushing
'John Wallis *ind'* merchant, with thirtie five lastes Danske rye £4 7s 6d'

The above entry, number *208* in this edition, can be taken as a fairly 'typical' (if short) port book entry, from which it is reasonable to deduce that the following ten pieces of information can usually be retrieved:

1. The date

This was almost certainly the date when the entry was made in the book (or in the officer's original documentation) rather that the date of arrival or departure of the ship.[16] The clerk might enter 'the same day' or *eodem die* (*eadem die* in the controller's book for 1613–14), or in some cases give no date at all, the assumption being that a new entry had the same date as the last mentioned. However, two or more entries might relate to the same ship and give different dates, either because two or more merchants were shipping cargo which was separately recorded (see, for example, entries *511* and *512*), or in the case of 'post entries'. These occurred when a merchant's declared cargo turned out, on examination, to consist of rather more than had been initially specified in the customs house. The resultant additional details were

[15] Cf. Hinton, *Boston*, pp. xix-xx.
[16] In the Boston port books, apparently, the date referred to the date of arrival or sailing – Hinton, *Boston*, p. xx; but cf. TNA PRO, *Descriptive List*, p. vi.

therefore appended, sometimes immediately after the relevant entry (or even at the end of it, as in entry *25*, for example, after the word 'more ...'), and occasionally a different date might be given. The extra details not infrequently appear to constitute a totally new entry some days later (see entries *219* and *222*). When explicitly labelled 'post entry' such details present no serious problem, but they can be confusing, and the dates, together with other details, must be studied carefully to be sure exactly what was intended. In one case (*13*), unaccountably, an additional item of cargo was given a date *before* that of the entry as a whole, although this may have been no more than a clerical error. Another entry (*841*) shows the clerk in two minds about when a post entry was actually made, writing 'the 28 or the 29 September'. There are also occasional discrepancies between the dates given in different parts of books, or in completely separate books, relating to what is essentially the same shipment, where wine details or new impositions have been recorded separately, but these only usually relate to differences of a few days, and they do reinforce the point that the dates given refer to the time when details were recorded rather than to the arrival or departure of ships.

2. The name of the ship

The ship's name was always recorded and, apart from irregular spelling, identifications are generally both consistent and logical, but there was still room for some variation. In entry *174* a ship was named as the *Mayde* but in *178* what appears to be the same ship, with cargo for a different merchant, was identified as the *Hollandes Mayde*. The *Night* and the *Nightingale* were clearly the same vessel (*36* and *37*), and in a similar way the *Unicorn* and the *White Unicorn* of Edam (*291, 313, 410*) were also one and the same. The *Garebonaventur* (*752*) might well be the same ship named elsewhere as the *George Bonaventure* (*914*). *Harry* and *Henry*, perhaps not surprisingly, often refer to the same vessel, particularly when the names of the homeport and the master are compared (see *220, 301, 375, 555, 583, 611,* and *789*) and there could be a similar confusion with *Old Harry* and *Old Henry*. The index to the text provides an initial guide to this kind of problem. It is also clear that a number of ships shared the same name, and they were not always from different home ports, although it would hardly be surprising to find the same name being used in different places. But there do appear, for example, to have been two Lynn ships called *Elizabeth* and two called *Martin*, one of 40 tons, skippered by John Denmark, and another of 80 tons under the command of William Morgan. Similarly there were probably two or even three vessels of Kirkcaldy named the *Margaret* and another two called the *William*.

3. The ship's home port

This information was also invariably given, but there may be some uncertainty about its precise meaning. Although the orders of 1564 laid down that there should be a record of 'of whence' each ship was, as well as 'from whence' or 'whither' it had come or gone, there was no clear elucidation of the criteria to be used in determining a ship's home port, and there were no official registers of shipping.[17] The easiest, and a generally reasonably, assumption might be that the place specified was the home port of the owner. However, a ship could well be in multiple ownership, with the various parties living in different places. Some King's Lynn wills, and references in legal disputes and other papers, often specify shares of anything from one half down to one sixteenth parts, in addition to recorded instances of outright single ownership.[18] In the more complex cases the home port could be either the place of residence of the principal, or majority, shareholder or even perhaps simply the home port of the ship's master. A further complication arises when the home port of a vessel appears to change (see, for example, entries *411* and *452*, which clearly refer to the same ship, the *Bark Allen*, under the master John Darcy, or Dawsey), which might indicate a change in the balance of ownership or equally might be no more than a clerical error. Even so, a single home port is usually given for each entry, with most of the named places being also trade ports; some were inland towns (Bolsward, Delft and Sneek in the Netherlands, for instance), albeit usually connected to the coast by water. Most are fairly comprehensible, although irregular, and probably phonetic, spelling can make identifications difficult. A few have defied firm identification altogether – 'Concra' (probably in Scotland), 'Mellquerne', 'St Marttyns' and 'Warnes' for example. There were, as one would expect, many ships 'of Lynn', and also a fair number from Wells and Burnham, but it is very clear that there was an abundance of vessels from both Scotland, mainly Kirkcaldy and then Anstruther, and also from the Netherlands, in particular Amsterdam and Enkhuizen. This was all a part of that great expansion of the carrying trade that was such a feature of seventeenth-century commercial

[17] A survey of Norfolk shipping compiled for the Lord Admiral in 1580 is to be found in *Bacon Papers*, vol. 2 (1983), pp. 143–149, and gives the names, tonnages and ownership of a number of King's Lynn vessels, along with those of Burnham, Wells and other Norfolk harbours. Some of the ships may still have been in service during the years covered by these port books.

[18] See, for example, the wills of Seth Hawley (PCC 67 Grey 1651, TNA PRO PROB 11/216/117), William Atkin (PCC 59 Swann 1623, TNA PRO PROB 11/141/471), and Matthew Clarke (PCC 42 Swann 1623, TNA PRO PROB 11/141/334); and TNA PRO REQ 2/165/180, and STAC 8/145/18. A local water toll account for 1610–11 records the additional tolls due on the *Charity* of Lynn 'for 1/3 that is not free being Mychellson' 1/3 of Wells' – NRO KL/C44/8. John Lead of Lynn had 1/8 shares in two ships, and the ramifications of this after his death were worked out by his brothers-in-law Valentine and John Pell in association with the shipmasters – see PCC 71 Harvey 1639, TNA PRO PROB 11/180/46, and CUL Pell Papers, P.P.1; the details are discussed in Metters, 'Rulers', vol. 1, pp. 359–362. Cf. V. Barbour, 'Dutch and English Merchant Shipping in the Seventeenth Century' in E. M. Carus-Wilson, ed., *Essays in Economic History*, i, 234; R. Davis, *The Rise of the English Shipping Industry* (1962), ch. 5, esp. pp. 82–88; A. R. Michell, 'The Port and Town of Great Yarmouth and its Economic and Social Relationships with its Neighbours on Both Sides of the Seas: an Essay in the History of the North Sea Economy', Cambridge PhD thesis (1978), pp. 220–223.

life and which was eventually to lead to considerable animosity towards the Netherlands from leading mercantile quarters in England.[19] It is remarkable that less (though still some) antagonism seems to have been directed towards the Scots, even though they were increasingly active in the carrying trade.[20]

4. The ship's tonnage

This is not a particularly reliable piece of information, the figures given being very rough approximations, frequently rounded up or down into tens, and some vessels were also given tonnages which could vary considerably, even allowing for the fact that the same name might (as indicated above) refer to more than one ship. Among the Lynn ships the *Amy* was recorded as being of 60, 70 and 80 tons, the *Joan* of 40 and 50 tons, and the *Pleasure* of 60, 70 and 80 tons. There was similar inconsistency among some foreign ships – the *John* of Kinghorn being variously of 20, 25 and 30 tons' burthen, the *Gift of God* of Kirkcaldy of 25, 30 and 40 tons, and the *Fortune* of Amsterdam of 30, 40, 50, 60 and even on one occasion of 80 tons (possibly more than one ship is involved, however). A few ships were given tantalisingly precise tonnages. The *Jacob* of Kircaldy was invariably recorded as being of 24 tons, the *William* of Kirkcaldy (under Robert Duncan) of 16 tons, while both the *Cock* of Flushing and the *Estrich* of Veere, both very regular visitors to Lynn and/or its creeks, were fairly consistently described as being of 15 tons. Other examples of such possibly believable precision included burthens of 17, 28, 34, 36 and 56 tons, but perhaps we should not try to read too much into this. Among the smallest vessels recorded in these port books were the *Ann* of Boston, at only 5 tons, and the *Margery* of Anstruther, of 10 tons, and the largest was, perhaps not suprisingly, a Dutch vessel, the *Red Lion* of Stavoren, at 180 tons. Other tonnages in excess of 100 were ascribed to a range of vessels from Edam, Enkhuizen, Hindeloopen, Medemblik and Vlieland, with two local ships, the *Golden Fleece* and possibly (there is some doubt) the *Emmanuel* of Lynn, apparently weighing in at exactly 100 tons, while the *Vineyard* of Ipswich, at 120 tons, was the biggest English ship. The average burthen would appear to have been about 40 tons, roughly the same sort of size as many of the heavy lorries that thunder along our present-day roads carrying commercial goods to and from vast container ports capable of handling a wholly different kind of cargo from that of previous eras, and in far greater quantities.

[19] T. Mun, 'England's Treasure by Forraign Trade', especially ch. 19, in J. R. McCulloch, ed., *Early English Tracts on Commerce* (Cambridge, 1852), pp. 191–204; J.R. [*sic*], 'The Trade's Increase', *Harleian Miscellany*, iii (1809), pp. 232–250.

[20] Contemporaries were sufficiently aware of this development to be able to use it as a platform for airing other grievances, such as the need to allow free transportation of corn to prevent the Scots from buying up the redundant English shipping that would follow from excessive restraint – *Bacon Papers*, vol. 4 (2000), p. 215.

5. The name of the shipmaster

In three of the main records (excluding those of the collectors of new impositions) the master of each vessel is always named. The spellings of these names were very variable, as one would expect at this time, and in the case of Scottish and foreign shipmasters the clerks often anglicised them as best they could, unless an individual was already well known (but even here there was often little consistency, even with some King's Lynn shipmasters). The index to thee text provides an initial standardised spelling of all names, both of shipmasters and merchants, with the various alternatives added in parentheses. A number of shipmasters, particularly those from Scotland and the Netherlands, entered cargoes in their own names and it is more than likely that they were acting as factors or agents for other merchants back home. In only one case (*224*) was this actually made explicit, when George Martin, master of the *Thomas* of Dunbar, was described as 'factor for one Mr Atkinson of Donnbarr.' However it does not follow that the absence of such details necessarily indicates that a master was always trading on his own account.[21]

A more significant feature is that such 'merchant-shipmasters' invariably traded either exclusively or overwhelmingly between Lynn and one other port, which was probably their own home port (and usually the home port of each of the ships involved). Among the most regular visitors to Lynn were the Scottish masters David Anderson, David Balfour, James Collier, John Cussen, Andrew Masterton, Henry Reynoldson and William Williamson, all apparently from Kirkcaldy, and the Dutchmen Jacob Bonis (who seemed to ply only between Veere and the creeks of Wells and/or Burnham), Cornelius Clawson (probably of Dordrecht), William Cornelius (of Amsterdam), Anthony Israel (Amsterdam), Simon Johnson (Dordrecht), and Garrard Nabbs (Flushing). As well as being responsible for the safe arrival of their ships in harbour, and for the maintenance of discipline on board throughout the voyage, such men were clearly important figures in the management of the whole business transaction that was involved in shipping a cargo. Whether or not they were trading in their own names they might well be the accounting officers for a complicated set of business arrangements both in King's Lynn itself and in whichever port they plied to or from.[22]

6. Where the ship was bound for or had come from

Trade ports were not recorded in either the customer's book for 1610–1611 or in the book of the collector of new impositions for the part-year 1613, but

---

[21] In the coastal coal trade inward shipments were always entered in the names of shipmasters, but they were invariably acting on behalf of other merchants – Metters, 'Rulers', vol. 1, pp. 209–235, 257–9; TNA PRO STAC 8/145/18 clarifies the ownership of some named coastal colliers.

[22] For a particularly good example of this see CUL Pell Papers, P.P.1.1 and P.P.1.4, relating to the winding up of the estate of John Lead of Lynn – Metters, 'Rulers', vol. 1, pp.360–362. Also Williams, *Maritime Trade*, pp. 203– 207.

they are given in all of the others. Again spellings varied very considerably, but most of the places can be relatively easily identified. The index to the text provides an initial standardised, and mostly modern, version of each name followed by (in parentheses) all the variants that appear in the documents (as both trade ports and ships' home ports). Amsterdam, which features very prominently in these records, was written either in its modern form or as 'Amstredam', sometimes in the abbreviated forms of 'Amster' and 'Amstr'', but it must not be confused with Anstruther in Scotland, which could also appear as 'Amster' and 'Amstr'' as well as 'Amstrother' and 'Anstrother' (see, for example entry *630*). Careful examination of corroborating details such as the names of the ship, the master and the merchant, together with the cargo items help to distinguish the one from the other. Bo'ness (Scotland) was written in a way more closely approximating to its fuller modern version of Borrowstounness. Cadiz in Spain was usually referred to as a variant of 'Cales', not to be confused with Calais. Enkhuizen (Netherlands) was invariably spelt very phonetically but is easily recognisable, while the modern Dutch port of Vlissingen was recorded as Flushing. Veere (Netherlands) was more generally known in the seventeenth century as 'Camphire'. Bergen in Norway was sometimes referred to as North Bergen, presumably to distinguish it from Bergen op-Zoom in the Netherlands. More troublesome have been some of the less obvious references, most of which have been covered in notes to the text. 'Lenkell' was probably the Scottish port of Limekilns, near Inverkeithing (itself referred to as 'Anverkeden'), while slightly more elusive still have been 'Normor' and 'Savor' in Norway, which were probably locations in the vicinity of the Romsdalfjord. A few, such as 'Kirrhen' (with variants) in connection with coal shipments from Scotland, have proved to be unidentifiable with any degree of certainty (it could possibly mean Carron or Carriden), and the same constraint applies to the very vague references to 'Soundwater', somewhere in Norway. 'Sanct Ovis in Portingale' may refer to Setubal but this identification remains speculative.

In only a small number of cases were no particular ports specified at all. A few entries simply recorded 'Norway' and one (*350*) indicated that a ship was going to put in at Boston first and then proceed to 'Scotland', one of the few instances of this kind of double-destination. There was no record at all of ships coming into Lynn via another port, although another isolated entry (*719*) explained that a ship was 'from Berghen in Norway bound for Rochell in France and by tempest of weather forsed one [*sic*] shore with the members of this porte'; it did not specify which minor harbour was involved (presumably neither of the principal creeks of Wells and Burnham, which one would expect to have been explicitly named). Shipments to and from Iceland never mentioned a port or haven, but very frequently the clerks added the detail that goods were for or from 'the Island fishing', even when part of an inward cargo might consist of live hunting birds. There always appeared to be some doubt as to whether the annual Iceland voyage was a fishing or a commercial enterprise; it appears to have been both. Sometimes different books, or sections of books, record different trade ports for what appears to be the same shipment. Thus entry *288* has a cargo of salt coming from Rotterdam while in *397* the wine associated with the same shipment is said to have come from Amsterdam. Exactly the same inconsistency has occurred with entries *445* and *679*, with general cargo from Rotterdam and Spanish wine from Amsterdam, although in this case there is the further complication that yet another separate wine entry has French wine also coming from Rotterdam (*660*). It seems likely that these were clerical errors.

7. The merchant's name

This was arguably one of the more important pieces of information to be recorded in the port books, along with the actual amounts of duty charged on cargo items, as somebody had to be made specifically responsible for the payment of the duties, and the officers, or the farmers' deputies, had to make sure that the money was collected. The orders of 1564 had laid down that goods were to be recorded in the name of the 'very owner' who was to subscribe the entry in the port book with his own name after the completion of the whole customs procedure.[23] However it is clear that by the seventeenth century the 1564 orders were not being followed to the letter, as no signatures appear in any of the documents and only one merchant's mark has been recorded (that of Thomas Snelling, subsequently 'of Lynn', in entry numbers *343* and *344*). We have also already seen that although on only one occasion was a Scottish shipmaster explicitly named as the factor for another merchant a good many Scottish and Dutch shipmasters, as well as some others, were readily entering cargoes in their own names even though they may not necessarily have been 'very owners'. Another way in which the prescriptions of the Elizabethan orders were allowed to lapse was that the home towns of merchants, or at least those pertaining to individuals not living in the headport itself, were no longer being recorded, which is another great loss to historians. Even as late as the 1590s many of the Lynn port books did include this valuable extra detail, which can be used as starting point for tracking down some of the inland connections with the port of Lynn.[24]

Nevertheless the name of a merchant is always given for every entry in the port books, and for the overwhelming majority of entries there is only one name. On two occasions (entries *65* and *140*) the clerks added 'and company' to the named merchants but without going into any more detail. In one entry (*49*) two merchants were explicitly named as partners, but there were clear hints elsewhere of other forms of apparent partnership or co-operation. In entry *203* a cargo was entered in the single name of William Atkin of Lynn,

---

[23] Hinton, *Boston*, pp. xv, xxiii–xxiv.
[24] See, for example, E190/431/2, 5, 7 and 432/1, 5, 13

but the associated wine entry (*387*) named both Atkin and his brother-in-law Gervase Wharton as the joint owners, at least of the wine. In entries *775* and *777* Thomas Slaney and Thomas Brewster had separately recorded cargoes but the post entry at *780* named the two merchants as joint owners of the additional cargo. Where wine details and new impositions were recorded in different sections of a book, or even in another book altogether, a number of other entries appear to suggest joint or confused ownership of cargoes which can still be understood, in each case, as single consolidated shipments – see, for example, the related entries *471, 667* and *682*; or *823* and *972*; or *859, 974* and *976*; or *774, 971* and *991*. There are other instances of this same feature, in some cases involving the shipmaster in addition to another named merchant, in others specifying two different 'genuine' merchants. Far more entries suggest yet another form of co-operation where two or more merchants had separately identified cargoes being carried in one ship. There are far too many to enumerate in detail, but the different ways in which this was recorded can be seen in entries *59, 119, 152* (involving no less than five named merchants); *290, 292* and *293* (where apparent new entries all relate to the same ship); *429, 431* and *432*; or *594, 595* and *596*. Two final entries are also suggestive in another way. On 3 October 1614 (entry *852*) John Sendall paid duty on some imported salt, 'whereof there is allowed unto the merchants that brought in this salte at their adventure fiftene wayes to be imployed at their adventure in this saide shipp for the Island fieshinge the next yeare *anno* 1614.' (The post entry of 22 October, in *862*, again named only Sendall). A little earlier, on 24 September, John Percival had exported a cargo of wax to Cadiz, and a post entry here (*947*) added: 'More entred the 28 of September of the goods of the saide merchantes in the caske afore saide, one hunderd waight of English waxe.' It is clear from these references that, although only one merchant had been named, others (unnamed) were somehow also involved in each transaction. The implications of this phenomenon will be discussed below in the section on **the merchants and their businesses**.

8. *The merchant's nationality*

The recording of each merchant's nationality was highly significant because aliens had to pay an additional levy of 25 per cent. Even so this detail is still sometimes, suprisingly, missing. After the accession of James I in England his fellow Scots ceased to be quite as alien as they had previously been and they were relieved of the liability for the extra duty. They tended to be recorded, in these port books, as 'Scots' (with variants),[25] to maintain the distinction from true native-born merchants who were described as English or 'indigenous' (the latter usually written in an abbreviated version of the latinised form of *indigenus*, although the rather clumsily anglicised 'inds' also

[25] In the Boston port books Scots might appear as 'British' – Hinton, *Boston*, p. xxii.

sometimes appears). Genuine foreigners were entered as 'strangers' or, more usually, as 'alien' (or simply as 'al'), which may have been intended to be in the latinised formulation *alienigenus* but which has been transcribed in the text in its anglicised form since one cannot be absolutely certain. An English merchant who was living abroad was also considered to be an alien for customs purposes, which is probably why Thomas Cremer was described as an alien in entry number *3*. Alternatively that could have been no more than a clerical error, of which there do appear to have been quite a number. Thus David Balfour was described twenty three times as Scottish but four times as English, John Cussen thirteen times as Scottish and once as English, Andrew Masterton sixteen times Scottish, once as English and once as *ind'*, while Garrard Nabbs appeared seventeen times as alien, once as a stranger and once as English. A whole host of other individuals who were consistently recorded (when the nationality was actually given) as either alien or Scottish put in the occasional appearance as English, but none of this implied that they had somehow become, however temporarily, indigenous. Even if they took up residence in Lynn (or elsewhere in England) they still retained their original nationality, including the liability for the alien, or strangers', custom of 25 per cent extra. A good example here was Erasmus Coates, the Dutchman who did become permanently resident in Lynn and acquired property there.[26]

9. The cargo details

Cargoes are usually described in some detail, in accordance with the very full itemisation of goods to be found in the books of rates, with their various values for the calculation of duty amounts. Thus we find strong beer being differentiated from ordinary beer, full details of the various kinds of cloth imported and exported, precise identification of skins and hides, both in terms of their animal origins and their condition (whether raw and unseasoned or fully or partly treated), and similarly precise details of fish, spices and even of the live hawks that regularly came in from Iceland (falcons, gerfalcons, merlins and tiercels). Even so the clerks could become either bored or lazy, and so we also find cargo items sometimes written down as 'sundry small wares' (*182*), 'and other commodities' (*185* and *186*), 'and other wares' (*189* and *190*), 'and other trifles' (*274*). One entry in the book of the collector of new impositions in 1613 (*691*) began to itemise with some care the spices which were also recorded elsewhere (*554*) but then collated the rest of the cargo as 'other petty grocery.' In general, though, the documents do give a very full indication of the kinds of goods passing through the port of Lynn.

Much more troublesome can be the numbers and quantities used in association with items of cargo. Particular difficulty arises with hundreds, and as a consequence (but much less frequently) with thousands. The word

[26] PCC 81 Hele 1626, TNA PRO PROB 11/149/196.

'hundred' is extensively deployed in these documents and so is the roman numeral 'C', but neither of these necessarily means the modern metric 100. In *avoirdupois* measurement of weight 'hundred' is more likely to mean the hundredweight of 112 pounds, while the same word could also mean the 'long hundred' of 120, depending on what precisely was being measured or counted. Only when the additional gloss of 'at five score *per cent*' appears (as in *218*, and *225*, for instance), or the simpler formulation 'five score' with another unit of measurement (*313, 942*), can one be absolutely certain that the metric hundred was intended. Sometimes further clarification is also given with the words 'at six score *per cent*' (*281, 428, 504*), but more generally it would seem that the long hundred was extensively understood to be the more usual meaning of 'hundred' and of 'C'. Accordingly for this edition the word 'hundred' has been retained as written in the original books and, whereas in dates and for lesser numbers roman numerals have been routinely translated into arabic notation, the 'C' and 'M' (for thousand) have been retained and transcribed as *C* and *M*, even when associated with another number (e.g. 2 *C* for 'ij C' or 4 *M* 6 *C* for 'iv M vj C'). Only where a more recognisably modern formulation of the roman numerals can be reasonably assumed to mean something that we today would recognise, as for some ships' tonnages and a few isolated cargo items, has a full translation into arabic notation been implemented (see, for example, entry numbers *189* and *770*). More generally, now obsolete units of measurement (lasts, coombs, weys, ells, chalders), along with the vaguer and more imprecise measures associated with containers (barrels, bags, firkins, puncheons), have also been transcribed as written and they are explained in *Appendix 1: Glossary*. Some entries give tantalising clues as to alternatives for some of these measurements, numbers *488* and *554* being particularly good examples.

10. The duties paid

The record of the amount of duty paid on each cargo imported or exported was arguably the most important piece of information of all. It had been needed initially for the customs officials to be able to clear their obligations when they presented their accounts to the exchequer each year, but even after the introduction of customs farming, and in particular the inauguration of the great farm in 1605, after which the farmers and their deputies appear to have kept their own books (see marginal comment to entry *470*), the exchequer still wanted its own returns, not least so that a check could be kept on whether the farmers' contracts were generating profits in excess of what had been expected. This would then determine the terms on which any new contract would be negotiated. Furthermore, the levies being collected remained royal taxes, whether or not (as in the case of new impositions) they had been voted by parliament, and even though the money was now going into private hands. The principal charges were the subsidies of tunnage (on wine imports) and poundage (on dry goods), and *ad valorem* duties which could change according to the values recorded in the variously reissued books of rates. In addition to this, as we have already seen, aliens had to pay a surcharge of 25 per cent, although the first document in this edition makes no mention of this at all as a separate levy. Indeed that particular port book simply provides one single sum for the entire duty levied on each cargo and does not break it down, as other books do, item by item. Finally there were the impositions, which were increasingly levied, amid much political uproar, after 1608. These are recorded in the main customer's and controller's books in additional columns down the right hand side of each page, alongside the more 'regular' levies. However, in order not to waste space on the printed page, in this edition such sums have been placed underneath the 'regular' duty amount for each relevant item after a + sign. Most of these amounts do tally with the separate record to be found in the books of the collectors of the new impositions, where these exist, although there are a few discrepancies, which have been pointed out in the notes to the text. Perhaps the most intriguing concerned the duties on forty imported wainscots which were charged by the controller (*807*) to the shipmaster, 'being an alien', at the rate of 3*s* 4*d*, while the separate recording of the imposition (*995*) charged it to the very English Thomas Snelling at 2*s* 8*d*. The controller also recorded the impost on exported beer in a rather different way, putting the extra amount immediately underneath the sum for the subsidy, rather than in separate columns – hence in the text (from entry *891* onwards) this second sum is printed without the + sign.

In addition to the basic details described above, two other kinds of supplementary information can also sometimes be found in port book entries:

11. Allowances

Some items were occasionally allowed to pass through the port duty-free, or at a reduced rate. One of the commonest reasons sometimes given in other port books was an allowance to the master and the ship's company for their own provision, usually called portage and store, but very few of these are to be found in the Lynn books for 1610–14. Only one entry (*470*) mentions store, in connection with a special warrant from the farmers, but the cargo items (including 340 pairs of short worsted stockings) seem rather strange if they were for the ship's company; and there have been no specific references to portage at all. Another entry (*339*) was endorsed as wholly 'freed by warrant from the farmores', and the cargo looks very much like a mixture of provisions for the Iceland fishing venture and some trade goods. Similarly a cargo of various kinds of cloth was also freed by special warrant from the farmers for the Iceland voyage (*916*), while the shipmaster-merchant Dennis Olley paid duty on 'tenn tonnes of stronge beare besides drinking beare for his fieshing vioage' (*912*). Much imported salt was allowed into the port at no charge when it was to be used for Iceland fishing. On one occasion *(288)* John Wallis, a very big man in Lynn's business and political life, seems to have had a heated altercation with the officials about this, as the port book records that 'this marchant refuseth to pay custome affirming yt to be wholy for his provision for the Island fishing next to come' and he seems to have got away with it. For another salt shipment *(489)* Wallis paid duty on part of the cargo, the remainder being freed, this time without demur. Such allowances may have been more generally a bone of contention with the customs men, as on Lady Day 1613 Henry Congham, a regular trader through Wells/Burnham, felt the need to back up his claim with a further warrant, 'by order from the greene cloth' *(522)*, which would appear to be a reference to the lord steward's department of the royal household.[27] The officials dutifully recorded the export of the same salt when the fishing expedition set off *(528* and *529)*.

An allowance could also be given when something had gone wrong. On Christmas Eve 1612 Erasmus Coates had the import duty on his fish reduced because part of the cargo had been 'currupted in the home comeing as by report of an officer' *(317)*, while on 6 October 1613 Nathaniel Maxey, who was himself a customs official, paid no duty on 'two hundred waight loaffe sugar which perished in the haven in the landing thereof' *(604)*. Occasionally an allowance might be given for no stated reason, as when an alien shipmaster-merchant *(861)* had one last of a cargo of 15 lasts of Dansk rye freed of custom; perhaps it, too, had suffered damage during the voyage to Lynn. More logically some goods were allowed out duty-free because customs had already been paid on them and they were being re-exported unsold or otherwise re-shipped – this can be seen in entries *346, 382, 588* (duty already paid in London), *642* and *645* (both referring back to details already contained in entry *638)*, *943*, and *951*. In all these cases the customs officers showed themselves to have been particularly assiduous in keeping an accurate record of precisely what had happened. They were equally careful to record the significant number of times key individuals managed to procure special licences or warrants to export goods at preferential rates, or even entirely duty-free. Thus we find that Sir George Bruce of Culross, in Scotland, an entrepreneur with powerful connections, was able to get a special licence for the export of peas and beans (entries *517–521, 563–566,* and *572–575* inclusive), while John Greene *(568, 571* and *576)*, the con-

---

[27] The lord steward was the principal officer of the royal household below stairs and thereby the senior member of the 'Board of Green Cloth.' After 1570, with one brief exception, the office was left vacant for forty-five years with the result that the direction of the household below stairs passed to the next senior members of the board of green cloth, the treasurer and comptroller - see *Office-Holders in Modern Britain* ('Provisional Lists 1485–1646' compiled by J.C. Sainty, June 1999), at the IHR website, URL: http://www.history.ac.uk/office/greencloth_clerk.html#5t, accessed on 28 November 2008. It is not clear why this merchant should have invoked such support, unless he was under contract to supply salt fish to the royal kitchen.

troller of the port, procured a similar privilege, and his fellow Lynn merchants Thomas March (*700*), Thomas Snelling (*621*) and Gervase Wharton (*622–623*, and *709*) all imported rye duty-free. Finally, many wine entries recorded allowances, both for the merchants named and also for shipmasters (possibly as a variant of portage) but without going into any further detail, and no sums of money were mentioned as the duties had been previously compounded for. A few also mentioned both prisage (*387, 389, 390* and *395*, and see Glossary) and other occasions when wine was freed for the royal butler (*964, 969* and *979*), although neither of these were really allowances to merchants in the more conventional way, more of a burden to them in fact.

12. Further 'unwitting testimony'

There have been clear hints in the outline given above of many of the additional nuggets of information that port book entries can sometimes yield, going well beyond the rather dry and tedious enumeration of ships, trade goods and the duties collected on cargoes. We have already seen that the business organisation underpinning the shipment of a cargo might well be more complicated than the simple recording of a merchant's name, quite apart from the role of shipmasters as possibly independent (and certainly very significant) commercial operators. The cargo details, invariably full and highly descriptive, and the allowances that were occasionally given can suggest both 'wheeling and dealing' by merchants and the concern of the officers to ensure that all relevant details (including internal cross-references) were put down in their books, even if this was because they had the farmers' deputies, like modern inspectors of various kinds, breathing down their necks. A few entries also provide information about otherwise unrecorded ship movements, particularly those relating to the Iceland fishing venture. Entries *981* and *982* go further than most, not only acknowledging the allowances on imported salt but also naming other ships scheduled for departure into northern waters: 'theirty wayes of Spannish salte allowed unto this marchant for the furnishinge of his shipps this yeare for Island, *videlicet* twenty *two* wayes for the Meane of Wells, whereof Robert Leeche master, for Island fieshinge, and more eight wayes for the John *de* Wells, Eliza King master, for Island *predicte*'; and 'theirty wayes of Spannish salte alowed unto this merchant for the furnishinge of his shipps for Island, *videlicet* into the Sara of Wells, Steven Leake master, for Island fieshing, aleaven wayes and more nyne wayes into the God Grace of Wells, Nicholas Dey master, for Island, and more into the Robert *de* Wells tenn wayes, whereof one John Tompsone master, for the Island fieshinge'. There were no other references to the departure, or the return, of these vessels, for the Iceland trade was always very erratically recorded in the port books, but involvement in this important part of Lynn's commercial life can be detected from such apparently casual and throwaway references. They also perhaps confirm that, within the limits of their competence and their jurisdiction, the customs officers and their clerks did take care in the compilation of their records, in spite of other evidence to the contrary (see below).

Conclusion: port book entries and 'shipments'

There could be significant variations from the standard pattern of the port book entry, as exemplified in entry *208* at the beginning of this section, some of which have already been touched upon. In particular, more than one merchant might be named in connection with a single cargo, or two or more merchants might have separately identified cargoes in the same ship. Similarly, one merchant's cargo might be recorded in more than one place, as suggested by the issue of the separate wine sections, and also in the case of 'post entries'. To try to maintain some kind of consistency in the analysis of port book data, therefore, entries usually need to be rationalised into 'shipments', a term that has already been used a number of times and which can now be more clearly and precisely defined as follows: 'A shipment of cargo, which may consist of more than one item, made in one ship by one merchant, or by a group of merchants clearly working in some kind of partnership, to or from one port.' This sometimes involves pulling together details of cargoes from different parts of a book, or even from another book altogether in the case of wine, and separating out cargoes belonging to different merchants but carried in the same ship, which was a not infrequent practice. The shipment might therefore be seen as a 'transaction' by one merchant or company, and it does correspond to the usual or normal port book entry for well over ninety five per cent of the cases. Nevertheless the distinction is important if we are to make any kind of sense out of what the port books contain and the way in which the information is presented.

Customs evasion and smuggling – are the port books essentially valueless?

Before considering what the port books might tell us about the nature and extent of the overseas trade of King's Lynn, we must go back to one of the motives for introducing a new set of customs records in the first place, the prevention of fraud, to clear up one of the principal objections to the use of port book data for any kind of serious historical purpose.[28] Over half a

---

[28] The first major note of caution had been sounded by G. N. Clarke, *Guide to English Commercial Statistics 1696–1782* (1938), pp. 52–55, although by then port books had already been used in a number of important pioneering studies: A. Friis, *Alderman Cockayne's Project and the Cloth Trade* (Copenhagen and London, 1927), N. S. B. Gras, *The Evolution of the English Corn Market from the Twelfth to the Eighteenth Century* (Cambridge, Mass., 1918), J. U. Nef, *The Rise of the British Coal Industry*, 2 vols. (1932), T.S. Willan, *The English Coasting Trade 1600–1750* (1938).

century ago, Neville Williams began a short contribution to *The English Historical Review* with these words: 'From the first introduction of duties until the establishment of a loyal and efficient customs service, if a merchant's primary concern was the safe arrival of his cargo at its point of discharge, his second was the evasion of the customs.' His note dealt with the illicit trading activities of one of the leading burgesses of late sixteenth century King's Lynn, Francis Shaxton.[29] Shaxton was no cheap or petty criminal; he was an alderman and mayor of the borough, but he was also described by Williams as 'the most notorious smuggler in eastern England'. For years, and in league with a number of others (a former clerk of the customs house, one or more of the customs officers, and a good many other notable Lynn merchants), Shaxton had apparently exported vast quantities of corn and other goods illegally. Use had been made of many of the established fraudulent devices, such as bribes to the officers, the entering of false destinations (usually a coastal rather than an overseas port, thereby avoiding the payment of duties), and persistent under-registration of cargoes. But in addition a new element had emerged in the form of counterfeit cockets (the parchment receipts for the payment of duties on export items) which were here written by the former customs clerk and sealed with a copy of the cocket seal – the official seal had somehow been 'borrowed' from the customs house so that a duplicate could be made. Between 1567 and 1573 Shaxton (who became mayor of Lynn in 1569) had received over 120 forged 'blanks' which could then be filled in and used at will; hence he could trade extensively without his name appearing in the customs records in a way that bore any relation to what he was actually doing.

We know all this, and more, because, perhaps inevitably, Shaxton and his accomplices were found out and hauled before the exchequer court – there had been an informer, someone who had probably wanted to be in on the corruption but found himself on the outside and did not like it. The detailed record that was then made of all the confessions and excuses, amounting to ninety pages of depositions[30] and dragging in many of the leading burgesses of the town, provided much of the evidence on which Neville Williams based his article and from which he drew this rather gloomy conclusion: 'Research into the trade of the East Anglian ports in the later sixteenth century has led the present writer to question the worth of his transcripts from the Port Books.' Even so he still went on to produce a brilliant thesis, which earned him his Oxford DPhil in 1952 (never published during his own lifetime – it did not appear as a monograph until 1988), and he also compiled the authoritative PRO listings of all of the port books and associated material. But in a

[29] N. J. Williams, 'Francis Shaxton and the Elizabethan Port Books', *EHR*, LXVI (1951), pp. 387–395, reprised in Williams, *Maritime Trade*, pp. 25–33. See also G. D. Ramsay, 'The Smugglers' Trade: A Neglected Aspect of English Commercial History', *Transactions of the Royal Historical Society*, 5th series, 2 (1952), pp. 131–157.

[30] TNA PRO E178/7273.

more general history of smuggling he reiterated his condemnation of early modern West Norfolk: 'Of all the outports, King's Lynn was at this time the worst.'[31]

Were things any better in the succeeding century? T. S. Willan once observed that the Elizabethans had been 'incorrigible liars'[32] and we cannot be certain that the Jacobeans were any more honest. A case before the exchequer court in 1604–5, though not as damning as Shaxton's, nevertheless reveals that some Lynn merchants were still up to their old tricks.[33] Thomas Garrard (of Lynn) had apparently been involved in some rather murky dealings of his own and when ordered to produce his account books for examination he deposed that: 'He neyther did nor dothe keepe anye such bookes, but saythe that he used to keepe shorte notes in loose papers touchenge those matters, which notes after His Majesties duties [were] satisfied he never regarded but did lose and teare them. And [he] further saythe that he keepes no bookes for such corne as he ladeth beyonde the seaes.' Was he telling the truth? It is worth noting that Thomas White, a Bristol merchant of roughly the same era, recorded in his will that: 'I have a greate booke, a little booke and a blottinge wherein is to be seene what I owe and what is owinge to me. I have alsoe a booke of my ventures at sea, where is to be seene what I have abroade. I have alsoe a booke of coppies of remembrances and letteres to such as are my factores, which hath reference to my booke of ventures and my book of ventures to it. I have alsoe a booke wherein is a particular inventorie of all my household stuff and plate. All which are in my counter.'[34] That sounds like more sensible business practice, and it is a major loss that we do not have more of this kind of evidence of merchant activity. So, why did Thomas Garrard not record his business activities in this way, or was he simply being deliberately obstructive? Lynn men perhaps worked more generally to a wholly different set of principles. Alderman John Spence, at that time mayor of the borough, admittted to the exchequer judges during the same enquiry that he had paid the searcher's man an additional sum over and above the usual fee for, as he put it, 'his dispatche in the custome house', a useful and probably fairly regular occurence which allowed underpaid officials and their clerks to supplement their salaries and their fees, and almost certainly made them more than just a little more compliant. A shipmaster also explained to the same judges how seven or eight days into a voyage from Lynn his ship, laden with rapeseed and linseed, was caught by contrary winds 'and theruppon she cam[e] backe agayne' – to be re-loaded by the merchants with corn, a far more valuable cargo and one

---

[31] N. J. Williams, *Contraband Cargoes: Seven Centuries of Smuggling* (Hamden, Conn., 1961), p. 43.

[32] T. S. Willan, *Studies in Elizabethan Foreign Trade* (Manchester, 1959), p. 160.

[33] TNA PRO E178/4250.

[34] P. McGrath, ed., *Merchants and Merchandise in Seventeenth-Century Bristol*, Bristol Record Society, vol. XIX (1955), p. xv.

that was supposed to be much more tightly controlled. On another occasion a little later, in 1614, the searcher of the port, Alderman Matthew Clarke, together with the deputy customer, was summoned to appear before the privy council to answer charges of failing to perform the duties of his office.[35] We know no more of his transgressions, but even this brief reference should put us on our guard. At the end of the day, it all reminds us that customs records cannot be taken simply at face value. As Willan has also pointed out, figures derived from port books, and from similar documents, might well vary very considerably according to the 'selective' nature of the smuggling activities that could be said to undermine them. Corn exports and any trade in other high-value commodities were probably particularly susceptible to sharp practice and evasion, with predictable but often unquantifiable implications. But, equally, he has very pertinently concluded: 'No doubt it is difficult to separate the statistical sheep from the statistical goats, but it may [still] be better to attempt that than to condemn them all to the slaughter.'[36]

The period for which we have quite a lot of information from this particular collection of documents does, at least, have one or two special advantages. It falls within what A. M. Millard once characterised as 'the twelve good years of James I' (1604–1615) in general commercial terms, a time when trade was good in the interval between two prolonged periods of European war.[37] Perhaps, in such circumstances, when profits could be made legally there would be less smuggling and customs evasion, although the periodic revisions of the book of rates and the introduction of the new impositions after 1608 might have provided further incentives for illicit trading. But then, to counter-balance that, the inauguration of the great farm of the customs after 1605 may have led to greater efficiency in the collection, and therefore the recording, of duties, the 'zeal of the farmers' and their agents making the port books more useful as sources for the commercial history of the period.[38] Whether or not this was true, finally, it would still be more likely that a greater volume of legal trade would be recorded in good years than in bad and if, taking the most pessimistic view, customs records only ever reveal the tips of icebergs, then at least we may expect to see bigger icebergs or more of them.

[35] *Acts of the Privy Council, 1613–14*, p. 318.

[36] T. S. Willan, ed., *A Tudor Book of Rates* (Manchester, 1962), p. xlviii.

[37] A. M. Millard, 'The Import Trade of London, 1600–1640', London PhD thesis (1956), ch. 3. See also R. H. Tawney, *Business and Politics under James I: Lionel Cranfield as Merchant and Minister* (Cambridge, 1958), pp. 13–18.

[38] R. Ashton, *The City and the Court 1603–1643* (Cambridge, 1979), pp. 31–33.

The general pattern of overseas trade and the role of the King's Lynn merchants in it – a brief overview

Lynn's overseas trade in earlier centuries has already been extensively investigated. Carus-Wilson outlined the essential features of the medieval trade of both Lynn and Boston, and her work can be supplemented with material from the researches of others, most notably Gras and more recently Owen.[39] The sixteenth-century pattern has been analysed in depth by Williams, whose work has already been mentioned.[40] The overall picture for the early seventeenth century was substantially a continuation of these earlier trends, with a concentration upon the trades with the northern half of Europe but with some commercial contacts with southern Europe as well (see *Map 1*). There were, perhaps, a few changes of emphasis, particularly with the rise of a really flourishing Scottish trade, but what we have is essentially the final flowering of the old pattern of commercial activity before the great seventeenth-century dislocations produced by, first of all, an acute depression, then prolonged European war and civil war, and finally a 'commercial revolution' which fundamentally altered the nature of English commerce as a whole and ultimately left King's Lynn behind.[41] The short period covered by these documents is a particularly good one in which to observe this pattern, since it was so untypically prosperous in general commercial terms. If there is something of a distortion introduced thereby, at least it is a known and consistent one; and, as we have already seen, the period's special character does present us with a number of advantages with regard to these particular sources.

Table 3 gives a breakdown of all of the 870 overseas shipments (i.e. the port book entries collated and amalgamated as necessary to create consolidated 'shipments' as defined above), inwards and then outwards, shown by year (at the top) and by region of trade: Scotland, which was still regarded as at least semi-foreign in spite of the personal union of the crowns in 1603; the Netherlands; Northern Europe (the old Hanseatic lands, including Norway); France, by which is meant northern and south-western, or Atlantic, France; Spain and Portugal; Iceland (which was something of a special case); and then 'other' and unknown ports, of which there were very few, apart from the first year, 1610–11, when the main record very inconveniently did not record trade ports at all. Towards the bottom right of the table the shipments for Wells and Burnham have been separated out in footnotes,

---

[39] E. M. Carus-Wilson, 'The Medieval Trade of the Ports of the Wash', *Medieval Archaeology*, 6–7 (1962–3), pp. 182–201; N. S. B. Gras, *The Early English Customs System* (Cambridge, Mass., 1918), especially ch. 9 and 11–15; D. M. Owen, ed., *The Making of King's Lynn: A Documentary Survey* (1984), pp. 41–51, 331–378.

[40] Williams, *Maritime Trade*, especially ch. 3.

[41] B. E. Supple, *Commercial Crisis and Change in England 1600–1642* (Cambridge, 1959), and R. Davis, *A Commercial Revolution: Overseas Trade in the Seventeenth and Eighteenth Centuries* (1967)

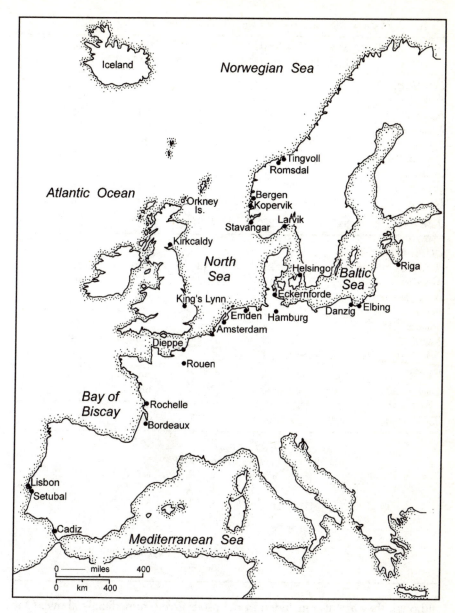

MAP 1 *The Foreign Trade of King's Lynn 1610–1614*

TABLE 3   *Overseas shipments, port of King's Lynn, 1610–1614*

	Xmas 1610–11	Xmas 1611–12	Xmas 1612–13	Xmas 1613–14	Totals
INWARDS					
Scotland	–	42[a]	67[a]	75	184
Netherlands	1	53[c]	42[f]	54[c]	150
N. Europe	–	16	11	51	78
France	4[a]	7	4	10[b]	25
Spain & Port.	–	1	5	1	7
Iceland	–	4[a]	4[c]	3	11
Other	–	–	–	1	1
Unknown	120	–	–	1	121
Total	125	123[d]	133[g]	196[d]	577
OUTWARDS					
Scotland	–	21	48	32	101
Netherlands	–	11[b]	23[d]	12[a]	46
N. Europe	–	6	7	18	31
France	–	3	1	1	5
Spain & Port.	–	1	1	1	3
Iceland	–	3	4[b]	1	8
Other	–	1	–	–	1
Unknown	98	–	–	–	98
Total	98	46[b]	84[e]	65[a]	293
Total shipments	223	169[e]	217[h]	261[e]	870

a. from ms.
433/12

Wells and Burnham:
[included in figures above]

a. 1	a. 2	a. 1
b. 3	b. 3	b. 2
c. 15	c. 4	c. 8
d. 17	d. 7	d. 10
e. 20	e. 10	e. 11
	f. 1	*[incl. 'Lynn*
	g. 18	*with W & B']*
	h. 28	

although they are also included in the totals given immediately above. One thing that is abundantly clear from this table is that the balance of trade in these years was overwhelmingly weighted in favour of imports, which by 1614 accounted for three quarters of all the shipments and overall exceeded exports by a factor of two to one.[42] The general decline in exports, compared

[42] This compares with import/export ratios (in numbers of shipments) of 103/172 for 1604–5, 124/220 for 1605–6, and 150/128 for 1607–8 – Metters, 'Rulers', vol. 1, p. 123.

to earlier years, can be explained largely by reference to one of the staples in Lynn's overseas trade. It has become almost customary to see English commerce as a whole mainly from the point of view of the port of London and to concentrate attention on the export of woollen cloth; but for Lynn this simply will not do. Cloth did feature in traffic through the port, both as an export and as an import, in the latter case from Scotland, the Netherlands, Northern Europe, France, and even from Iceland. But Lynn was essentially a grain exporting port, possibly the greatest in the kingdom and certainly the greatest in eastern England.[43] The Ouse basin was one of the leading wheat and barley producing regions, and it has been suggested that more than half of the country's entire grain exports were sent out from East Anglian harbours.[44] In an account of the marketing of corn in Norfolk, written in about 1630, Lynn, with its creek of Burnham, was portrayed as the only port especially equipped to handle vast quantities of grain.[45] And it was precisely this specialisation that made Lynn's export trade so susceptible to great fluctuations from year to year, partly as a result of legal constraints imposed artificially from outside, but mostly because of the state of the harvest in the agricultural hinterland.

Merchants might be able to get round, or simply ignore, government policy with regard to the shipping of corn, but there was very little they could do about harvest failure, a phenomenon which, as Hoskins pointed out many years ago, was 'a hundred times more important' for producers and consumers (and, he might have added, for merchants trading through a port such as Lynn) than fluctuations in the cloth trade.[46] A good deal is now known about harvest qualities, thanks to the pioneering work done by Hoskins and subsequently by Bowden and Harrison.[47] Harvests were apparently good in the period 1604–06; 1607 was less good, particularly for wheat; 1608 was a relative disaster for wheat, though quite good for barley; 1609 was deficient in barley but otherwise average-to-good, and 1610 more generally average-to-good; harvests for 1611–13 were on the whole poor, getting progressively worse. Allowing for the time-lag between harvesting and the possible shipping of corn, we have here a plausible explanation of the general shape of Lynn's export trade in the early-seventeenth century and particularly for the apparent

[43] T. S. Willan, *Studies in Elizabethan Foreign Trade* (Manchester, 1959), p. 72; Williams, *Maritime Trade*, pp. 35–37, 55–61, 150–161; N. S. B. Gras, *The Evolution of the English Corn Market from the Twelfth to the Eighteenth Century* (Cambridge, Mass., 1915), p. 176 and appendices C and D.

[44] A. Everitt, 'The Marketing of Agricultural Produce' in J. Thirsk, ed., *The Agrarian History of England and Wales, IV, 1500–1640* (1967), p 526.

[45] J. Thirsk and J. P. Cooper, eds, *Seventeenth Century Economic Documents* (Oxford, 1972), p. 344.

[46] W. G. Hoskins, 'Harvest Fluctuations and English Economic History 1480–1619', *Agricultural History Review*, XII (1964), p. 29, n. 3.

[47] Hoskins, 'Harvest Fluctuations', pp. 28–46; P. Bowden, 'Statistical Appendix', in J. Thirsk, ed., *Agrarian History*, p. 820; C. J. Harrison, 'Grain Price Analysis and Harvest Qualities 1465–1634', *Agricultural History Review*, XIX (1971), pp. 135–155.

TABLE 4 *Ship movements through Lynn: overseas 1610–1614*

Year	Inwards	Outwards	Total
1610–11	104	90	194
1611–12	104	43	147
1612–13	112	70	182
1613–14	164	58	222
	484	261	745

collapse of exports after 1610. After grain, and less directly dependent on harvest qualities, beer and skins also featured prominently among exports, and other commodities included various re-exports. The merchants clearly had to have other strings to their bows when the staple commodity was unobtainable. Imports were perhaps much more in line with the national pattern, particularly since Lynn supplied a vast hinterland with goods from abroad and also developed something of a function as an *entrepot* in its own right.[48] The goods involved in particular areas of trade are discussed below.

As a measure of the total volume of trade through the port, a table based on shipments might not be considered to be the most helpful for making meaningful comparison with the situation in other ports, so the overall totals given in *Table 3* can be further adjusted to reflect the movement of ships, by consolidating shared-ship cargoes and eliminating other duplications. On the basis of these revised figures, shown in *Table 4*, an interesting comparison can be made with shipping through the neighbouring port of Boston.[49] Over the seventeen years for which port books are extant in the period 1601–1640 Boston had 520 ships passing inwards and 235 outwards, 755 altogether, or about the same number as those clearing the port of Lynn in less than a quarter as many years. It seems reasonable to surmise, therefore, that Lynn's overseas trade may have been some four times greater than that of its near neighbour, which had clearly seen better days. Indeed these Lynn figures are much more comparable with those of Chester, with its 234 ships (91 inwards, 143 outwards) in 1602–1603, or even Bristol, with 220 ships (121 inwards, 99 outwards) clearing that port in 1600–1601.[50] Lynn was still a commercial centre of the first rank among the outports and fully deserving of its more general placing in the various urban 'league tables' of early-modern century towns.[51]

[48] The hinterland perhaps comprised 'a fifth of England' – Williams, *Maritime Trade*, p. 55, echoing D. Defoe, *A Tour Through the Whole Island of Great Britain* (Everyman edition, 1962), vol. 1, pp. 73–74; see also Bodleian Library, Gough MSS, Norfolk 29, first part (description of the town *circa* 1710–14). Metters, 'Rulers', vol. 1, pp. 207–208, for the pattern of re-exports, particularly across the Wash to Boston.

[49] From the published port books - Hinton, *Boston*.

[50] D. M. Woodward, *The Trade of Elizabethan Chester* (Hull, 1970), p. 131; P. McGrath, ed., *Merchants and Merchandise in Seventeenth Century Bristol*, Bristol Record Society, vol. XIX (1955), pp. 279–281.

[51] W. G. Hoskins, *Local History in England* (1959), p. 177; D. H. Sacks and M. Lynch, 'Ports 1540–1700' in P. Clark, ed., *The Cambridge Urban History of Britain, vol. 2, 1540–1840* (Cambridge, 2000), p. 384.

How much of the trade was carried on in the names of King's Lynn merchants? It is relatively easy to identify the individuals who can be said to have 'belonged' to the port, from the register of the borough's freemen. This can be cross-referenced to the corporation hall books, the minutes of the governing body, which had to agree to all admissions to the freedom and whose membership is also readily discernible.[52] The town's rulers might be expected to have been co-terminous with the leading members of the merchant community, as there was a strong tradition of mercantile domination of virtually everything in Lynn. The medieval borough had boasted an extraordinarily rich and powerful guild merchant, the Trinity Guild, in whose hall (still a part of the municipal town hall) the borough government met and which had often been the town's creditor.[53] After the dissolution of guilds and chantries in the mid-sixteenth century the ghost of the Trinity Guild had continued to haunt the place in the re-constituted form of the 'Company of Merchants'. This still represented the political and commercial elite of the town and was a body which anyone with aspirations of any kind wanted to join, to the extent sometimes of taking up a second freedom of the borough as a merchant while already free in another trade.[54] As a consequence there were at any one time a very considerable number of 'merchants of Lynn'. The index to the text of this volume highlights the known freemen, including members of the borough corporation both at the time and subsequently, whose names can be found in the port books for 1610–1614, and further details are provided in *Appendix 2.A*. A few of these individuals, such as Nathaniel Maxey or Thomas Slaney, were not actually freemen of Lynn during the years covered by the port books but they did take up the freedom shortly afterwards and can therefore be counted as 'emerging' Lynn men, particularly as they subsequently rose to high municipal office. Equally, though, the alien merchant Erasmus Coates also eventually became a Lynn resident, acquiring property in the town, so the issue can become even more complicated.[55] He is not counted as a Lynn merchant for the purposes of this discussion.

The general levels of merchant activity, as measured by the number of shipments per individual (for *all* of those named in the port books and not just the Lynn men), were remarkably low, an average of about three shipments per man. Within this, however, there were big variations. The vast majority of the names appear only once or twice, while at the other end of the spectrum are to be found much more prolific commercial operators such

---

[52] See Appendix 2.

[53] Owen, *Making of King's Lynn*, pp. 60–63, 295–330, 383–408; E. M. Beloe, *Our Borough, Our Churches* (Cambridge, 1899), pp. 6–9; *Report on the Manuscripts of the Corporations of Southampton and King's Lynn*, Historical Manuscripts Commission, Eleventh Report, Appendix, Part III (1887), pp. 185–203; A. S. Green, *Town Life in the Fifteenth Century*, vol. 2 (1894), pp. 402–426; C. Gross, *The Gild Merchant*, vol. 2 (Oxford, 1890), p. 151.

[54] As, for example, John Greene did – see Appendix 2.A.

[55] See note 26 above.

as William Atkin (with 14 shipments), John Greene (10), Robert Hayes (12), Thomas March (10), Nathaniel Maxey (14), Thomas Slaney (15), Thomas Snelling (26), Robert Thorey (12), John Wallis (16), and Gervase Wharton (14), all of them 'of Lynn', whose activities sat alongside those of the Scotsmen David Balfour (31 shipments), Sir George Bruce (11), John Cussen (18), Andrew Masterton (26), Henry Reynoldson (10), and William Williamson (15), together with the aliens Jacob Bonis (17), Simon Johnson (10), and Garrard Nabbs (21), and the 'other English' merchants Henry Congham (19 shipments, mainly through the creeks) and Cornelius De Wild (10). Overall, the identifiable King's Lynn merchants comprised less than a fifth of all the merchants trading and they accounted, in their own names, for just over a quarter of all the recorded shipments. However there were some significant differences across the various European markets.

The most buoyant branch of King's Lynn's overseas trade at this time was with Scotland (*Map 2*) but interestingly the Lynn merchants themselves were not much involved in it directly. The Scottish trade was dominated by Scotsmen and Scottish shipping, as it had been in the Elizabethan period.[56] Indeed at certain times of the year the port of Lynn must have been overrun with Scots (along with Geordies engaged in the coastal coal trade). The bulk of the exchanges were with the ports of the Firth of Forth, and the most important by far was Kirkcaldy, both for imports and exports. After Kirkcaldy the most frequently mentioned places were Culross, Leith and Anstruther, with occasional shipments to and from Bo'ness and Kinghorn. Outside the Firth of Forth, Dundee and Montrose were the most significant ports, but their trade with Lynn was relatively slight. Five shipments of coal were also recorded from the uncertain port of 'Kirrhen', which may have been Carron or Carriden, again on the Firth of Forth, although that identification remains speculative. The other goods that the mainly Scottish merchants brought in included salt (usually described as 'white salt' to distinguish it from 'bay', French or Spanish salt), fish, cloth and yarn and they took out barley and malt, some wheat and also peas and beans. But the most interesting commodity taken away was beer, which was shipped north in vast quantities and provides evidence of a thriving brewing industry in the Jacobean town, for which there is much additional evidence.[57]

More important than Scotland for the Lynn merchants, and more generally important in terms of wealth-generation, were the trades with the Netherlands and Northern Europe. Of the Dutch ports (*Map 3*), Rotterdam and Enkhuizen had been the most important immediately before the period covered by these documents[58] but after the conclusion of the truce between

[56] Williams, *Maritime Trade*, pp. 80–85.

[57] Metters, 'Rulers', vol. 1, pp. 320, 331–334, 343–351; G. A. Metters, 'Business and Politics in the Reign of James I: the Careers of John and William Atkin of King's Lynn', in A. Longcroft and R. Joby, eds, *East Anglian Studies: Essays presented to J. C. Barringer on his retirement* (Norwich, 1995), pp. 181–190.

[58] Metters, 'Rulers', vol. 1, pp. 138–144; cf. Williams, *Maritime Trade*, pp. 69–80.

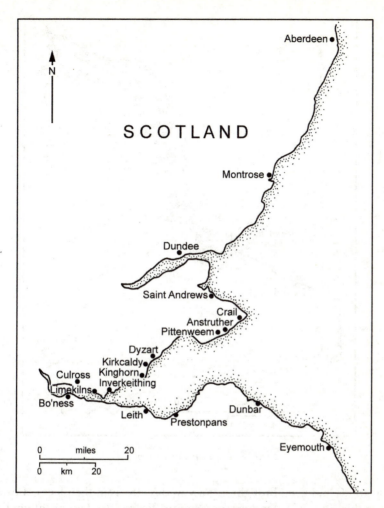

MAP 2 *The Scottish Ports*

the Dutch rebels and the King of Spain in 1609 the major new entrepot of Amsterdam rapidly rose to prominence and completely outshone all the other Dutch ports. Exports to the Netherlands consisted of foodstuffs with a little cloth, and in return the Lynn men and others, including a remarkable number of Dutch shipmasters, brought back a wonderful variety of goods which fully reflected the growth of Dutch commercial enterprise at this time – Spanish and French salt, Baltic rye and timber, Iceland fish, wines, spices, paper, glass, kettles and pots, bricks and tiles, and so on. It really was like returning from a vast European hypermarket where anything that anyone might want was on offer, and it is worth noting that before 1609 many of

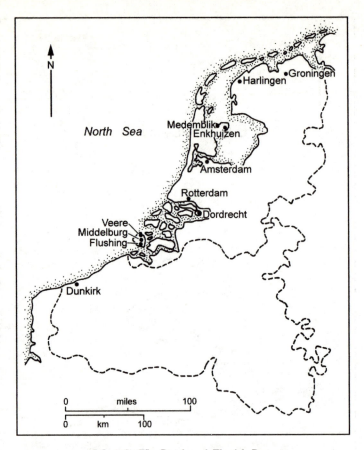

MAP 3 *The Dutch and Flemish Ports*

these goods had been brought into Lynn directly from the places of production rather than via Amsterdam. A more limited trade with other Dutch ports did continue, however, particularly with the more southerly commercial centres at Flushing, Middelburg, Veere (particularly important for Wells and Burnham), and Dordrecht. Two transactions involving this last port are particularly interesting because some of their wider commercial ramifications can be traced. In February 1611 (entry *10*) John Wallis paid duty of £3 15s 0d on seven and a half lasts of hempseed, to be taken out in the *Griffin* of Dordrecht by the shipmaster Cornelius Clawson, a very regular visitor to Lynn. The destination was not actually recorded but it was almost certainly Dordrecht, given the regular pattern of Clawson's movements. In April the ship returned (entry *119*) with twenty millstones, two hundredweight of aniseed and three reams of copy paper, duty on the entire cargo being £3 5s 0½d. The stones were sold by Wallis to the borough corporation to supplement its millstone stock and the account of that transaction is recorded in the town's millstone account.[59] The stones were cullenstones, sixteen 'fifteeners' and four 'fourteeners', and had cost Wallis £91 8s 2d in 'Holland'. His other charges included £7 3s 4d for custom and entry at Lynn, £6 for freight, £2 10s for his adventure and ten shillings to the porters for cranage. In addition the corporation paid out seventeen shillings towards the cost of dinner at a Mr Gooding's, when the negotiation of the sale of the goods was conducted. Interestingly, too, in both of these shipments John Wallis of Lynn was sharing cargo space with two Dutchmen, in the case of the export with the shipmaster, Cornelius Clawson, and for the import with the shipmaster-merchant Simon Johnson. Wallis clearly had some important Dutch business connections and had no doubt spent time in the Netherlands, as he admitted while giving evidence to the court of star chamber in 1610 that he was fluent in the Dutch language.[60]

A number of Lynn merchants traded with Northern European ports, in a continuation of the formerly important Hanseatic connection: Bergen and Romsdal in Norway; Emden and Hamburg on the North Sea coast of Germany; and with Elbing and Danzig in the Baltic.[61] From Norway they brought vast quantities of timber (masts, spars, clapboards, deals etc) and also tar and fish, but they apparently had relatively little to sell in return and so that trade was very one-sided. The Emden/Hamburg trade was virtually an extension of the Netherlands trade, and there were some similarities too between these and the trade with the Baltic ports. From Danzig were brought rye, fish, timber, pitch and tar, flax, hemp, cloth and glass, while to Elbing went mainly vast quantities of skins and leather, together with a little cloth. The export of hides to the Baltic was, however, perhaps the most notable feature: sheep's leather, lambskins, coney and rabbit skins, and catskins – not even felines could feel safe in Lynn's hinterland. One of the principal merchants in this trade was Thomas Snelling, a citizen of London according to his memorial in St Nicholas' Chapel (and a member of the Skinners' Company), who subsequently became mayor of the borough at the age of only thirty eight but then tragically died during his year of office.[62] He

[59] NRO KL/C44/18, account for 1610–11.

[60] TNA PRO STAC 8/59/6.

[61] There had once been a Lynn merchants' residence in Bergen, and the Norfolk town still boasts a Hanseatic warehouse, recently celebrated and re-dedicated – Williams, *Maritime Trade*, p. 100; V. Parker, *The Making of King's Lynn: Secular Buildings from the 11th to the 17th Century* (London and Chichester, 1971), pp. 114–116; K. Friedland and P. Richards, eds, *Essays in Hanseatic History: the King's Lynn Symposium 1998* (Larks Press, 2005), especially pp. 7, 51–66, 115–116. See also J. K. Fedorowicz, *England's Baltic Trade in the Early Seventeenth Century: a Study in Anglo-Polish Commercial Diplomacy* (Cambridge, 1980), pp. 61–69.

[62] See Appendix 2.A; also E. M. W. Hovell, *Complete List of the Inscriptions on the Tablets, Slabs and Monuments in the Chapel of St Nicholas, King's Lynn, Existing in the Year 1937* (King's Lynn, 1937), pp. 3, 61; B. Mackerell, *History of King's Lynn* (1738), p.104. And see note 100 to the text.

was, almost certainly, the 'Thomas S— of Lynn' who also appears in the Boston port books shipping rye from Danzig in 1618.[63]

The other northern trade with which Lynn men were intimately concerned was the Iceland venture[64] – the annual fishing and trading voyage which set out in the spring and returned in the late summer or early autumn with fish, train oil, falcons and the strange Icelandic cloth called *wadmal* (or, as the customs clerks invariably recorded it, 'woodmole') either in its raw state or woven into stockings or mittens.[65] Unfortunately, because there always seemed to be a certain amount of confusion over whether the Iceland venture was a purely fishing expedition or a commercial enterprise, it was very erratically recorded in the port books and so it is difficult to piece together very much of a picture of precisely who was taking part in it. Tobias Gentleman, writing in 1614, was in no doubt about its importance: 'Then is there Lynn, a proper gallant town for seafaring men, and for men for Iceland; this is a rich town, and they have some twenty sail of Iceland ships, that they yearly send for cod and lings....'[66] As we have already seen, apart from the few clearly recorded shipments, we have to rely on other oblique references to merchants being allowed to import their salt from France, Spain or Amsterdam duty free because it was to be employed in the Iceland voyage. The will of John Wainford (or Wentforth), made in 1612, also throws a little more light on the issue, but only to reinforce the point that the Iceland trade is very poorly represented in customs accounts.[67] It refers specifically to his venture to Iceland in the *Martin* of Lynn, in which he owned a share, and to the stock which would return upon the completion of the voyage. The relevant port book has no record of this, unless, of course, the vessel returned to a different Norfolk, Suffolk, or other English port, because a good deal of fish did come into Lynn coastwise. We have here a lot of hints that Lynn merchants took part in the Iceland trade, without any way of even beginning to quantify it accurately.[68]

There was a most intriguing commercial link between Lynn and Dieppe in northern France which is worth mentioning even though none of the Lynn merchants had anything to do with it – it was handled by men from other ports and consisted of fairly regular consignments to Dieppe of old bones of various kinds, ox-horns, broken glass and old shoes, presumably an early example of waste recycling. It had been a feature of Lynn's trade in the

---

[63] Hinton, *Boston*, pp. 160–161.

[64] E. M. Carus-Wilson, *Medieval Merchant Venturers* (1954), ch. 2; Williams, *Maritime Trade*, pp. 85–96.

[65] A piece of this cloth was found during an excavation in Lynn in the 1960s - H. Clarke and A. Carter, *Excavations in King's Lynn 1963–1970* (1977), p. 376 – however, the reference there to the commodity dropping out of the post-medieval trade into Lynn is not supported by the evidence of these port books.

[66] Tobias Gentleman, 'England's Way to Win Wealth', *Harleian Miscellany*, iii (1809), p. 243.

[67] PCC 102 Fenner 1612, TNA PRO PROB 11/120/336.

[68] For further details see Metters, 'Rulers', vol. 1, pp. 156–161.

Elizabethan era and the contemporary commentator Fynes Morrison had remarked on it with a certain amount of astonishment.[69] The Lynn merchants, particularly the brothers-in-law William Atkin and Gervase Wharton, did, however, have serious trading links with the ports of south-west France, Bordeaux and Rochelle. This was mainly an import trade based on salt and wine, together with prunes which, we are assured, the Elizabethans at least had consumed in great quantities;[70] there were also imports of honey, vinegar, feathers and rosin. In addition to the inevitable wheat, barley and peas, Lynn exchanged smaller amounts of fish, coal, pitch and tar, timber, wax and cloth.

In the best harvest years, when supplies of grain had been abundant in the hinterland, Lynn merchants had conducted a thriving export trade to southern Europe and beyond. It was founded on the export of wheat, with smaller amounts of barley and also some of the various goods sent to south west France, and it had taken them to Lisbon, Seville, San Lucar, to Marseilles and Leghorn in the Mediterranean and also to Barbary (North Africa).[71] A good deal of this southern traffic had been trans-shipped at Harwich, Tilbury, Gravesend or London, and the cargoes completed their journeys usually in London ships.[72] This indicates some fairly extensive business connections of the Lynn merchants, another significant aspect of their commercial world. They did not apparently import anything directly from Barbary or the Mediterranean but they did bring back from Spain and Portugal considerable quantities of salt, and also wine, figs, raisins, apples, sugar, almonds, liquorice, pepper, and on one occasion even some cloth. The evidence of these port books reflects a very truncated version of these trades, with the emphasis clearly on imports, and King's Lynn men were particularly prominent in them.[73]

The merchants and their businesses

Nearly all of the shipments recorded in the port books were entered in the names of single merchants. Just a few recorded 'and company', and a few more indicated two or more merchants working together. As we have already seen, William Atkin appears to have traded in collaboration with his brother-in-law Gervase Wharton, while a number of port book entries record the

[69] Williams, *Maritime Trade*, p. 114.
[70] Williams, *Maritime Trade*, p.176.
[71] Williams, *Maritime Trade*, pp. 122–135; Metters, 'Rulers', vol. 1, pp. 167–175.
[72] Metters, 'Rulers', vol. 1, p. 168, and vol. 2, Appendix E.1.
[73] John Greene, John Spence and John Wallis, were the most prominent in the Spanish trade, the first two of whom (along with eight other identifiable Lynn merchants) may have become members of the Spanish Company. However John Wallis, the most prolific of them all, apparently did not – Metters, 'Rulers', vol. 1, p. 175.

sharing of ship space for cargoes belonging to more than one named merchant. However, that was not quite the end of the story. The salt shipment entered in the name of John Sendall (*852*) went on to indicate that other unnamed merchants were also involved in that cargo and equally were going to be involved in the forthcoming Iceland voyage; and the same kind of reference occured in the post entry to number *947*. It is more than likely, therefore, that a single named merchant was simply the lead figure in a much more complex set of business arrangements, just as there was often fragmented and shared ownership of trading vessels, which spread the risks in a way that constituted much sounder business practice than the potentially suicidal activities of, for example, Shakespeare's merchant of Venice.[74] The profits may have been less but they would have been considerably more secure. This might also help to explain why so many 'Lynn merchants' were so conspicuously absent from the port book record; they may well have been sleeping partners in the ventures entered, for customs purposes, in the names of other individuals. *Appendix 2.B* identifies the actual members of the corporation during the years 1610–1614 whose names never feature at all in these port books, along with those of other 'absentees' who later joined the governing body but were already free, mostly as merchants, at that time. Among this group was Alderman Matthew Clarke, himself the searcher of the port and the son of a former searcher who, we know from his will, owned his own ship, the *Thomas* of Lynn,[75] which may have been the vessel named in entries *169* and *283*. Similarly *Appendix 2.C* lists all those other individuals who became freemen of the borough *as merchants* during the whole decade 1604–1614, whom one might expect to feature as maritime traders but who do not. They cannot all have been engaging in the kind of activity for which Francis Shaxton had made their port notorious in the previous reign, although that does still remain a possibility.

A good many of the smaller merchants may have engaged in the coasting trade rather than in much more expensive and risky overseas ventures, and this could be why they are missing from these port books. It is also clear that some of those whose names do appear may have been relatively young men, still 'on the make' and perhaps associates of other businessmen, possibly more established or even semi-retired. Thomas Snelling and Thomas Slaney seem

[74] P. McGrath, *Merchants and Merchandise in Seventeenth-Century Bristol*, pp. xiii-xviii; Williams, *Maritime Trade*, pp. 200–207. The issue is explored at length in Metters, 'Rulers', vol. 1, ch. 5 and 6; and also in A. Metters, ' Mixed enterprise in early-seventeenth century King's Lynn', in C. Rawcliffe, R. Virgoe and R. Wilson, eds, *Counties and Communities: Essays on East Anglian History presented to Hassell Smith* (Norwich, 1996), pp. 225–240. See also, for the wider context: J. Kermode, *Medieval Merchants: York, Beverley and Hull in the Later Middle Ages* (Cambridge, 1998); P. Spufford, *Profit and Power: the Merchant in Medieval Europe* (2002); F Braudel, *Civilisation and Capitalism 15th-18th Century, vol. 2 - The Wheels of Commerce* (1982); R. Grassby, *The Business Community of Seventeenth-Century England* (Cambridge, 1995).

[75] On his general business activities see Metters, 'Rulers', vol. 1, pp. 351–357, and Metters, 'Mixed Enterprise', pp. 233–237; his will is at PCC 42 Swan 1623, TNA PRO PROB 11/141/334.

to come into this category and they were both highly successful in the longer term, joining the political elite of the town and rising to senior municipal office. They made 'good' marriages, Snelling marrying Margaret, the daughter of Alderman Matthew Clarke, and Slaney marrying Joanna, a daughter of Alderman John Atkin, no doubt an important factor in the ultimate success of both men.[76] Many such dynastic connections can be identified, such as those involving the Wormells and the Leightons,[77] and it is a pity that we do not have any surviving private business records for this period to be able to flesh out with more certainty the commercial organisations that were established to underpin their various activities. Family was clearly very important in the establishment of a business house, particularly when the arrangements often remained informal.

However, there was a range of other businesses that merchants could engage in quite legally without their names appearing in customs accounts at all, and these made up much of what N. S. B. Gras once characterised as the 'traditional functions' of the 'sedentary merchant'.[78] They included wholesaling, retailing, shipping, warehousing, money-management of various kinds, production, and investment in property, and many of them constituted, together, a fairly comprehensive package of commercial services which were provided by the borough and port of King's Lynn in its capacity as a thriving business centre – a much scaled-down English provincial version of Antwerp in its heyday or London or Amsterdam, and very much, as it was later called, 'the Metropolis of Marshland and the Fens.'[79] Of these various activities perhaps the most important, and the most lucrative, was domestic wholesaling, a logical undertaking for the leading burgesses, given their special position as the chief beneficiaries of established charter rights and the time-honoured doctrine of 'foreign bought and foreign sold.'[80] We have already seen that goods were both brought into the port and taken out by 'merchant-strangers', especially by the busy Scottish and Dutch shipmasters who were such frequent visitors. While it is true that certain English 'merchant-strangers' might pass through the port unhindered, as long as they did not bring their goods on to dry land, anything that was actually landed in Lynn for sale or brought there for export, by strangers of any description, had to pass through the hands of a freeman; and this was a right which the

[76] For Snelling's marriage, see the register of St Nicholas Chapel, NRO PD39/83(S); for Slaney see the wills of John Atkin (PCC 2 Meade 1617, TNA PRO PROB 11/131/13) and William Atkin (PCC 59 Swann 1623, TNA PRO PROB 11/141/471).

[77] There were many similarities in the trading activities of the brothers Bartholomew and John Wormell, and for the Leightons (Alderman Thomas Leighton and his sons Thomas, Francis and Stephen) see in particular TNA PRO STAC 8/92/3 and REQ 2/233/30 – Metters, 'Rulers', vol. 1, pp. 288–289.

[78] N. S. B. Gras, *Business and Capitalism* (New York, 1939), pp. 75–77

[79] W. Richards, *The History of Lynn* (King's Lynn, 1812), vol. 1, p. 32.

[80] For a more extended discussion see Metters, 'Rulers', vol. 1, pp. 308–313.

corporation defended fiercely and tried to enforce rigidly. Outsiders who tried to infringe the privilege got very short shrift, and there was clearly ample scope for the more substantial burgesses to make profits as wholesaling middlemen, buying and selling at the quayside, without the extra worry of adventuring to sea on their own accounts. Participation in the corn, salt and coal trades (the last an offshoot of the highly important coastal trade[81] and not so obviously apparent from these port books) is particularly well documented, but perhaps one specific example will suffice. An extant municipal toll account of 1618–19 records the additional local dues on salt, coal and corn brought into the port by strangers and details twenty eight entries relating to salt imports, particularly from Scotland.[82] No less than twenty four of these shipments, ranging in size from sixteen weys to fifty weys and amounting to 888 weys in all, were sold to 'Mr Adkin', almost certainly Alderman William Atkin, from the respectful formality of the reference. The quantities involved would appear almost to single him out as something of a specialist in the salt trade, but it was still only a part of his overall business.

The other business activities which could be intimately related to the details to be found in port books were shipping and warehousing, both of which could be hired out for use by other businessmen and thereby turned to a profit. Reference has already been made to shipping and there were many ships 'of Lynn' recorded in the customs accounts, by no means all of them used by Lynn merchants, as a close examination of the text of this edition, with its index, will readily reveal. Equally we know from Vanessa Parker's work on the buildings of the town that warehousing was in ample supply, with much rebuilding taking place in the late-sixteenth and seventeenth centuries.[83] Some of this storage space was muncipally owned and there are extant borough accounts, for example for the Common Staithe Quay, that record its use by 'foreign' merchants, but much of it remained in private hands. There had been considerable outrage when, in 1584, the corporation had issued a restraining order prohibiting the storing of strangers' goods in private warehouses, apparently in retaliation against infringements of other corporate privileges by some Cambridge merchants; and from then until the final settlement of the dispute in 1597 the situation became particularly acrimonious.[84] Robert Wallis became a leading spokesman for Cambridge (as he did in a similar dispute about the salt patent) and complained bitterly of what he called 'a mallicious and injuryous president such as hath not byne offered to anie Christian marchantes in anie parte of

[81] 572 shipments from Newcastle alone in 1607–8 and 422 in 1608–9, with a further 89 and 53 shipments from Sunderland in the same years, almost all of coal although a few specified 'white salt' – from TNA PRO E190/433/9, 10; Metters, 'Rulers', vol. 1, pp. 198–200.
[82] NRO KL/C44/9.
[83] V. Parker, *The Making of King's Lynn*, p. 119.
[84] NRO KL/C7/7, ff. 293–294, and KL/C7/8, ff. 10, 24; NRO King's Lynn Borough Archives, uncatalogued documents relating to disputes with Cambridge.

Cristendome or Turkye.'[85] Warehousing was clearly both a sensitive and a highly profitable business for both sides. Everyone seemed to be mightily relieved when the quarrel was finally settled and things could return to normal; and by the early-seventeenth century it would appear that the business was again proceeding much as before.

The customs house and the customs officers

Probably the best known public building in King's Lynn, the one most often reproduced as a kind of emblematic symbol of the town, is what is now called the Custom House on Purfleet Quay, which brings us conveniently back to the people who were responsible for compiling the port books. Unfortunately they had absolutely nothing to do with that particular building, which was first erected, to the design of the local worthy Henry Bell, as a merchants' exchange in the reign of Charles II. It only finally became the customs house, exclusively rather than in shared occupation, in 1717, although it did subsequently fulfil that function for some time.[86] A hundred years earlier the customs house was located in a muncipally-owned building further north along the quay, between the Tuesday Market Place and the Common Staithe Yard. A local account recording revenues derived from the Common Staithe Quay noted in 1607–8 that H.M. Customer paid a rent of ten shillings for two chambers used for the customs house, while at the same time the deputies to the farmers of H.M. Customs paid no less than forty shillings for the rent of the Tollbooth Court House – a timely reminder, perhaps, of the attitude of the Lynn bigwigs towards the customs farmers (or it might simply have meant that their accommodation was bigger).[87] Presumably this was the property referred to in the lease to Thomas Sidney, customer, and William Ashwell, controller, for ninety nine years and dated 15 November 1573: a 'chamber over the Tolbth Court house and the little chamber adjoining over the gatehouse to the Common Stath Yarde, with free egress and regress at the uttermost door of the Tolbth Court house towards the Tuesday Market Place.'[88] Some years later, on 2 September 1621, a new lease was sealed to John Cook, customer, and John Williamson, controller, to run for a further ninety nine years from 29 September 1620.[89] It provides a slightly fuller description of the property concerned, which may have been a newer replacement on the same site: a 'chamber lately new built, divided into two chambers containing together in length within the walls 26 feet on

[85] 'Replication of Wallis' in the uncatalogued collection above.
[86] P. Richard, *King's Lynn* (Chichester, 1990), p. 11.
[87] NRO KL/C44/8, p. 2.
[88] NRO KL/C51/34.
[89] NRO KL/C51/35.

the east side next the street, over the south gatehouse and entry leading into Common Stathe Yard and over a certain little shop or warehouse next the gatehouse and entry and abutting on Tuesday Market Stead towards the east, with free entry ... up and down the chamber by the uttermost door towards the Tuesday Market, for use as a custom house.' Whether this more detailed description refers to the building in use between 1610 and 1614 or to another one, as shown in a sketch by Henry Bell and copied in the nineteenth century by Rev. Edward Edwards,[90] there was clearly a two-storey edifice involved throughout the period and this helps to make sense of the casual reference, in a star chamber case of 1610, to merchants (and magistrates) sitting *under* the customs house at the time when the Dutch shipmaster, Simon Johnson, a regular visitor to Lynn, first made his angry complaint about sexual misconduct by a senior member of the borough corporation.[91]

One of the men in attendance on that occasion was the customer, Thomas White, who gave his age at the time of his deposition as 52. He had been appointed customer on 22 December 1605,[92] and was presumably the same man who had been elected to the common council of the borough in 1601 (see *Appendix 2.A*). The corporation seemed to be very keen to keep customs officials on their side, either by securing the appointment of men who were already members of the governing body or by electing them to municipal office following their appointment by the crown (they even elected John Cook, mentioned above, straight to the aldermanic bench, in 1623, without any previous service as a member of the common council).[93] White died at some time in 1610, which may account for the apparent confusion in the format of the first document in this edition, although his successor, Edward Blunt, had been appointed on 20 August 1610[94] and so there was plenty of time for him to become familiar with all the procedures and to oversee the compilation of the port book entries. Perhaps he had some difficulty with the farmers' deputies and that accounts for the unusual nature of the surviving book. At any rate, Blunt, who never even became a freeman of the borough, remained in office until 1618, when he was succeeded by John Cook.[95]

The controller of the port in 1610 was probably still Robert Ashwell, first apppointed on 4 April 1593,[96] although none of his port books has survived.

[90] See D. Higgins, *The Antiquities of King's Lynn: From the Sketchbooks of the Rev. Edward Edwards* (King's Lynn, 2001), p. 28; and *idem*, *The ingenious Mr Henry Bell, His Life, His Work, His Legacy, His King's Lynn* (King's Lynn, 2005), pp. 43–44.

[91] TNA PRO STAC 8/59/6. For the progress and outcome of that particular incident see Metters, 'Rulers', vol. 1, pp. 42–48.

[92] TNA PRO IND 1/17351, p. 265 – Calendar to the Fine Rolls of the Chancery, where the patents of office were formally enrolled.

[93] Metters, 'Rulers', vol. 1, pp. 33, 414.

[94] TNA PRO IND 1/ 17351, p. 307.

[95] TNA PRO IND 1/17351, p. 375.

[96] TNA PRO IND 1/17351, p. 181.

His successor was John Greene, appointed on 17 March 1614,[97] and presumably the common council member, first elected to that body in 1597. He was the only official to subscribe a surviving port book with his name. He resigned from the corporation in 1618, because he claimed to be resident in the country, and the John Williamson named in the second lease cited above probably took over the controllership in January 1619.[98] He was succeeded, in turn, by Roger Bungay, appointed on 27 February 1626,[99] who did have one shipment recorded in the port book for 1614 (entry *962*) and even later also became a member of the borough corporation. The searcher throughout the period covered by these port books was Alderman Matthew Clarke, who had succeeded his father, Alderman Richard Clarke, on 26 January 1602, and remained in office until 12 June 1620, when Nathaniel Maxey took over.[100] Maxey features as an active trader in the port books for 1610–14, importing spices and exporting worsted stockings in considerable quantities, and he appears to have been a deputy officer of some kind during that period (see entry *951*); like the Clarkes he, too, was ultimately to serve as an alderman of the borough and as mayor.[101] None of the searchers' books for 1610–14, however, has survived.

Conclusion

Even allowing for the fact that we must be both careful and cautious in using port books as a basis for any kind of statistical work on patterns of trade (they perhaps yield 'figures' rather than proper statistics), they still remain invaluable sources for the commercial history of the periods for which they survive. Those for the times when customs farming was in operation may be more revealing and reliable than others, while more prosperous and profitable conditions probably resulted in the recording of a significantly greater amount of legitimate trade than times of depression, and the port books in this volume meet both of these criteria. Even though they can only ever be a starting point for the investigation of merchant activity and business organisation, we can nevertheless derive from them a general picture of the shipping and the goods involved in overseas trade, and the names of at least some of those

---

[97] Not found in the Calendar to the Fine Rolls, but his appointment is recorded in the *Calendar of State Papers Domestic, 1611–1618*, p. 227.

[98] Also not found in the Calendar to the Fine Rolls, but the appointment of a John Williamson to the controllership of *Lyme* Regis on 16 January 1619 is recorded in the *CSPD, 1619–1623*, p. 5. The name of the port must be a misreading for Lynn Regis, a not uncommon mistake.

[99] TNA PRO IND 1/17351, p. 433. He was admitted to the freedom of the borough in 1613–14 by apprenticeship to Alderman Matthew Clarke – see *Appendix 2.A*.

[100] TNA PRO IND 1/17351, pp. 243 (Clarke) and 394 (Maxey). See also *CSPD, 1619–1623*, p. 149, for Maxey's appointment in succession to Clarke.

[101] See *Appendix 2.A*.

who were active in commercial operations. There is still plenty of evidence
to work on here.

THE KING'S LYNN PORT BOOKS
1610–1614

E190/433/13: Customer: Christmas 1610 – Christmas 1611

f. 1r
Outwardes
The 29 day of *Decembris* [*sic*] 1610
[1] In *le* William of Kercaudie[1] *predict'*
William Lassells, 4 lastes malte and 8 tonnes of beere   £6 13s 4d

Quarto die Januarii 1610
[2] In *le* Harte of Flushinge[2]
Adrian Martynson alien, 24 lastes and sixe combes of barley   £20 5s 0d

The 15 day
[3] In *le* Fortune of Snetcham[3]
Thomas Creamer alien[4], nyne lastes and eight combes of barly   £6 5s 4d
More three tonnes of beere   £1 10s 0d

The 18 day
[4] In *le* William of Hitcham[5]
Frauncis Guibon, 13 lastes and 18 coombes barles [*sic*]   £9 5s 4d

The 28 day
[5] In *le* Cocke of Flushinge
Jarratt Nabbs, master, alien, 7 lastes and 12 coombes hempseeds,
halfe a hundred sheeps lether tawed   £4 15s 11¼d

The 31 day
[6] In *le* Emanuell of Kercaudie
James Fillin, master, Scott, 40 *C* wheight of barke and three
tonnes of beere   £1 12s 4d

[7] In *le* Thornback of Flushinge *predict'*
Adrian Absollon alien, 5 lastes and 14 combes barlley   £4 15s 0d

Primo die Februarii 1610
[8] In *le* Guifte of Lynne *predict'*
John Wallis *ind'*, 3 lastes and tenn combes of barley   £15 13s 4d

The 4 day
[*9*] In *le* William & John of Black[*eney*][6]
Thomas Fairefax, 18 lastes and 4 combs wheat, and sixe lastes
of barly   £22   4s   0d

f. 1v
The 12 day of *Februarii* 1610
[*10*] In *le* Griffen of Dordreight[7] *predict'*
John Wallis inds [*sic*], 7 lastes and a halfe of hempseed   £3   15s   0d
Cornellius Clawson, master, alien, 18 lastes of barley   £15   0s   0d

[*11*] In *le* Annes of St Marttyns[8]
Elias Dowsnett *ind'* *, 13 lastes *et di'* of barlley   £11   5s   0d

The 16 day
[*12*] In *le* David of Pettywembs[9]
Robert Wallis, 23 lastes and a *di'* of wheat and sixe lastes of beanes £27   10s   0d

The 18 day
[*13*] In *le* Charittie of Creylle[10]
John Otter, master, Scott, 5 tonnes of beere, 2 *C* sheeps lether
tawed and 2 quarters of pease entred the 12 of February[11]   £2   17s   0d

The 22 day
[*14*] In *le* Elizabeth of Lynn
John Greene *ind'*, 18 lastes and tenn combes barlley and mallt   £12   6s   8d

The 23 day
[*15*] In *le* Barbara of Lynne
Robert Hayes, master, inds, 8 whitte shorte clothes, 20 northen
kers[*ey*]s, 14 lastes and sixteene combes of barlley   £14   15s   1½d

The 26 day
[*16*] In *le* Margerry of Amstrother[12]
Andrew Smyth, master, 5 tonnes and a halfe of beere, 5 *C* barrels
of hopps   £2   15s   6d

[*17*] In *le* Joye of Amstrother
William Burnntside, 6 tonnes and 5 barrels of beere and 4 *C*
barrels of hopps   £3   8s   9d

The 28 day
[18] In le William Bonaventure de Leith
Archball Gibson, master, Scott, 3 tonnes of beere   £1 19s 0d

The 27 [sic] day
[19] In le Guifte of Burneham predict'
John Tayllor, 16 lastes & 3 coombes barlley   £10 15s 4d

[20] In le Barbara of Lynne, Robert Hayes master
The master ind', 20 northen k[ersey]s, 20 hamshire & northen
k[ersey]s, 24 shorte clothes   £8 0s 0d

The 18 [sic] day
[21] In le Judeth of Lynne
John Robson, 22 lastes and 7 combes barley   £14 18s 0d

f. 2r
Primo die Martii
[22] In le Clemence of Lynne predict'
Franncis Guibon inds, 16 lastes and 5 combes of barlley   £10 16s 8d

Quinto die
[23] In le Diamonnd of Burnham
Robert Dr[e]wry, 14 lastes and 18 coombes of barlley   £9 18s 8d

Sexto die
[24] In le John of Wells predict'
Henry Congham, master, 16 lastes and 4 coombes of barlley   £10 16s 0d

Septimo die
[25] In le Blessinge of Concra'[13]
Thomas Marchellory, 30 quarters of barley, 8 tonnes of beere,
more halfe a tonne of beere   £5 12s 9d

The 9 day
[26] In le Anne of Lynne predict'
Jarvic[e] Whartton inds, 7 combes barlley meale, 7 combes white
pease, 13 combes barlley, one laste of rye, 2 lastes et di' of malte,
3 tonnes of beere, 5 C wheight of unwrought iron, di' a way
Spanish salt, 2 C wheight et di' of Flemish hopps, 2 dossens
et di' shorte kersey stockings and 4 C wheight of unwrought iron   £5 3s 0d

The 11 day
[*27*] In *le* Swann of Camphire[14]
John Gallanc, master, alien, 9 lastes 10 combes of barlley   £7 18s   4d

The 13 day
[*28*] In *le* Mary Katherine *predict'*
Andrew Masterton, master, 4 loads of oaken tymber, 6 tonnes of beere £2 17s   7d

The 14 day
[*29*] In *le* Mary Katherine
John Gray inds, 3 tonnes of beere   £1 10s   0d

The 15 day
[*30*] In *le* Fortune of Lynn *predict'*
Erassmus Coates[15] alien, *di'* a tonne of beere, 2 *di*[16] shorte cloths,
one waye of Spanish salt, 23 gallons aquavite, 12 dozen horsseshooes,
2 barrels rye meale, 25 goads of cottons   [*no sum given*]

f. 2v
The 17 day of *Marcii* 1610
[*31*] In *le* John of Colchester *predict'*
Gabriell Myles inds, 7 lastes and 8 coombes of malte   £4 18s   8d

The 18 day
[*32*] In *le* Jane of Scarborough
Christopher Reade, 17 lastes and 4 coombes of barlley   £11 9s   4d

[*33*] In *le* Katherin of Lynn *predict'*
Franncis Guibon, 16 last and 12 combes of barlye   £11 1s   4d

The 27 of Marche
[*34*] In *le* Delight of Hitcham *predict'*
Ralphe Hargatte, 14 last 18 combes barlye
more 1 last barly, 2 tons of beere   £11 12s   0d

[*35*] In *le* Clement of Lynne *predict'*
Henery Robinson, 17 last 2 combs of barlye   £11 8s   0d

The 29 of March
[*36*] In *le* Nightingale of Flushinge *predict'*
John Greene *ind'*, 8 last 4 combes of barlie   £5 9s   4d

[37] In *le* Night [*sic*] of Flushinge *predict'*
Adrian Dansker alie[n], 5 last and nine combes of barlie   £4 10s 10d

The 30 of March
[38] In *le* Fortune of Lynne *predict'*
Robarte Coolte *ind'*, 2 shorte clothes in remnantes, 20 goades of
cotten , one Bridgwater read[17]   18s   4d

The second of Aprill
[39] In *le* Rose of Burnham *predict'*
Robart Drewrye, 14 last 12 combes barlie   £9 14s   8d

f. 3r
The thirde of Aprill
[40] In *le* John of Lynne *predict'*
John Atkine *ind'*, 10 last and five combes of barlie   £6 16s   8d

The same day
[41] In *le* Grayhound of Roterdam *predict'*
Simon Johnsone alie[n], 18 last and 10 combes of barlie   £15 7s   4d

The fourth of Aprill
[42] In *le* Angell of Breame[18] *predict'*
John Addamsone, 13 tone and a *di'* of beere   £6 15s   0d

The same day
[43] In *le* Guifte of Lynne *predict'*
John Taylor, 16 last 3 combes of barlie   £10 15s   4d

The 6 of Aprill
[44] In *le* Angell of Amstrother
William Ellysone *ind'*, 4 penistones, 20 yardes of penistone frized,
17 yardes of bridgwaters and 16 yardes of broad clothe, 50 yardes
of holmes[19] fustian, 6 felte hattes   £1   6s 10½d

The 19 [*sic*]
[45] In *le* William of Hicham *predict'*
Francis Guibon, 13 last 7 combes of barly   £8 18s   0d

The same day
[46] In *le* Diamonde of Burneham *predict'*
Thomas Wattes, 14 last and 16 combes of barlie   £9 17s   4d

The 10 of Aprill
[*47*] In *le* Unitie of Burnham *predict'*
Clement Hoe, 23 last of barlye   £15   6s   8d

The 15 day
[*48*] In *le* Fortune of Dordreighte *predict'*
John Wainford, 7 last 10 combes barlye   £5   0s   0d

f. 3v
The same day
[*49*] In *le* Flyinge Harte of Roterdam *predict'*
Gabriell Myles and John Tendringe Inglish, 14 lastes and 15 combes
of barlie   £9   16s   8d

[*50*] In *le* Swan of Camphere *predict'*
John Gallannce alie[*n*], 8 last 6 combs barly   £6   15s   10d

The same day
[*51*] In *le* George of Lynne *predict'*
John Perkins *ind'*, three last of maulte, five tone of beere, one
hogshead of veniger   £4   10s   7d

The 16 of Aprill
[*52*] In *le* Dolphin of Lynne *predict'*
Thomas Snellinge, 2 thowsannd of seasioned blacke conyskins,
12 *C* blacke rabit skins, thirteen *C* gray conieskins tawed,
4 *C* tawed catskins, 24 foxskins, nine rawe otter skins   £3   17s   6½d
The ship master and companie, 8 *C* of sheepeleather   12s   0d
William Atkine, one thowsannd sheepeleather   15s   0d
Thomas Snellinge, 32 thowsand of gray conieskins seasioned,
35 thowsand gray conie stagers,[20] three thowsand 6 *C* of mortkins
untawed, more 18 *C* and a *di'* of sheepe and lambsleather tawed,
one last of somer herringes shotten   £10   14s   9d

The 29 of Aprill
[*53*] In *le* Fortune of Flushinge *predict'*
Dericke Fredricksone, 8 last 2 combes barlye   £16   15s   0d

[*54*] In *le* Fortune of Dordrighte *predict'*
Simon Jonsone alie[*n*], 23 last five combes barly   £19   7s   6d

[*55*] In *le* Guifte of Burneham *predict'*
Jo[*h*]n Taylor, 16 last 3 combes barlye   £10   15s   4d

The first of May
[56] In *le* Emanuell of Kircaudye *predict'*
John Staffourd, 6 tone of beere   £3   0s   0d

[57] In *le* Blew Lion of Breame *predict'*
John Jacobson alie[n], 75 last of maulte   £62 10s   0d
                                                                  [*sic*]

f. 4r
The same day
[58] In *le* Cocke of Flushinge *predict'*
Jarrett Nabes alie[n], 7 last 12 combes barlye   £7   1s   4d

The third of May
[59] In *le* Mary Katherin *predict'*
Andrew Mrasterton [*sic*] *ind'*, 24 tones of beere   £12   0s   0d
John Fargoson, 20 *C* of mortlambskins, 1 *C* of white leather tawed   9s   0d

The 7 of May
[60] In *le* Grace of God of Kircaudye *predict'*
John Cuisen *ind'*, three tone of beere   £1 10s   0d

The 7 of May
[61] In *le* Griffin of Dordreighte *predict'*
Simon Johnsone alie[n], 23 last five combes of barlie and maulte,
more 12 combs barly   £19 17s   6d

The 8 of May
[62] In *le* Barbary [*sic*] of Lynn *predict'*
Robarte Hayes, 16 last of hempeseede   £8   0s   0d

The 11 of Maye
[63] In *le* William of Hitcham *predict'*
Francis Guibon, 11 last 4 combes barlye   £7   9s   4d

[64] In *le* Swan of Camphere *predict'*
John Gallannce alie[n], 8 last 6 combes barly   £6 15s 10d

The 15 day
[65] In *le* Elizabeth Katherine *predict'* of Lynne
Edward Russell & company, 3 tone of beere   £1 10s   0d

The 24 of May
[66] In *le* Jacob of Kircaudye *predict'*
David Ballfourd, 12 tone of beere   £6   0s   0d

The 8 of June
[*67*] In *le* Mary Katherine *predict'*
Andrew Masterton, thre[*e*] tone and a *di'* beere   £1 15s 0d

f. 4v
The 10 of June
[*68*] In *le* Cocke of Flushinge *predict'*
Garrat Nabs, 3 lastes 6 combes hempeseed and lynseede   £2 1s 3d

[*69*] In *le* Fortune of Flushinge *predict'*
Cornelius De Wilde, five last fifteene combes hempeseed and linseed,
27 *C* of oyle cakes, more halfe a last of seedes   £3 5s 2d

The 19 of June
[*70*] In *le* John of Lynn *predict'*
William Atkyn, 69 barrelles of beere, besides the allowance   £5 15s 0d

[*Change of hand*][21]
The 9 of July
[*71*] In *le* Cocke of Fl[*ushing*] *predict'*
Garratt Nabbs Inglish[22], 8 lastes of hempeseede   £4 0s 0d
Nicholas Ashwood, 4 *C* wheight of horsehaier and 12 tonns rape oyle   14s 0d

The 26 day
[*72*] In *le* Guift of God of Kircaudy *predict'*
William Atkin, 8 tonns of beere   £4 0s 0d

The 3 of August
[*73*] In *le* Emanuell of Kircaudy *predict'*
James Fellen Inglish, one tonn of beere   10s 0d

[*74*] In *le* Barbara of Lynn *predict'*
Roger Scarbrough *predict'*,[23] 9 clothes containing 28 yardes per
cloth' and two k[*ers*]is, 4 *M* 6 *C* of sheepe & lambes lether tawed,
16 combes of hempseede, 9 dornix coverliddes   £8 4s 8d

The 14 of August
[*75*] In *le* Mary Katherin *predict'*
The master Inglish, 3 tonnes of beare   £1 10s 0d

The 20 of August
[*76*] In *le* Cocke of Fl[*ushing*] *predict'*
Cornelius De Wyld, 6 lastes 5 combes hempseed   £3 2s 6d

The 27 day
[77] In *le* Grace of God of Kircaudy
James Browne Inglish, 5 tonns of beere   £2 10s 0d

f. 5r
The 6 of September 1611
[78] In *le* Fortune of Lynn *predict'*
Gervis Wharton, 6 *C* wheight of Inglish waxe   10s 0d
6 nor[*thern*] k[*ers*]is and twoe shorte clothes   £1   7s 4d

[79] In *le* Peter of Fleland[24] *predict'*
Cornelius De Wyld, 3 lastes 15 combes rapeseede, 20 *C* smale oyle
cakes, 30 groce oyle cakes, 60 pare of worsted stockinges, 3 tonns
and a *di'* of beare   £4 10s 0d

The 19 of September
[80] In *le* Jacob of Kircaudy *predict'*
David Balfourd Inglish, 9 tonns of beere   £4 10s 0d
Thomas Cowey Inglish, 3 tonns of beere   £1 10s 0d

The 25 day
[81] In *le* Margrett of Kircaudy *predict'*
Archbald Davison, 15 tonns of beere   £7 10s 0d

The 8 of October
[82] In *le* Pellican of Aberdyn *predict'*
Archbald Davison, 12 tonns of beere   £6   0s 0d

[83] In *le* Mary Katherin *predict'*
Andrew Masterston, 17 tonns of beere   £8 10s 0d

The 18 day
[84] In *le* John of Kircawdy *predict'*
William Wyth, tenn tonns of beere, more twoe tonns of beere   £6   0s 0d

[85] In *le* Guift of God of Kirkawdy *predict'*
John Masterton, 24 tonns of beere   £12 0s 0d

The 11 November
[86] In *le* Mary Ann of Lynn
Sterman Bird, 18 tonns of beere   £9   0s 0d

The 21 [*sic*]
[*87*] In *le* Elizabeth of Aberdynn *predict'*
Thomas Perry, 7 tonns of beere   £3   10s   0d

[*88*] In *le* Blessing of Amstrother *predict'*
John Gibsonn, 12 tonns and a *di'* of beere   £6   10s   0d

[*89*] In *le* Prescilla of Lynn *predict'*
Arnold Fydew, 2 *C* and a *di'* of wax, *di'* 1 *C* Norwaye deales   15s   7½d

f. 5v
The 5 of December 1611
[*90*] In *le* Mary Catherin of Kircaudy *predict'*
David Ballfourd, 4 tonns of beere   £2   0s   0d

The 16 of December
[*91*] In *le* Pidgeon of Rotterdam *predict'*
Cornelius De Wyld Inglish, one last 12 combes hempeseede,
15 hundred of oyle cakes and 1 *C* wheight of feathers,
15 *C* smale oyle cakes   £1   4s   6d

[*92*] In *le* Fortune of Hambro[*ugh*][25] *predict'*
The master, 18 *C* of Norway deales   £5   12s   6d

[*93*] In *le* Promised Land of Encuson[26] *predict'*
The master alien, 7 wayes and a *di'* Spanish salte, and *di'* a last of
full white herringes   17s   6d

[*94*] In *le* Fortune of Hambro[*ugh*] *predict'*
The master alien, tenn tonnes of beere   £5   0s   0d

f. 6r   [*Blank*]
f. 6v   [*Blank*]
f. 7r
Inwardes [*in original hand*]
The 29 day of *Decembris* 1610
[*95*] In *le* Hunter of Dorte[27], Petter Williamson master from Dortt
Symon Johnson alien, 18 waies Spanish salt, 4 *C* pottes cast uncovered,
one laste of large quernne stoones, 15 *C* wheight reisonns of the sonne,
2 *C et* 4 quarters wheight whitte suger, 25 p[*iece*]s of Malliga[28] reisons,
7 *C* wheight and a *di'* of hoppes   £4   13s   6d

Secundo die Januarii 1610
[*96*] In *le* Guifte of Wells
John Lane master inds, 18 waies Spanish salt allowed unto this merchaunt   nill
More 2 barrels great bonnd tarr, 6 barrels small bond pitche,
11 *C* wheight of cable yarne   8s   9d

The 16 day
[*97*] In *le* Emanuell of Kirca[*ldy*]
James Fillin, master, Scott, 26 waies white salt, 54 ells lynnen cloth   £1   16s   1d

The 30 day
[*98*] In *le* William Bonaventure
Rowland Bradforthe inds, 2 tonnes of prounes   £1   0s   0d

Quinto die Januarii [*sic*] 1610
[*99*] In *le* Charity of Creeile
John Otter, master, Scott, 8 lastes and 9 barrells of herrings, 20 barrells
of codfishe, one barrells [*sic*] conger, 8 *C* of codfishe, 1 *C et* 3 quarters
of linges and one hundred of colefishe   £4   3s   7d

[*100*] In *le* Blessinge of Conrac'[29]
Thomas Mackel Roye, 32 waies of whitte salt, 2 *C* yards of tickinge,
2 *C* wheight of Scottish yarne and 32 ells of lynnen cloth   £2   11s   3½d

f. 7v
The 11 of *Februarii* 1610
[*101*] In *le* Robert of Welles, Robert Leeche master
The master inds, halfe a hundred of Luckes[30] coales, 20 *C* of cables
and tarred roopes   17s   4d

The 15 day
[*102*] In *le* William of Kercaudie
John Graye, 40 waies white salte, 3 *C* ells of lynnen cloth,
80 *li'* wheight of Scottish yarne   £3   3s   1d

The 16 day
[*103*] In *le* Joy of Amstrother
William Burntsyde Scott, 7 lastes & a halfe of whitte herringes, 2 lastes
of great bonnd tarr, 4 barrels coddfishe and 40 ells of lynnen cloth   £2   7s   10d

The 18 day
[*104*] In *le* Margery of Amstroth[*er*]
Andrew Smyth, master, nyne lastes white herringes, one laste of
coddfishe   £2   13s   0d

The 19 day
[105] In *le* Mary Katherine *predict'*
Andrew Masterton, master, 4 waies whitte salte, 90 yards of tickinge,
1 *C* 20 elles of lynnen cloth, *di'* a *C* wheight of yarne   £3   2s   6d

[106] In *le* Diamound of Burnham *predict'*
Richard Barrett inds, 1 *C* [*?weight*] *et di'* of Luckes cooles   12s   0d

The 22 day
[107] In *le* Unity of Burneham
Clemen[t] Hoo inds, 5 *M* of brickstoones, 4 *C* pavinge tyles, halfe a
hundred of Norway deales, 2 barrells small bond tarr, 52 reams
printinge or coppie paper, one thowsand of thacke tyle[31]   10s   6½d

The 28 day
[108] In *le* Guifte of Lyme [*sic*] *predict'*
John Wallis inds, 10 *C* wheight of cable and sixe halfe chestes of
Renish glasses   14s   2d

Septimo die Martii 1610
[109] In *le* Swann of Camphire
John Gallanc, master, alien, 8 *C* of colefishe, 2 *C* wheight of hopps   11s   10½d

[110] In *le* Alice of Welles
John Greene inds, 6 *C* wheight of muscouathoes [*sic*] sugar   £1   0s   0d

f. 8r
The 12 day of *Martii* 1610
[111] In *le* Grace of God of Cattens[32]
Edward [*blank*], master, Scott, one laste of whitte herringes   2s   6d

The 18 day
[112] In *le* Greyhound of Rotterd[*am*]
Simon Johnson alien, 22 waies of Spanish salt   £1   16s   8d

[113] In *le* Elizabeth of Lynne *predict'*
John Wormell, 18 waies Spanish salt, 26 *C* wheight of corke,
18 *C* wheight of whitte muskavadoes sugers   £4   7s   0d

The 21 day
[114] In *le* Angell of Amstr[*other*][33]
John Addamson, 2 *C* wheight of yarnne, 1 *C* 60 ells of lynnen cloth,
9 score yards of tickinge, tenn skore quishones, 7 bedd coverings, one

needleworke carpett, one vallennce of a bedd, 96 ells of lynnen cloth,
2 *C* and 3 quarters of Norway deales, 20 pounds gunpowder and one
laste of greate bonnd tarr £2 4s 7½d

[*115*] In *le* Fortune of Dorte *predict'*
Symond Johnson, 7 *C* bundles of browne paper, one laste small
querne stoones, one hundred and a halfe of Luckes cooles,
30 *C* wheight of roopes, one copper still, one barrel of soape and
one barrell of ottmeale £4 10s 7½d

The first of Aprill
[*116*] In *le* Barbara of Lynn
Robarte Hayes, 8 *C* and a *di'* of clapholte, 4 cheest of Rhenishe
grasses [*sic*], 1 *C* bundles of browne paper, 30 cakes of rossen,
3 fagottes steele *vocat* longe steele whainge 2 *C* and a *di'* wheight,
4 *M* 5 *C* wheight of cordage, 2 *C* wheight of candle weeke,
30 poundes of nuttmegges & 18 po[*u*]ndes of maces £3 6s 7d

f. 8v
The same day
[*117*] In *le* Hope of Breame *predict'*
George Poppye alien, 5 *C* Norwaye deales, 6 wayes of Renishe glasse,
3 *C* wheight of course flaxe undrest £2 12s 10d

[*118*] In *le* John of Welles *predict'*
Henery Congham *ind'*, 15 wayes of Spanishe salte which was allowed
him for his provision for Ilandes[34] fishing nil
More half a *C* [*?weight*] of Flemishe cooles, 1 *C* wheight of reasons
sonne, *di'* a *C* of browne paper 7[*s*] 5d

The 11 of Aprill
[*119*] In *le* Griffen of Dordreighte *predict'*
John Wallis *ind'*, 20 milstones, 2 *C* wheight of anisseedes, three reames
of coppie paper £3 5s 0½d
Simon Jonsone alien, thre[*e*] milstones, *di'* a laste of greate
quernestones, 1 laste of smale quernestones, 1 *C* of Norway deales,
1 peace of Holland clothe, 1 featherbedd ticke £1 0s 2d

The 20 of Aprill
[*120*] In *le* Emanuell of Kircaudye *predict'*
James Fellen, 20 chalders of seacooles, more tenn chalder *per*
poest entry £1 0s 0d

[*121*] In *le* Mary Katherin of Kircaudye *predict'*
Andrew Masterton, 30 waye of white salte, more 6 wayes white salte,
1 combe of wheate £2 16s 2d

The 24 day
[*122*] In *le* Cocke of Flushinge *predict'*
Jarratt Nabs alie[n], 10 wayes of Spanish salte, one chest white
Burgandy glasse, 10 *C* wheight tarred ropes £1 7s 6d

f.9r
The 26 of Aprill
[*123*] In *le* Clemence of Lyme [*sic*] *predict'*
Jo[h]n Robson, one pece of blacke serege, 1 dozen of velvet laces,
6 ownces of Venis gold and silver, thre[e] po[u]nd and a *di'* of sisters
threed[35], 1 *C* thirtie and eight yeardes of bone lace 11s 0½d
The shipmaster, 2 *di'* chestes of Burgandy glasse and 28 yardes of
tickinge 2s 11d

The thirde of Maye
[*124*] In *le* Grace of God of Kircaudye *predict'*
John Cussen, 24 wayes of white salte, *di'* a *C* yardes of tickinge,
50 elles of lynen cloth £2 15s 4½d

The 6 day
[*125*] In *le* Caine and Abell *predict'*
Simon Jonsone alie[n], 5 thowsand Norwaye deales, more 8
C Norwaye deales *per* a poest entry £18 2s 6d

The 11 of May
[*126*] In *le* Swan *de* Camphere *predict'*
John Greene, 2 wayes and a *di'* of Spanishe salte 3s 4d

The 15 of May
[*127*] In *le* Neptune of Hambrow *predict'*
Walter Cornellis alie[n], 8 *C* Norwaye deales, more 20 *C* Norwaye
deales, more 4 *C* and a *di'* of Norway deales *per* a poest entry £10 3s 1d

The same day
[*128*] In *le* Grayhound of Roterdam *predict'*
Simon Johnsone alie[n], 3 *C* Norwaye deales, 3 *C* bundles of browne
paper, 2 *C* cast of pottes uncovered, 1 *C* and a *di'* of Luke cooles £2 9s 4½d

The 16 day
[*129*] In *le* Jacob *de* Kircaudye *predict'*
David Balfourd, 20 chalders of cooles & 40 yardes of tickinge   14s 8d

f. 9v
The 23 day of May
[*130*] In *le* Angell *de* Amsterdam *predict'*
Stephen Zelley *ind'*, 21 *C* of Norway deales, 50 balkers[36] containing
1 *C* and a *di'* feete, 60 capranens[37], 80 bome sparres, 1 *C* and a *di'* of
sparrs   £5 10s 4d

[*131*] In *le* Grufte [*sic*] of Burneham *predict'*
John Spurne, 1 *C* and a *di'* of Lukes cooles, *di'* a *C* of cant spars, *di'* a
C of Norwaye deales, 4 Turney tyckes for fetherbeddes   19s 4d

[*132*] In *le* Rose of Burneham *predict'*
Richard Goulder *ind'*, 2 *C* of Lukes cooles   16s 0d

The same day
[*133*] In *le* Margaret *predict'*
David Anderson, 20 wayes of white salte, more 6 wayes of white salte,
16 quarters of wheate, and three score yardes of tickinge   £2 2s 0d

The 29 of May
[*134*] In *le* Ann of Lyne *predict'*
Jarvac[*e*] Wharton, 22 *C* Norwaye deales, five fathum of firrewode   £5 11s 3d

[*135*] In *le* Cocke of Flushinge *predict'*
Jarrett Nabs, five wayes of baye salte   6s 3d

[*136*] In *le* Nightingale of Akerslote[38] *predict'*
Clawse Cornellisone, master,
Thomas Swan *ind'*, 50 last of Danske rye   £6 5s 0d

[*137*] In *le* Mghtingale [*sic*] of Ankerslott *predict'*
Clawse Cornellisone alie[*n*], 6 last smale band pitche, 34 boate oares,
28 wainescotes   18s 7½d

The first of June
[*138*] In *le* Guifte of God of Dunde[*e*] *predict'*
James Smithe, 6 last of wheate   £1 0s 0d

The thirde of June
[*139*] In *le* Mary Katherin *predict'*
Andrew Masterton, 20 chalders of cooles, 1 last and a *di'* of wheate   18s   4d

f. 10r
The 4 of June
[*140*] In *le* Barbarra of Lynne *predict'*
Robarte Hayes and company, 57 pound of pepper, 4 *li'*
of mase, 57 *li'* of ginger, 19 poundes of cloves, 6 pond of sinomon,
19 pond nutmeges, 1 *C* 6 *li'* fine sewgar, 1 dozen of houreglasses,
60 pond of sewgar, more 30 pond of sewgar, 1 *C* 6 bundles browne
paper & 2 reames white paper, 2 *C* cast pottes uncoverd, 6 *C* clapholte,
2 last of greate band pitche, 2 thousand of walenuttes, 29 *li'* of peper,
19 pond of sinomon, 9 *li'* and a *di'* of maces, 10 fetherbed tickes,
9 *li'* & a *di'* of cloves   £2 19s   5d

The 7 of June
[*141*] In *le* Cicellye of Lyne *predict'*
John Bassett, 10 last of Danske rye, five last of wheate   £2   1s   8d

[*142*] In *le* Grace of God of Kircaudye *predict'*
John Cossen, 3 lastes of oates, 7 last of wheate   £1   9s   4d

[*143*] In *le* William *de* Kircaudye *predict'*
John Collyer, 30 chalders of seacooles   £1   0s   0d

[*144*] In *le* James *predict'*
John Lynsey, 30 & 6 chalders cooles, 2 waye of salte   £1   6s   8d

[*145*] In *le* Emanuell of Kircaudye *predict'*
James Fellen, 30 chalders of cooles   £1   0s   0d

[*146*] In *le* Fortune of Amsterdam *predict'*
Walter Clapham, *di'* a *C* cast of earthen pottes uncovered, 2 *C* wheight
Englyshe hopes, *di'* a *C* wheight frying pans   3s   1½d
Thomas White, 11 last of wheate, 4 last rye, 1 Danske cheest
vall[*ued*] at 10s   £3 12s   2d

The 17 of June
[*147*] In *le* Guifte of God *predict'*
William Atkin, 14 last of wheate, more 1 last and a *di'* wheate   £2 11s   8d

The 18 day
[*148*] In *le* Joane of Lyne *predict'*
Horsebrooke Myett, 9 *C* Norway deales, 12 p[*iece*]s of firre tymber,
24 smale baulkes, 4 fathom of firre wood, 2 cuttinge boardes for
showmakers   £2   8s 11d

f. 10v
The same day
[*149*] In *le* Cocke of Flushinge *predict'*
Jarrat Nabes alie[*n*], 3 lastes of meslin, more 3 combs of the same
corne, 6 waies of bay salt, 15 *C* of tarred roapes   £1 11s 6¼d

The 26 day
[*150*] In *le* Providence *de* Kircaudy
James Lawe, 55 waies of salt, 1 last Scot[*c*]h wheat   £3 16s 8d

The first of July
[*151*] In *le* Hope *de* Breame *predict'*
Jarvis Wharton, 6 *C* of Norwaye deales, 3 *M* 6 *C* 38 foote of fir
tymber, *di'* a *C* of Norway deales
[*In a different hand – to end of document*][39]   £3 15s 6d
More halfe 1 *C* of Norway deales   2s 6d

[*152*] In *le* Mary Katherin of Kircaudy *predict'*
Andrew Murton Inglish, 20 chalders of coales, one last of wheate
and *di'* a last of oates   17s 8d
John Tate Inglish, 4 *C* of yarne, 3 dosin and a *di'* of cusheons   6[s] 9d
James Mellin, 5 hundred elles of Sco[*t*]ch cloth   15s 0d
Archebould Davison, 1 *C* wheight of yarne, 4 *C* elles of lynnen cloth 12s 0d
Cuthbert Urynn, 7 *C* elles of lynnen cloth   £1   1s 0d
Edward Hartley, 5 *C* elles and a *di'* of lynnen cloth   16s 6d

The second of July
[*153*] In *le* Seahorse *predict'*
Lewes Hope Inglish, 8 *C* Norway deales, 6 *C* smale spars, tenn smale
mastes for shipps, 36 smale balkers, 20 boate oares, *di'* 1 *C* of
Norway deales   £3   4s 7½d

[*154*] In *le* Guift of God of Kircawdy *predict'*
William Atkin, *di'* a last of wheate   1s 8d

The 5 of July
[*155*] In *le* George of Lynn *predict'*
John Perkin, 4 *M* Norway deales   £10   0s   0d

[*156*] In *le* John of Blackney *predict'*
William Girdlston, *di'* a tonn of fish oyle   3s   0d

[*157*] In *le* William of Kircaudy *predict'*
John Collyer Inglish, 40 wayes of salt   £2 13s   4d

[*158*] In *le* Guift of God of Kircaudy *predict'*
James Balkanquill, 36 wayes of salt   £2   8s   0d

f. 11r
The 6 of July
[*159*] In *le* Jacob of Kircaudy *predict'*
David Balfourd Inglish [*sic*], 9 lastes wheat, 4 wayes of white salt   £1 15s   4d

[*160*] In *le* Grace of God of Kircaudy *predict'*
John Cuisen, 8 lastes of oates, twoe lastes & a *di'* oatemeale,
1 *C* elles of Sco[*t*]ch cloth, 6 combes of oatemeale   £2 16s   4d
More twoe lastes of oates   4s   0d

The 10 of July
[*161*] In *le* William of Lynn *predict'*
Henery Violett, one tonn & a barrel of fish oyle   7s   0d

[*162*] In *le* Jacob of Kircaudy *predict'*
David Balfourd, one way of white salt   1s   4d

The 19 day
[*163*] In *le* John of Kinghorne[40] *predict'*
William Atkin, 15 lastes oates, 4 lastes of oates   £1 18s   0d

[*164*] In *le* John of Lynn *predict'*
William Atkin, 7 lastes 12 combes wheat   £1   5s   4d

The 20 day
[*165*] In *le* Elizabeth Katherin *predict'*
Thomas Miller Inglish, 42 chalders of coales   £1   8s   0d

[*166*] In *le* Elizabeth Katherin *predict'*
John Pitt Inglish, 4 packes Irr[*ish*] yarne and 23 rawe cowehides   £1   5s   9d

[*167*] In *le* Grayhound of Staverne⁴¹ *predict'*
John Peterson, 1 *C* and one quarter of Norway deales, 11 *C* 60 foote
of firr timber   £1   9s   1d
John Waynfourd Inglish, 3 quarters of Norway deales, more 3 *C*
Norway deales   18s   9d
More three thowsand 4 *C* 64 foote firr timber   £2 10s   5d

The 27 day
[*168*] In *le* Emanuell of Kircady *predict'*
James Fellen, 28 chalders of coales   18s   8d

[*169*] In *le* Thomas of Lynn *predict'*
John Hookes, one tonn and a *di'* of fish oyle   9s   0d

f. 11v
The first of August
[*170*] In *le* Cicelley of Lynn *predict'*
John Leade Inglish, 15 lastes of Danske rye   £1 17s   6d
Richard Greenwood, 3 *C* and a *di'* of candlweeke and 15 chaires   2s   4d

[*171*] In *le* William of Lynn *predict'*
Thomas Feazer Inglish, 3 barrels & a *di'* of fish oyle   3s   6d

The 8 of August
[*172*] In *le* Mary Katherin *predict'*
Andrew Masterton Inglish, 20 chalders of coales   13s   4d

[*173*] In *le* Cock of Fl[*ushing*] *predict'*
Cornelius De Wyld, 4 lastes of rye, 3 lastes of maslin, one last and
a *di'* of wheate   £1   3s   9d

The 12 of August
[*174*] In *le* Mayde of Mellquerne⁴² *predict'*
Thomas Finch Inglish, 12 cagges of sturgeon and 60 water glasses   5s   3d

[*175*] In *le* Ciceley of Lynn *predict'*
Robert Bouch Inglish, dyvers petty wares   3s   2d

[*176*] In *le* Ann of Lynn *predict'*
Jarvis Wharton Inglish, 19 *C* one quarter Norway deales, *CC* [*sic*] wheight
of tallowe, one last great bonnd tarr & 2 *C* wheight of tallowe   £5 16s   3d

The 15 of August
[*177*] In *le* Providence of Kircawdy
James Lawe Inglish, 55 wayes of white salt and 14 combes of wheate £3 15s   8d

[*178*] In *le* Hollandes Mayde of Mellquerne *predict'*
John White Inglish, 13 lastes great band tarr, more 16 lastes of great
band starr [*sic*], more twoe lastes of smale band tarr, 5 lastes of great
band tarr, with many other wares   £10   0s   4d

[*179*] In *le* Grace of God of Kircaudy *predict'*
James Wyth Inglish, 25 chalders of coales and one hundreth elles of
lynnen cloth   19s   8d

f. 12r
The 18 of August
[*180*] In *le* Lyon of Lynn *predict'*
John Cockett, one cast jerfalkon, 3 terselles   5s   0d

[*181*] In *le* Peter of Fleland *predict'*
Thomas Snelling, 20 cagge girkeinges   1s   2d

The second of September
[*182*] In *le* Barbara of Lynn *predict'*
Roger Scarbrough *predict'* [*sic*], sundry smale wares   £1 15s   4d

The 19 of August
[*183*] In *le* Peter *predict'*
Thomas Snelling, 49 lastes great band pitch, 2 lastes and a *di'* smale
band tarr, 49 *C* and a *di'* clapholt, 8 lastes smale band pitch,
20 cagges girkeins[43]   £11   2s   6d

[*184*] In *le* Angell of Kircaudy *predict'*
Archbould Davison, 4 *C* elles lynnen cloth and a *di'* [*sic*]   13s   4d

[*185*] In *le* Franncis of Lynn *predict'*
Erasmus Coates, 5 *C* linges, 6 *C* coddes, 2 *C* stockfish and other
comodityes   £3   10   6½d

The 20 August
[*186*] In *le* Franncis of Lynn *predict'*
Robart Colt Inglish, 1 *C* of linges, 2 *C* of Island coddes, 1 *C* and a
di' of stockefish & other comodityes   14s   3d

[*187*] In *le* Lyon of Lynn *predict'*
Henery Ellis, 4 barrels traine oyle, one dosin of slopps   7s 3d
Edmund Pye Inglish, 4 hogsheadi [*sic*] traine oyle   4s 6d

The 3 of September
[*188*] In *le* Lyon of Lynn *predict'*
John Webster, 7 jerfalkons & 6 terselles   14s 6d

[*189*] In *le* Barbara of Lynn *predict'*
John Tayler Inglish, 127⁴⁴ poundes of pepper, 17 *li'* of sistres thridd
and other wares   [£]2 1s 10d

The 4 September
[*190*] In *le* Barbara of Lynn *predict'*
Abdy Mason, 57 brushell tiles, 3 p[*iece*]s tufted ca[*mbric*], 27 peeces
of cambr[*ic*], 8 dosin and a *di'* damaske napkins, 16 damaske napkins,
44 p[*iece*]s cambr[*ic*] and other wares   £13 16s 3d

f. 12v
The 4 of September
[*191*] In *le* Jacobb of Kircaudy *predict'*
David Ballfourd Inglish, 24 way whitsalt, more 5 wayes and 1 *C* elles
of lynnen cloth   £1 16s 3d

[*192*] In *le* Pellican of Aberdynn *predict'*
Patricke Guerdon *predict'* [*sic*], 4 *C* Norway deales, 3 lastes & a *di'* of
great band tarr, 6 barrels of smale nuttes, one barrel and a *di'* of
traine oyle   £1 14s 8d

[*193*] In *le* Mary Catherin of Lynn *predict'*
Andrew Masterton, 40 wayes of salt   £2 13s 4d
Alexander Nicolles, 13 *C* 60 elles Sco[*t*]ch cloth   £2 0s 6d
Franncis Maye Inglish, 1 *C* elles Scotch cloth   3s 0d
More 15 elles of Slecia⁴⁵ cloth   5½d

The 7 of October
[*194*] In *le* Grace of God of Kircawdy
John Marchaunt, 35 wayes white salt   £2 6s 8d

[*195*] In *le* John of Kircaudy *predict'*
William Williamson, 30 wayes whitsalt, 1 *C* 60 elles of lynnen cloth   £2 4s 6d

The 28 [sic]
[196] In le William of Kircawdy predict'
John Moore Inglish, 55 wayes of whitsalt, 20 dosins course cusheons
woven in Franns   £4   1s   4d

The 28 of October
[197] In le Blessing of Amstrother predict'
John Gibson Inglish, 4 C one quarter Norway deales, 1 C wheight
Sco[t]ch yarne, 8 score 8 elles of Sco[t]ch cloth, 1 C of dryed codd
and one Sco[t]ch coveringe   £1 11s   2½d

The 11 of November
[198] In le Elizabeth of Aberdynn predict'
Thomas Perry Inglish, 10 barrels of somer herringes, 2 C of colefish,
12 C of Sco[t]ch coall, 5 barrels of barrel fish   £2   8s   8d

[199] In le William of Kircaudy predict'
John Moore Inglish, 6 wayes of whitsalt   8s   0d

[200] In le Presella of Lynn predict'
John Younge, 4 C wheight of French proins[46]   2s   0d

f. 13r
The 23 of November 1611
[201] In le Mary Katherin of Kircawdy predict'
David Ballfourd Inglish, 42 wayes of white salt   £2 16s   0d

The 25 of November
[202] In le Emanuell of Kircaudy
James Fellen, 30 chalders of coales   £1   0s   0d

[203] In le Providence of Kircawdy predict'
William Atkin, 15 puncheons of proins, di' a tonn of French honny[47] £3   6s   4½d

[204] In le Pidgeon of Rotterdam predict'
Cornelius De Wyld, 3 lastes of rye, 17 pockett Flemish hopps,
4 di' peeces cambrickes, one last of smale querne stones, and
1 C wheight of flaxe   £3   5s   3d

[205] In le Angell of Kircawdy predict'
Robart Donckame, 44 wayes whitsalt   £2 18s   8d

The 4 of December
[206] In le Harry of Kircawdy predict'
Henery Lyle Inglish, 24 wayes of salt   £1 12s 0d

The 6 of December
[207] In le Lyonn of Lynn predict'
Robart Waters, 40 wayes Spanish salt, 28 C wheight of hopps,
5 C wheight of Iland woade   £4 3s 10d

E190/433/12: Customer : Christmas 1611 – Christmas 1612

f. 1r
/Lynn Regis
Inwardes/
The entries of all goods and marchandize brought into this porte and members
thereof from beyonde the seas for all which His Highnes subsidies, customes and im-
postes have been duely received in this porte and members therof for one whole
yere begonn at the feast of the nativity *alias* the 25 of December *anno* 1611 and
ended at the same feast next following *videlicet* 1612

The 26 daye of December 1611
[208] In the Fortune of Amsterdam [?]60 tonn, John Johnson master,
from Flushing
John Wallis *ind'* merchant, with thirtie five lastes Danske rye   £4 7s 6d

The 30 of December
[209] In the Cocke of Flushing 15 tonn, Garrard Nabbs master,
from Flushing[48]
The same Garrard alien merchant, with five waighes and a half
baye salte   5s 6d
                                                                      +7s 0d[49]
Foure pockettes hoppes containing 14 C waight   14s 0d
                                                                      +7s 0d
Half hundred waight batterie unwrought   18d
                                                                       +18d
Six iron potts containing eightie pounde vallued at 2d *per* pot   8d
                                          Strangers custom   5s 5d

The third of Jannuary
[210] In the Falkon of Amsterdam 50 tonn, Roger Johnson master,
from Amsterdam
Samuell Newgate *ind'* marchant, with twentie twoe waighes
Spaynish salte   29s 4d
Tenn lastes white herringes   50s 0d

The 7 of Jannuarie
[*211*] In the Marie Katherin of Kercaudie 30 tonn, David Balfore
master, from Curras[50] in Scotland

The same Davide Scot marchant, with fortie two waighes white salte	56s	0d
Three quarters wheate		12d

The 9 of Jannuarie
[*212*] In the Jacobe of Kercaudie 20 tonns, Thomas Cowey master,
from Kercaudie in Scotland

The same Thomas Scot marchant, with twentie eight waighes white salte	37s	4d

The 20 of Jannuarie
[*213*] In the Hope for Grace of Disert[51] 64 tonn, Alexander
Manck master, from Burdeux in France[52]

Rowlande Bradford *ind'* marchant, with six peeces prewnnes containing one tonn *di'* waight	15s	0d
	+7s	6d
Three tonns vinager	7s	0d
	+7s	0d

f. 1v

The 28 of Jannuarie
[*214*] In the Tomazin of Lynn 30 tonns, William Ja[r]vice master,
from Amsterdam

Roger Scarrbrough *ind'* marchant, with fiften waighes Spaynish salt	20s	0d
Twoe lastes wheate	6s	8d

The 30 of Jannuarie
[*215*] In the Sheepe of Midlbrough[53] 40 tonn, Joas Penn master,
from Midlbrough[54]

The same Joas Penn alien marchant, with five sackes hopps containing 15 *C* waight	15s	0d
	+7s	6d
Twoe punchions containing 15 *C* waight French prewnes	7s	6d
	+3s	9d
Thirtie pounde peper	2s	6d
	+2s	6d
Strangers custom	6s	3s

Eodem die
[*216*] In the [?]Sara' Ann of Lynn 50 tonns, Thomas Walker master,
from Rotterdam

Josua Greene *ind'* marchant, with nynten lastes oates	38s	0d

Twentie waighes Spaynish salte which this marchant had free of
custome for his provision for the Island fishing   nil

The thride [*sic*] of Februarie
[*217*] In the Marie Ann of Lynn 30 tonn, William Hebden master,
from Leith in Scotland
St[ur]men Burd *ind'* marchant, with three lastes oates   6s   0d

The 4 of Februarie
[*218*] In the [?]William of Kercaudie 40 tonn, John Collier master,
from Kercawdie in Scotland
The same John Collier Scot marchant, with fortie twoe waighes
white salte   56s   0d
One hundred yards course tiking at five score *per cent*   3s   4d
One hundred waight of Scottish yarne   15d

Eodem die
[*219*] In the William of Kercaudy 18 tonn, Henrie Reynoldson master,
from Curras in Scotland
The same Henrie Scot marchant, with twentie waighes white salte   26s   8d

The 6 of Februarie
[*220*] In the Harry of Kercaudie 24 tonn, Davide Wilson master,
from Kercaudie in Scotland
The same Davide Scot marchant, with sixten chalder Scottish coales 10s   8d

The 17 of Februarie
[*221*] In the Cocke of Flushing 15 tonn, Garrard Nabbs master,
from Flushing
The same Garrarde alien merchant, with foure lastes meslen *alias*
wheate and rye   11s   8d
Twoe hundred buntches onions   10d
Tenn barrells loose onions   8d
Fourten hundred waight tarrd ropes and cordage   9s   4d
Fowre bagges Flemish hopps containing 9 hundred waight   9s   0d
                                                                                 +4s   6d
                                            Strangers custom   7s 10½ d

f. 2r
The 18 of Februarie
[*222*] In the William of Kercaudie 18 tonn, Henrie Reynoldson
master, from Curras in Scotland
The same Henrie Scot merchant, *per* post entry twoe waighes white salt   2s   8d

The 19 of February
[*223*] In the Margerett of Kercaudye 24 tonn, James Simpson master, from Abberdyn in Scotland

The same James Scot marchant, with fowerten lastes oates	28s	0d
Two lastes more oates entred the 22 Februarie	4s	0d
Half a last more oates entred 26 of Februarie		12d

The 20 Februarie
[*224*] In the Thomas of Donnbarr 60 tonns, George Martin master, from Preeston[55] [in] Scotland
The same George Scot marchant, factor for one Mr Atkinson of

Donnbarr, with thirty chalders seacoles	20s	0d
Twoe baggs Flemish hopps containing 6 *C* waight	6s	0d
	+3s	0d
One hogshead mellasses	2s	6d

The 22 of February
[*225*] In the William of Kercaudie 50 tonn, John More master, from Kercaudy in Scotland

The same John More Scot merchant, with thirty chalders of seacoales	20s	0d
Three lastes *di'* oates	7s	0d
One last of wheate	3s	4d
One hundred waight Scot yarne		15d
One hundred yards tiking at five score *per cent*	3s	4d
One waigh more white salte		16d

The 24 of February
[*226*] In the Margerett of Kercaudie 25 tonn, Gilbert Omant master, from Curras in Scotland

The same Gilbert Scot merchant, with thirtie twoe ells tiking		13½d
Twentie eight waighes white salt	37s	4d
Twentie pound Scot yarne		3d
One barrell oatmeale containing two bushells *di'*		5d

The 7 of March
[*227*] In the William of Kercaudie 50 tonn, John More master, from Kercaudie in Scotland

The same John More Scot marchant, *per* post entry fowre chalders coales	2s	8d

The 12 of March
[*228*] In the Fortune of Amsterdam 50 tonns, Anthony Izerell master, from Amsterdam

The same Anthony alien merchant, with eleaven waighes Spaynish salte	14s	8d

Two lastes great bond pitch, one last great bond tarr	10s	0d
Foure waighes Reynish glasse	10s	0d
Strangers custom	8s	8d

f. 2v

[229] In the shipp last before said one hunderd Norway deales	5s	0d
Twoe pockettes Flemish hopps containing five hundred waight	5s	0d
	+2s	6d
Thirtie six pound peper and fifty pound wheight Indian ginger[56]	4s	8d
	+4s	8d
Tenn pounde maces	3s	4d
	+3s	4d
Tenn pound nuttmeggs		18d
	+18d	
Twentie seaven yards Eastcountrey tiking		11½d
Strangers custom	5s	1½d

The 19 of March
[230] In the Barrbara of Lynn 30 tonns, Robert Hayes master,
from Amsterdam[57]

The same Robert ind' merchant, one hundred [sic] Spaynish salte containing eleaven waighes di'	15s	4d
Sixtie bundles browne paper	3s	0d
	+3s	0d
Half a last of smale bonnd tarr		12d
Twelve hundred waight cordage	8s	0d
One last smale bonnd pitch	2s	0d
Entred the 24 of March more two waighes Spaynish salte	2s	8d

The 25 of March
[231] In the Marye Katherin of Kercaudie 30 tonn, David Balfore
master, from Kercaudi in Scotland

The same Davide Scot marchant, with sixten waighes white salt	21s	4d
Fortie quarters wheate	13s	4d
Six lastes oates	12s	0d
Foure quarters mault		12d
Half hundredwaight yarne		7½d
Three score ells lynen cloth		18d

The [blank] of March predict'
[232] In the Blewe Pidgeon of Amsterdam 30 tonn, Cornelius
Williamson master, from Amstredam

The same Cornelius alien merchant, with sixten lastes rye	40s	0d
Strangers custom	10s	0d

The 26 of March 1612
[*233*] In the Mary Katherin of Kercaudie 30 tonn, David Balfore
master, from Kercaudie in Scotland
Andrewe Leighton Scot merchant, with two smale trusses containing
4 *C* waight Scot yarne   5s 0d

Eodem die
[*234*] In the Jacobe of Kercaudie 24 tonns, John Cuisen master, from
Kercaudie in Scotland
The same John Cuisen Scot marchant, with twentie six waighes
white salte   34s 8d
Half hundred waight Scot yarne   7½d

The 27 of March
[*235*] In the Margerett of Kercaudie 24 tonn, William Williamson
master, from Kercaudie in Scotland
The same Williamson Scot marchant, with twentie fowre waighes
white salt   32s 0d

Eodem die
[*236*] In the Falkon of Amsterdam 50 tonn, Roger Johnson master,
from Amsterdam
Samuell Newgate *ind'* merchant, *per* post entry foure waighes
Spaynish salt   5s 4d

f. 3r
The last of March
[*237*] In the Marye Katherin of Kercaudie 30 tonn, David Balfore
master, from Kercaudy in Scotland
The same David Scot merchant, *per* post entry one last oates   2s 0d

The 16 Aprill
[*238*] In the Cocke of Flushing 15 tonn, Garrard Nabbs master,
from Flushing[58]
The same Garrard alien merchant, with two lastes messlen *alias* wheate
and rye mingled   5s 10d
Foure lastes French rye   10s 0d
Three pocketts Flemish hopps containing [*illegible*] *C* waight   5s 0d
                                                                      +2s 6d

Tenn iron potts and six iron ketles containing [*illegible*] *C* waight
valued 13s 4d *per cent*   16d
Twoe hogsheads vinager   14d
                                                                      +14d
                                          Strangers custom   5s 10d

The 20 of Aprill
[239] In the Guift of Lynn 40 tonn, Brady *alias* Robert Brady [*sic*]
master, from Amsterdam

Cornelius De Wilde *ind'* marchant, with eleaven lastes Danske rye	27s	6d
Eleaven lastes oates	22s	0d

The 22 of Aprill
[240] In the Marye Katherin of Kercaudy 30 tonns, Andrewe
Messterton master, from Kercaudie in Scotland

The same Andrewe Scot merchant, with eighten lastes oates	36s	0d
Three lastes oates more the 24 of this month entred	6s	0d

The 23 of Aprill
[241] In the Crabbe of Saredam⁵⁹ 40 tonn, Cornelius Cornelison
master, from Amstredam

Cornelius De Wilde *ind'* marchant, with twentie lastes Danske rye	50s	0d

The 24 of Aprill
[242] In the Jacobe of Kercaudy 24 tonns, John Cuisen master, from
Aymoth⁶⁰ in Scotland

The same John Scot marchant, with tenn lastes oates, two lastes barly	25s	0d

The 12 of May
[243] In the Andrewe of Sanct Andrewes 50 tonns, William Wattson
master, from Romsdale⁶¹ in Norway

The same Wattson Scot merchant with 16 *C* Norway deales	£4	0s	0d
Entred deales more [*sic*] the 14 of May after, 4 *C* Norway deales		20s	0d

The 20 of May
[244] In the Mary Katherin of Kercaudie 30 tonn, Andrewe
Messterton master, from Kercaudy in Scotland

The same Andrewe Scot merchant with eighten lastes oates and more one last *di'* entred the 22 May next after	39s	0d

The 25 of May
[245] In the Guifft of God of Disert 34 tonn, Alexander Wilkey
master, from Disert in Scotland

The same Alexander Scot merchant, with thirtie foure tonns of Scot seacoales containing 24 chalders	15s	4d

f. 3v

The first of June
[*246*] In the William of Kercaudie 56 tonns, John More master, from Curras in Scotland

The same John More Scot merchant, with thirty chalders seacoales	20s	0d
One last of oates	2s	0d

The second of June
[*247*] In the Jacobe of Kercaudy 20 tonns, John Cuisen master, from Kercaudy in Scotland

The same John Cuisen Scot marchant, with eleaven lastes oates	22s	0d
Two lastes barlie	5s	0d

The third of June
[*248*] In the Elzabeth [*sic*] of Lynn 40 tonn, Thomas Skynner master, from Amsterdam

Thomas March *ind'* marchant, with twentie nyne lastes oates	58s	0d

The 4 of June
[*249*] In the William of Kercawdy 16 tonns, Robert Donnckan master, from Kercaudy in Scotland

The same Robert Donckan Scot merchant, with twentie waighes white salt	26s	8d

The 11 of June
[*250*] In the Margerett of Kercaudie 60 tonns, John Williamson master, from Lawrwick[62] in Norway

The same Williamson Scot marchant, with sixten hundred Norway deales	£4	0s	0d

The 13 of June
[*251*] In the same shipp, master and marchant from Norway by post entry

Three hundred and a half Norway deales	17s	6d

The 22 of June
[*252*] In the Mary Katherin of Kercaudy 30 tonn, Andrewe Messterton master, from Kercaudy in Scotland

The same Andrewe Scot merchant, with fortie twoe waighes whyte salt	56s	0d
Three hundred ells Scot lynen cloth, and more one hundred ells lynen	12s	0d
Halfe a packe of Scot yarne	2s	6d

Eodem die

[*253*] In the Margerett of Kercaudie 30 tonn, David Balfore master,
from Kercaudy in Scotland

The same David marchant, with twentie six waighes white salt	34s	8d
Two hundred ells lynen cloth	6s	0d

The 23 of June

[*254*] In the Fortune of Amsterdam 50 tonn, Anthony Izerell master,
from Amsterdam

The same Anthony alien marchant, with eleaven waighes *di'*

Spaynish salt	15s	4d
Twoe lastes smale bannd pitch, one last great bonnd tarr or pitch	7s	4d
Foure hundred clapholt	3s	0d
Twoe waighes Reynish glasse	5s	0d
Strangers custom	7s	8d

Eodem die

[*255*] In the same shipp and master from Amsterdam
Robert Hayes *ind'* marchant, with[63]

Twoe lastes great bonnd tarr, twoe lastes smale bonnd pitch	10s	8d

Eodem die

[*256*] In the Martin of Lyn 80 tonn, William Morgan master, from
North Berghen[64] in Norway
Henrie Wattson alien merchant, with 9 *C* Norwaie deales, 14 *C* smale
sparrs, foure *C* 36 cant sparrs, 2 *M* band staves hoopes for caske
valued 10d *per cent*, one hundred nynty twoo foot firr tymber
valued 3d *per* foote[65]

	£4 7s	5d

f. 4r

The 25 of June

[*257*] In the Fortune of Amsterdam 50 tonns, Anthony Izerell master,
from Amsterdam
John Ditchffeild *ind'* marchant, with one butt currents containing
besides tare and all wayte[66] 7 *C* waight

	10s	6d
	+23s	4d

The 30 of June

[*258*] In the Fortune of Amsterdam *ut predict'*
Robert Thory *ind'* marchant, with two bagges currents containing
net two hundred and quarter

	3s	4½d
	+7s	6d
Foure large mapps valued at 30s		18d

The second of Jully
[259] In the Martin of Lynn *ut predict'* from North Berghen in Norway
Henry Wattson alien by post entry thirtie peeces firr tymber

containing 4 *C* nyntie foote 6 score *per cent* valued 3d *per* foote	6s	9½d
Twentie six Norwaie deales		13d
Strangers custom		23½d

The thirde of Jully
[260] In the Adventer of Warnes[67] 120 tonns, James Lewis master,
from Danske[68]

Nicholas Lynnley *ind'* marchant, with eighti and eight hundred clapholt	£3	0s	6d
Tenn cheestes Burgundy glasse		20s	0d
One hundred waynscots		8s	0d
		+8s	0d
Two barrells Spruce[69] ells		4s	0d
Fiften lastes great bonnd pitch		50s	0d
Eight lastes smale bonnd pitch		16s	0d
Eight lastes great bonnd tarr		26s	8d

The 8 of Jully
[261] In the Adventer of Warnes 120 tonns, James Lewis master,
from Danske

Nicholas Lynnley *predict'* with one last great bonnd tarr and half a last great bonnd pitch	5s	0d

The [?]9 of Jully[70]
[262] In the [?]Margerett Ann of Lynn [?]80 tonns, Richard Gittinges
master, from Danske

John Wallis *ind'* marchant, with fortie lastes Danske rye	£5	0s	0d
One thousand clapholt and half a hundred Spruce deales		15s	0d

The 14 of Jully
[263] In the John of Kercaudy 30 tonns, William Williamson master,
from Kercaudie in Scotland

The same Williamson Scot merchant, with thirtie waighes white salt	40s	0d
Foure hundred ells lynen cloth	12s	0d

The 17 of Jully
[264] In the Jacobe of Kercaudie [blank] tonns, John Cuisen master,
from Kercaudy in Scotland

The same John Cuisen Scot marchant, with twentie five waighes white salte	33s	4d

f. 4v

The 18 of Jully

[*265*] In the Margerett Ann of Lynn 80 tonn, Richard Gittinges
master, from Danske

Thomas Snelling *ind'* merchant, with seven lastes Danske rye	17s	6d
Eight hundred clapholt	6s	0d
Two hundred more clapholt freed [*in*] regard of 12 Spruce deales over entred in this shipp as *per* entry taken the 9 of this instant[71]		nil
*2 *C* waight candleweeke		16d
		+16d*

Eodem die

[*266*] In the Mary Katherin of Kercaudie 30 tonns, Andrew
Messterton master, from Kercaudy in Scotland

The same Andrewe Scot merchant, with fortie twoe waighes white salte	56s	0d

The 20 of Jully

[*267*] In the Dolphen of Lynn 55 tonn, Robert Constable master,
from Danske

Briand Loupton *ind'* merchant, with tenn lastes great bonnd pitch, five lastes smale bonnd pitch, six lasts and half great bonnd tarr	£3	5s	0d
Twoe lastes Danske rye		5s	0d
Sixten half cheestes Burrgundy glasse		16s	0d
Foure hundred clapholt		3s	0d
Fiften hundred waight undreest flax		11s	3d
Half hundred candlweeke			4d
			+ 4d

The 22 of July

[*268*] In the Margerett of Kercaudie 20 tonn, David Balfore master,
from Kercaudi in Scotland

The same David Scot marchant, with twentie twoe waighes white salte	29s	4d
Three tonns of coales		12d

Eodem die

[*269*] In the William of Kercaudie 16 tonns, Robert Donnckan
master, from Kercaudy in Scotland

The same Robert Scot marchant, with twentie waighes white salt	26s	8d
One hundred waight Scot yarne		15d
One Edward Harknes Scot marchant entred in this shipp five hundred ells lynen cloth	15s	0d

The 27 of Jully
[*270*] In the William of Lynn 70 tonns, Edmond Houckes master,
from the Island fishing
Grave Vylett *ind'* merchant, with twoe barrells *di'* of trayne oile   2s   6d

f. 5r[72]
The 29 of Jully
[*271*] In the Barrbara of Lynn [?]30 tonn, Robert Hayes master,
from Amsterdam
The same Robert *ind'* merchant, with fiften lastes Danske rye   37s   6d
One last great bonnd pitch   3s   4d

The 30 of Jully
[*272*] In the Crabbe of Saredam [?]40 tonns, Cornelius Cornelison
master, from Amsterdam
Nicholas Astwoode *ind'* marchant, with eighteen waighes bay salt   18s   0d
Foure lastes rye   10s   0d
One hundred [and] three quarters candleweeke   14d
                                                                         +14d
[*Illegible*] barrell [?]currentts containing 2 *C di'*   3s[?]9d
                                                                         +8s   4d
*Twoe [*illegible*] waighes bay salt, 10 August   2s   0d*

Eodem die
[*273*] In the same shipp and master from Amsterdam
Cornelius Cornelison alien the shipp master, with one last Danske rye   2s   6d
Five waighes bay salte and three quarters more entred 10 of August   5s   9d
One barrell c[urre]ntts [containing] one hundred three quarters   2s   3½d
                                                                         +5s   10d
                                           Strangers custom   [?]3s   7d

Eodem die
[*274*] In the Barrbara of Lynn 30 [tons], Robert Hayes master,
from Amsterdam
Peter Brenble alien marchant, with six [?pic]tures, certayne glasses
and other triffles [of] that kind [*words illegible*]   3s   0d
                                           Strangers custom   9d

The 31 of Jully
[*275*] In the Barrbara of Lynn 30 tonn [Robert Hayes master from
Amsterdam][73]
The same Roberte *ind'* merchant [*words illegible*] waight currants   6s   0d
                                                                         +13s   4d

Three peeces Holland cloth containing [*words illegible*]   5s   7d
                                                                        +5s   7d

The thirde of August
[*276*] In the Lion of Scarrbrough 40 tonns, James Moise master,
from Stavenger in Norway
Thomas Coultson *ind'* merchant, with eighteen hundred Norway
deales   £4   0s   0d

The 7 of August
[*277*] In the Lion of Lynn [*sic*] *ut predict'* [? *words illegible*]
Thomas Coultson [*illegible*] *per* post entry with [*illegible*] hundred [*?di'*]
Norway deales   12s   6d

The [?]15 of August
[*278*] In the Mary Katherin of Kercaudy 25 tonns, Andrewe
Messterton master, from Kircaudy in Scotland
The same Andrewe Scot merchant, with fortie twoe waighes white salt   56s   0d
Two hundred waighes Scot yarne   2s   6d
Three score ells Scot lynen cloth   18d

Eodem die
[*279*] In the same shipp and master from Kercaudy in Scotland
Robart Chreestie *ind'* merchant, with four hundred ells of Scotch
lynen clothe   12s   0d

f. 5v
The last of August
[*280*] In the [*illegible*] of Edam 150 tonns, Peter Claw[?son] master,
from Noremor[74] in Norway
John Peterson alien marchant, with three hundred Norway deales   15s   0d
Three score and six peeces firr tymber great and smale containing
one thousand three hundred and sixtie foot valued at 3d *per* foote   17s   0d
                                             Strangers custom   8s   0d

Eodem die
[*281*] In the Martin of Lynn 70 tonns, William Morgan master,
from Savor[75] in Norway
Jarvase Wharton *ind'* marchant, with twelve hundred of Norwaie
deales   £3   0s   0d
Thirtie three smale masts   5s   6d
One hundred cant sparres   20d

Two hundred tenn peeces firr baulkes great and smale containing
tenn hundred and fortie foote at 6 score *per cent* valued at 3d *per* foote   15s 6d
One hundred smale sparrs   12d

Eodem die
[282] In the Jacobe of Kircaudie 24 tonns, Thomas Cowey master,
from Kercaudy in Scotland
The same Thomas Scot marchant, with twentie and six waighes white
salte   34s 8d

First of September
[283] In the Thomas of Lynn 70 tonns, John Barack master, from
the Island fishing
Jason West *ind'* marchant, with three jerfalkons and three tercells   6s 6d
          +6s 6d

The seconnd September
[284] In the Simon of Lubeck 80 tonns, Micheale Clawson master,
from Danske
Thomas Snelling *ind'* marchant, with twentie six hundred clapholt   19s 6d
Twelve lastes smale bonnd pitch, twentie six lastes great bond tarr   £5 10s 8d
Three lastes great bonnd pitch   10s 0d

The thirde of September
[285] In the Guifft of Lynn 40 tonns, Robert Brady master, from
Amsterdam
John Wallis *ind'* marchant, with fiften waighes baye salt   15s 0d
Thirty foure bundles browne paper   20½d
          +20½d
Six lastes Danske rye   15s 0d
Three lastes smale bonnd pitch   6s 0d
Twoe lastes great bonnd tarr   6s 8d
Three lastes great bonnd pitch   10s 0d

Eodem die
[286] In the Simon of Lubeck 70 tonns, Michaele Clawson master,
from Danske
James Ritches *ind'* merchant, thirty bagges gerckins valued at fourten
pence *per* gerckin   21d

f. 6r
The thirde of September
[287] In the Franncis of Lynn [*illegible*] tonns, Richard Broughton
master, from the Island fishing

Henry Ellis alien marchant, with fiftie yards woadmole		22½d
Two hogsheads two barrells trayne oile	5s	0d
Three hundred stockfishe *vocat'* titling		12d
Strangers custom		23½d

The 7 of September
[288] In the Margerett Alley of Lynn 20 tonns, John Gerdleston master, from Rotterdam[76]
John Wallis *ind'* marchant with te[n] waighes Spaynish salte for which this marchant refuseth to pay custome affirming yt to be wholy for his provision for the Island fishing next to come   nil

Eodem die
[289] In the Katherin of Lynn 12 tonn, Nathaniell Scott master, from Rotterdam

The same Nathaniell *ind'* marchant, with fifty bundles browne paper	2s	6d
	+2s	6d
Seaven hundred bunches onions	2s	11d

The 7 of September
[290] In the Vyneyarde of Ipswich 120 tonns, Bartholemewe Fuller master, from Danske

Thomas Snelling *ind'* merchant, with twoe cheests and three packes containing three thousand and eightie ells hinderland lynen	40s	10d
	+20s	5d
Seaven hundred and eightie ells browne Slecia'	28s	1½d
	+28s	1½d
Twentie foure peeces Slecia' lawnes	4s	0d
	+4s	0d
Sixtie six lastes and a half Danske rye	£8 6s	3d
Thirtie five bundles Spruce hempe undreest containing fiftie eight hundred and sixtie six [?peeces]	39s	0½d
Twoe thousand 8 *C* and eightie waight [*sic*] Spruce flax unwrought	21s	6½d
The same marchant entred the sixten of September next after foure peeces silver plate parcell gilt containing 25oz	5s	7½d

The 9 of September
[291] In the Unicorne of Edam 140 tonns, Peter Clawson master, from Normor in Norway

William Doughtie *ind'* marchant, with six hundred Norway deales	30s	0d
One hundred twenty six firr baulkes containing twoe thousand seaven hundred twenty six foote of timber valued 3d *per* foot	34s	0d

Eodem die
[292] In the Vyneyarde of Ipswich as abovesaid from Danske
William Tayte Scotshman merchant, with foure hundred ells
hinderlands lynen white and browne

               5s 4d
              +2s 8d

Twelve Slecia diaper table clothes containing thirtie seaven yards

               2s 9d
              +2s 9d

Eight score and tenn yards Eastcuntrey tiking   5s 8d
Six peeces of Slecia' diaper nappkining containing forty eight yards   14½d
              +14½d

f. 6v
The 9 of September
[293] In the Vyneyarde of Ipswich *ul* [*sic*] *predict'* from Danske
William Tayt Scot merchant, with twentie pe[eces] of Slecia lawnes   3s 4d
              +3s 4d

The 11 of September
[294] In the Fortune of Amsterdam 40 tonns, Anthony Izerell master,
from Amstredam
The same Anthony alien marchant, with foure lastes great bonnd tarr[77]   13s 4d
Eleaven waighes Spaynish salte   14s 8d
Twoe cheests Burgundy glasse   4s 0d
One hundred Norway deales   5s 0d
         Strangers custom   9s 3d

Eodem die
[295] In the Margerett of Kercaudy [*illegible*] tonns, William
Williamson master, from Kircaudy
George Hackett Scot marchant, with twentie tonns Scot coales
containing [?]13 Lynn chalder   8s 8d
Twe [*sic*] thousand ells of Scot lynen cloth   £3 0s 0d

The 14 of Septemb[e]r
[296] In the John of Kircaudy 30 [*tons*], William Williamson master,
from Curras in Scotland
The same Williamson Scot merchant, with thirty one waighes whyte salte 41s 4d

The 17 of September
[297] In the Reed Hand of Groning[78] 28 tonns, Elkay Peterson master,
from Groning
Rowland Leyloffe alien merchant, with twoe hundred and half
waynskotes

              20s 0d
             +20s 0d

Twoe hundred Norway deales   10s   0d

           Strangers custom   7s   6d

The 5 of October

[298] In the Mary Katherin of Kercaudy 30 tonns, Andrewe
Messterton master, from Kircaudy [in] Scotland

The same Andrewe Scot merchant, fortie twoe waighes of white salte   56s   0d

The tennth of October

[299] In the George of Dortt 30 tonns, Hybert Johnson master,
from Dortt

Simon Johnson alien marchant, with foure lastes smale querne stones   4s   0d

Twentie pound pudding tobacco   10s   0d

           +20s   0d

           Strangers custom   3s   6d

The 27 of October

[300] In the Margerett of Kercaudy 24 tonns, James Simpson master,
from Kercaudy in Scotland

The same James Simpson Scot marchant, with twentie and six waighes
white salte   34s   8d

f. 7r

The 29 of October

[301] In the Henry of Kercaudy [?]25 tonns, David Wilson master,
from Kercaudy in Scotland

The same David Scot marchant, with sixten chalder of Scot seacoales   10s   8d

The same daye

[302] In the Answere of Hull 80 tonn, Richard Sheiffeild master,
from Amsterdam

Barnaby Charnley *ind'* marchant, with foure fats brasse kettles and
one fatt brasse panns containing 4 *M* waight   £6   0s   0d

           +£6   0s   0d

One baskett frying panns containing 7 *C* waight   7s   0d

           +7s   0d

Three hundred waight wispe steele   2s   0d

           +2s   0d

Thirties waighes Spaynish salte   40s   0d

A quarter of the hundred Norway deales   15d

More entred the 13 of November next after *per* same merchant one
thousand waight croapp madder   13s   4d

           + 6s   8d

The seconnd of November
[303] In the White Swann of Enchusan 80 tonn, Cornelius Ivason
master, from Enchusan

Mathias Johnson alien merchant, with thirty waighes of Spaynish salt	40s	0d
Five hundred clapholt	3s	9d
One hundred Norway deales	5s	0d
Five lastes great bonnd tarr[79]	16s	8d
Foure lastes great bonnd pitch	13s	4d
Twoe waighes Reynish glasse	5s	0d
Three quarters of a hundred waynscotes	6s	0d
	+6s	0d
Entred the 24 November after 4 C waight cordage	2s	8d
Strangers custom	23s	1d

The third of November
[304] In the Answer of Hull ut predict' from Amsterdam

Henry Buckston ind' marchant, with three hundred Island lings and five hundred codfish	21s	8d
Tenn jerfalkons and foure tercells	17s	8d
	+17s	8d

/ This entry freed by warrannt from the farmeres /

The 4 of November
[305] In the Answer of Hull ul [sic] predict' from Amsterdam

Erasimus Cootes alien merchant, with nyne score of wattlings valued at 3s 4d per score		18d
Seaven score yards waodmoale	5s	3d
One hundred tenn payre waodmole stockens valued £3 6s 8d	3s	4d
Strangers custom	2s	6d

f. 7v

The 7 of November
[306] In the Jacobe of Kercaudy 24 tonns, Thomas Cowey master,
from Kercaudy in Scotland

The same Thomas Cowey Scot merchant, with eighten waighes white salte	24s	0d
Tenn hundred coddfish, half hundred coalfishe	23s	10d
Eight barrells herringes	3s	4d

The 9 of November
[307] In the Mary Katherin of Kercaudy of Kercaudy [sic] 30 tonns,
Andrewe [no surname] master, from Kercaudy in Scotland

The same Andrewe Scot marchant, with forty two waighes white salte	56s	0d

Eodem die

[*308*] In the John of Kercaudy [?]30 tonn, William Williamson master, from Kircaudy in Scotland

The same Williamson Scot merchant, with thirty waighes white salt	40s	0d
One waighe more white salte		16d

The 11 of November

[*309*] In the Andrewe of Amstrother 12 tonns, William Richardson master, from Amstrother in Scotland

The same William Scot marchant, with fourten waighes white salt	18s	8d

The 13 of November

[*310*] In the Lion of Lynn 100 tonns, Robert Waters master, from Danske

Henry Ramsey *ind'* merchant, with eight lastes great bonnd tarr and seaven lastes smale bonnd pitch	40s	8d
Fowre hundred waynscotes	32s	0d
	+32s	0d
Twentie foure hundred clapholt	18s	0d
Twentie half cheests Burrgondy glasse	20s	0d
One hundred Spruce deales	15s	0d
Three barrells *di'* Spruce *ells* conteyned in 15 firkins	7s	0d
Six kagges sturrgeon	2s	0d
	+2s	0d

The 19 of November

[*311*] In the John of Kinghorne 25 tonns, John Tompson master, from Kinghorne in Scotland

The same Tompson Scot marchant, with twentie five tonns Scot coales	8s	4d

The 28 November

[*312*] In the Dolphen of Lynn 55 tonns, Robert Constable master, from Burdeux in Frannce[80]

William Atkin *ind'* marchant, with eighten half punchions prewnes containing foure hundred six pounds net *per* puncheon	36s	4½d
	+18s	2¼d
Twentie cakes royson containing 20 hundred	5s	0d

The thirde of December

[*313*] In the White Unicorne of Edam 120 tonns, Peter Clawson master, from Sanct Ovis[81] in Portingale

The same Peter alien marchant, with five score waighes Spaynish salte	£6	13s	4d
Strangers custom		33s	4d

f. 8r

The 7 of December

[*314*] In the Barrbara of Lynn 30 tonns, Robert Hayes master, from Amsterdam[82]

The same Robert *ind'* marchant, with twoe lastes of great bonnd pitch, one last great bonnd tarr	10s	0d
Two lastes smale pitch	4s	0d
One hundred clapholt		9d
Six thousand waight cordage	40s	0d
A dosen toppnetts figgs	18s	0d
	+18s	0d

Eodem die

[*315*] In the same shipp and master from Amsterdam

John Marshall *ind'* marchant, with twoe punchions prewnes containing one thousand waight	5s	0d
	+2s	6d
One baile of cropp madder containing 4 *C* fortie eight pounds	6s	3½d
	+3s	2d
Twoe trusses printing paper containing 40 reames	5s	0d
	+2s	0d
One barrell *solis* reasens containing one hundred twelve pounds		12d
		+12d
Six toppnets figgs		9d
		+9d
One barrell containing 3 peeces Malagae reasens		18d
		+18d

The 9 of December

[*316*] In the Griffin of Dortt 40 tonns, Cornelius Clawson master, from Dorte

The same Cornelius alien marchant, with nyne millstones	30s	0d
	+30s	0d
One hundred eightie bundles browne paper	9s	0d
	+9s	0d
Two dosen chayres trymed with leather valued at 3s 4d a peece	4s	0d
One great hundred Luke coales valued at £8	8s	0d
Strangers custom	12s	0d

The 24 of December

[*317*] In the Answer of Hull *ut predict'*

Erasmis Cootes alien merchant, with three hundred Island lings accepted for one hundred *di'* being currupted in the home comeing as by report of an officer	5s	0d

Foure hundred Island coddfish accepted for 2 *C* for the cause abovesaid   4s 8d

Strangers custom   2s 5d

f. 8v [*Blank*]
f. 9r
/ *Wells cum Burnham*
Inwards/[83]
The entries [? of all goods] and marchandize brought into the creekes and [?members]
of this porte for [?which] His Highnes dueties of subsidy, custome and impost have
[?bene] duely received in [?one] whole yere begonn at the feast of the Nativity
[? *alias* the] 25 of December 1611 and ended at the same feast [?next] following *videlicet*
1612

The 30 of December 1611
[*318*] In the Griff[en] of Amsterdam [50 tonns], [?]My—ver
Egbertson master, *a predict'* [84]

Samuell Newgate *ind'* marchant, with [?39] waighes Spaynish salte	48s	0d
Five lastes Danske rye	12s	6d

The 11 of January
[*319*] In the same shipp and [master from] Amsterdam

The same marchant by post entry eight waighes Spaynish salte	10s	8d

The first of Februarie
[*320*] In the Swann of Flushing 40 tonns, John Elders [master],
from Flushing[85]

Sir Henry Sidney knight,[86] with thirtie five waighes Spaynish salte	46s	8d

The third of March
[*321*] In the Robert of Wells 30 tonns, John Tompson master,
from Rotterdam

Robert [?]Morey *ind'* marchant, with twentie foure waighes Spaynish salte for which he paid noe duties it beinge for provision for his Island fishing		nil
Three quarters of a great hundred Luke coales	6s	0d
Twentie hundred waight [?]tarrd rope	13s	4d
One cooper kettle valued [*remainder illegible*]	5s	0d

The 10 of March
[*322*] In the Fortune of Amsterdam 60 tonns, Bernard Albert master,
from Amsterdam[87]

Henry Congham [*ind'*] marchant, with fortie foure waighes Spaynish salt of which he hath paid noe custome for 14 affirmeng yt to be for his Island provision	nil

Soe custome paid for 30 waighes Spaynish salt	40s	0d
Three hundred waight pr[ew]nes		18d
		+9d
Two hundred waight [rea]sons *solis*		22d
		+22d
One great mast, a quarter hundred bome spars and half a hundred smale spars		23d

f. 9v

The 10 of March

[323] In the John of Wells 30 tonns, John Curson master, [from] Amsterdam[88]

Henry Congham *ind'* marchant, with [?twenty] two waighes Spaynish salt for which this merchant hath paid noe custome but deteyneth yt as free of custome for his Island fishing — nil

Five hundred waight of tarrd [ro]pes	3s	4d
Foure peeces great reasons	2s	0d
	+2s	0d

The 12 [of] March[89]

[324] In the Grayhownd of Amste[rd]am 30 tonns, Nicholas Jacobe master, from Amsterdam

Richard Goldsmith *ind'* merchant, with thirty waighes Spaynish salt for which he [?likewise] hath paid noe custome but claymeth yt as free of custome for his Island fishing — nil

One smale mast, three hundred *di'* smale spars and half a hundred Norrway deales	6s	6d
Eight hundred waight tarrd ropes	5s	4d

The 6 of Aprill

[325] In the Alice of Wells 20 tonns, William Tatsale master, from Aymoth in Scotland

John Greene *ind'* marchant, with thirteen lastes oates and barly *videlicet* th'one half barly th'other oates	30s	3d

The 21 of Maye

[326] In the Estrich of Camphire 20 tonns, Jacobe Bonis master, from Camphire[90]

The *said* Jacobe Bonis alien merchant, with fowre hundred waight hopps	4s	0d
	+2s	0d
One last of rye	2s	6d
Strangers custom		19½d

The 28 of Jully
[327] In the Estrich of Camphire 18 [sic] tonns, Jacobe master [sic],
from Camphire

The same Jacobe alien merchant, with foure lastes Danske rye	10s	0d
Foure hundred waight currents	6s	0d
	+13s	4d
Two hundred di' waight great reasons		20d
	+20d	
Strangers custom	4s	5d

The first of August
[328] In the Griffin of Dorte 40 tonns, Cornelius Clawson master,
from Dorte

Henry Congham ind' merchant, with three great hundred of Luke coales valued at £8 per cent	24s	0d
Twoe hundred waight white suger	6s	8d
	+10s	0d
Foure peeces great reasons	2s	0d
	+2s	0d
Two hundred bundles browne paper	10s	0d
	+10s	0d

f. 10r
The thirde of August
[329] In the Griffin of Amsterdam 40 tonn, Clawze Jacobson master,
from Amsterdam[91]

The same Jacobson alien marchant, with one great hundred et di' Luke coales	12s	0d
Foure hundred Norway [?deales]	20s	0d
Three hundred clapholt	2s	3d
Seaven hundred waight iron	2s	5d
Strangers custom	9s	2d

The 14 of August
[330] In the Adventer of Amsterdam 40 tonns, Freedrick Cornelison
master, from Amstredam[92]

Henry Congham ind' marchant, with nyne lastes rye and tenn lastes di' oates	43s	6d
Twoe hundred clapholt		18d
Two hundred waight prewnes		12d
	+6d	

The third of September
[*331*] In the Great Harry of Wells 70 tonns, Thomas Bunting master,
from Island
John Webbster *ind'* marchant, with eleaven jerfalkons and seaven tercells   21s 2d
                                                                   +21s 2d

The 16 of September
[*332* In the Susan of Wells 36 tonns, William Tatsale master,
from Rotterdam
John Greene *ind'* marchant, with two great hundred of Luke [*coals*]
valued *ut predict'* [*sic*]   16s 0d
Three hundred *di'* waight [*sic*] cordage   2s 4d

The 10 of November
[*333*] In the Estrich of Camphire 15 tonns, Jacobe Bonis master,
from Camphire[93]
The same Jacobe alien merchant, with five hundred waight prewnes   2s 6d
                                                     +15d
Three hundred *di'* waight cheese   14d
                                    Strangers custom   11d

The 14 of December
[*334*] In the Estrich of Camphire 15 tonns, Jacobe Bonis master,
from Camphire[94]
The same Jacobe alien merchant, with three lastes rye   7s 6d
Five hundred waight of prewnes   2s 6d
                                                     +15d
                                    Strangers custom   2s 6d

f. 10v [*Blank*]
f. 11r
/ *Lynn Regis*
Outwards /
The entries of all goods and marchandize shipped from this porte and the members
overseas for all which His Highnes duties of subsidie, custom and impost have
bene duely received for one wholle yere begonn at the feast of the nativity *alias*
the 25 of December *anno* 1611 and ended at the same feast next following *videlicet*
the 25 of December *anno* 1612

The 14 of Jannuary 1611
[*335*] In the Cocke of Flushing 15 tonn, G[arra]rd Nabbs master, to
Flushing
The same Garrarde alien marchant, with [*illegible*] lastes fiften combs
hempseed   £3 7s 6d

Foure combs lynnseed	2s	0d
Strangers custom	17s	4½d

The last of Fe[br]uary
[*336*] In the Cocke of Flushing 15 tonn, Garrarde Nabbs master,
to Flushing

Cornelius De Wylde marchant, with [twoe] lastes hempseed and half a last lynnseed	25s	0d
Ny[ne] hundred oile cakes val[ued] at 6s [8d] *per cent* and five hundred smale oile cakes [? at the like value]	4s	8d
Three [*illegible*] French [?hony] for which the dut[ie]s were paide in this porte as *per* entry taken the [25] November last[95]		nil

The [?14] of [Mar]ch
[*337*] In the Martin of Lynn [? 40 tonns], [*illegible*], to Island
Erasm[us] Coa[tes] [? alien merchant with three unfrized] penistones,

[*illegible*] containing [? forty foure] yards [?whereof] halfe short cloth want foure yards	6s	8d
Three kirsies which make one short cloth	13s	6d
Seaventy five goades cotton	2s	6d
Two runlets *aqua [?vite]* containing forty foure gallons		16d
One hundred *di'* unwrought iron		7d
Strangers custom except the cloth		13d

Eodem die
[*338*] In the Martin abovesaid, John Denmarke master, to Island

William Haucer *ind'* [?merchant], with eleaven yards *di'* violet cloth	3s	2½d
Twelve yards [?]blue cloth [?acce]pted for a [northern] dosen single	3s	4d
Two [*illegible*] kersies [? 8 yards] *per* peece	3s	5d
Twelve goads narrow cottons [?coloured]		4½d

f. 11v
The 19 of March
[*339*] In the Martin of Lynn as aforesaid, John Den[ma]rke master,
to Island
/ [*In a different hand:*] *This was freed by warrant from the farmores*/

Henry Buckston *ind'* marchant, with one tonn stronge [?beer]	18d	
	+8s	6d
Two barrels biskett containing 2 *C* waight valued at 14s *per cent*		17d
Eighten firkins barly meale containing two barrells *di'*		7½d
Half a waigh baye salt		8d
Three score yards cotton [?estimated] at 36 goades		7d
Thirty yards kersies in remnantes accepted for *di'* short cloth	3s	4d

One bridgwater *videlicet di'* short cloth	3s	4d
One northern dozen sengle	3s	4d

The 23 of March
[*340*] In the Fortune of Amsterdam 40 tonns, Anthony Izerell master, from[96] Amsterdam

The same Anthony alien marchant, with foure combs hempseed	2s	0d
Strangers custom		6d

Eodem die
[*341*] In the same shipp, master and marchant suffered to passe from this port for which the duetyes have bene here paid as *per* entry taken the twelvt[h]e daie of March last, tenn pounds maces, tenn pounds nuttmegges, fifty pounds West India ginger, *30* six pounds peper, twenty seaven yards feather beed tiking[97]   nil

The first of Aprill
[*342*] In the Mary Katherin of Kercaudy 30 tonn, David Balfore master, to Kercaudy in Scotland

Andewe Leighton Scot marchant, with thirty foure groce creuell gerdling and gartering, 12 dosen *per* groce	22s	8d

The thride of Aprill
[*343*] In the Margeret of Lynn 70 tonn, Richarde Gittings[98] master, to Elbing in th'East Cuntrey[99]
/Mark [+ *merchant's mark*]/[100]

Thomas Snelling *ind'* marchant, eight thousand gray conyskynes seazoned and seaven thousand stage	38s	4d
One trusse containing one thousand seazoned blacke cony skynes	26s	8d
Eight hundred blacke rabitt skynes accepted 2 to a skyne at 9d *per cent*	6s	0d
Eight hundred gray rabit skynes tawed, two to skyne *videlicet* 4 C	2s	8d
Three packes of gray conyskynes containing nyne thousand seazond and five thousand stage	38s	4d
Three packes mortkins untawed containing two thousand and more five hundred	12s	6d
One trusse dornix containing 31 peeces	10s	4d

The 9 of Aprill
[*344*] In the same shipp, master and merchant to Elbing in th'East Cuntrey
/No. 1, no. 2 [*with a further mark*]/

Twoe roules and a trusse gray conyskynes cont[aining] 6 thousand seazoned and five thousand stage	28s	4d

f. 12r

/No. 4, no. 5, no. 6, no. 7 [*with repeated merchant's mark*]/

Foure roules gray [*illegible*] cony skynes containing 7 thousand seazoned and tenn thousand stage	40s	0d
Two trusses untawed mortkins containing fourten hundred	7s	0d
Foure packes mortkins untawed containing two thousand nyne hundred	14s	6d
Sixten dosen shortt worrstead stockens	25s	7d
One shortt broad cloth	6s	8d

[*345*] In the same shipp, master and merchant entred the [*illegible*] of Aprill

One rowle and a trusse gray conyskynes [?containing] three thousand seazoned and foure *di'* stage	17s	6d
Two trusses mortkins containing six hundred	3s	0d

The 10 of Aprill

[*346*] In the Martin of Lynn 80 tonn, William Morgan master, to [?Norbarne] in Norway

Jervase Wharton *ind'* marchant, with eight northern dosens sengle and three northern kersies	33s	4d
Twelve goads cotton		4¹/₂d
Twoe chalders grindlstones		16d
Two more northern dozens	6s	8d
One hogshead decayed French wyne for which the dutie was paid sence Michaelmas		nil

The 18 of Aprill

[*347*] In the Margerett of Lynn 80 tonns, Richard Gittings master, to Elbing

Robert Atkin *ind'* marchant, with twoe short Suffolke cloathes	13s	4d
Six dosen shortt kersey stockens	3s	0d
One thousand mort lambskynes	5s	0d

The 28 of Aprill

[*348*] In the Cocke of Flushing 15 tonns, Garrard Nabbs master, to Flushing

The same Garrard alien, with one last lynnseed	12s	6d
Three tonns stronge beere, subsidy and impost *per* statute	5s	7¹/₂d
	+30s	0d

Eodem die

[*349*] In the Dolphen of Lynn 50 tonns, Robert Constable master, to Danske in th'East Cuntrey

Briand Loupton *ind'* marchant, with five thousand sheeps leather tawed	£3	15s	0d
Tenn northerne kersies whereof one for wrappers		17s	10d

Two smale trusses containing 16 *C* mortlambskynes	8s	0d
More one trusse white leather tawed *per* post entry *eodem die* containing one thousand	15s	0d

f. 12v

The 30 of Aprill

[*350*] In the Ann of Boston 5 tonns, John Lancaster master, to [?Boston]
John Forgasson Scotsh marchant, to [?Boston] and hence for Scotland,
with one thousand m[ort] lambskynes and one hundred gray conyskynes   5s   4d

The 5 of May

[*351*] In the John of Kercaudy *alias* the [*illegible*][101] 20 tonns, John
Cuisen master, to Kercaudy in Scotland
The same John Scot[tish] marchant, with foure tonns beere   6s   0d
    +24s   0d

The 12 of May

[*352*] In the Crabbe of Amsterd[am] 50 tonns, Cornelius De Wild
alias Cornelison[102] [*sic*] master, to Amsterdam
Cornelius De Wilde *ind'* marchant, with 12 *C* smale oile cakes valued
at 2s *per cent* and nyne hundred great oile cakes valued at 5s *per cent*   3s   5½d

The 13 of May

[*353*] In the Phenix of Dover 20 tonns, Robert Fleming master, to Dover
Silvester Rochier alien, from Dover to Deepe in Fraunce, with thirty
dosen old shues and five hundred scale bones   12½d

The 25 of May

[*354*] In the Mary Katherin of Kercaudy 30 tonns, Andrewe Messterton
master, to Norway
The same Andrewe Scot marchant, with three tonns stronge beere,
besides his drincking beere   4s   6d
    +25s   6d

The 17 of June[103]

[*355*] In the Jacobe of Kercaudy 24 tonns, John Cuisen master, to
Kercaudy in Scotland
The same John, with foure barrells stronge beere
[*356*] In the William of Kercaudy 16 tonns, Robert Donckan master,
to Kercaudy in Scotland   3s   0d
The same Robert, with three barrells stronge beere   +17s   0d
[*357*] In the Gifft of Disert 34 tonns, Alexander Wilkey master, to
Kercaudy
The same Alexander, with foure barrells stronge beere

The 17 of June
[*358*] In the Mary Katherin of Kercaudy 30 tonns, Andrewe
Messterton master, to Kercaudy in Scotland
The same Amdrewe [*sic*] Scot marchant, with two tonns stronge beere   3s 0d
   +17s 0d

Two thousand band staves to make hoopes for caske for which the
duties have bene lately paid in this porte as by entry taken the
23 of June last appeareth[104]   nil

f. 13r
The seconnd of Jully
[*359*] In the Martin of Lynn 80 tonns, William Morgan master, to
Norway
Henry Wattson alien marchant, with five northerne dozens sengle
and [?foure] kersies and a half   58s 0d

The 25 daie of Jully
[*360*] In the Mary Katherin *predict'*, Andrewe Messterton master, to
Kercaudy in Scotland
The same Andrewe Scot marchant, with two tonns strong beere   3s 0d
   +17s 0d

The thirde of August
[*361*] In the William of Kercaudy 16 tonns, Robert Donckan master,
to Kercaudy in Scotland
John Cuisen Scot merchant, with one load oaken [?barke] valued at 30s   18d

Eodem die
[*362*] In the Jacobe of Kercaudy 24 tonns, John Cuisen master, to
Kercaudy in Scotland
The same John Cuisen Scot marchant, with one load barke valued at
thirty shillinges   18d

Eodem die
[*363*] In the Margerett of Kercaudy 20 tonns, David Balfore master, to
Kercaudy in Scotland
The same David Scot marchant, with foure tonns stronge beere   6s 0d
   +34s 0d

The 22 of August
[*364*] In the Crabbe of Saredam 40 tonns, Cornelius Cornelison
master, to Amsterdam
The same Cornelius alien merchant, with five lastes rapseed   50s 0d

Nynten combs hempseed	9s	6d
Five hundred smale oile cakes at 2s *per cent*		6d
Six hundred great oile cakes a[t] 10s *per cent*	3s	0d
Eight hundred waight Flemishe hopps for which the duties were paid in this port a yere already past[105]	8s	0d
Strangers custom	17s	9d

The 27 of August
[*365*] In the Seale of Deepe 16 tonns, James Goshen master, to Deipe in France

The same James alien marchant, with one hundred fifty dosen old shues	3s	0d
Six thousand shancke bones valued at 6s 8d *per* thousand	2s	0d
Seaven barrells broken glasse valued at 2s *per* barrell		8½d
Six barrells paringes of lether valued at 3s *per* barrell		11d
Fiften hundred ranmes hornes		18d
Six hundred cowes and oxhornes		18d
Seaven barrells of slipp[106]		14d
Strangers custom	2s	8d

f. 13v

The 4 of September
[*366*] In the Mary Katherin of Kercaudie 30 tonns, Andrewe Messterton master, to Kercaudy in Scotland

The same Andrewe Scot merchant, with [?two] tonns stronge beere	3s	0d
	+17s	0d

The 8 of September
[*367*] In the Dolphen of Lynn 50 tonns, Robert C[on]stable master, to Burdeux in France

William Atkin *ind'* marchant, [with] twentie northerne kersies wherof twoe allowed for wrapp[ers]	40s	0d
Eleaven hundred waig[ht] Englishe waxe	44s	0d
Enterd by the same m[a]rchant the twelvth of September eight hundred English w[ax]e	32s	0d

The 17 of September
[*368*] In the Jacobe of Kercaudy 24 tonns, Thomas Cowey master, to Kircaudy in Scotland

The same Thomas Scot marchant, with three tonns *di'* stronge beere	5s	3d
	+25s	6d

The 21 of September
[*369*] In the same shipp, master and marchant to Kercaudy in Scotland

The same Thomas, with one tonn *di'* stronge beere	2s	3d
	+12s	9d
One bagge English hopps containing 2 *C* waight	2s	0d

The 23 of September
[*370*] In the Margerett of Kercaudy 20 tonns, William Williamson
master, to Kircaudy in Scotland

The said Williamson Scot marchant, with one tonn stronge beere		18d
	+8s	6d
Foure peeces of frize containing 32 yards *per* peece	6s	5d
One northern dosen sengle *et di'*	5s	0d
Six barrells onions		5d

The 24 of September
[*371*] In the Fortune of Amsterdam 40 tonns, Anthony Izerell master,
to the parts beyond the seas
The same Anthony alien suffered to passe with foure lastes tarr and
one hundred Norway *deals* which have paid the duties in this port and
could not be sold, as *per* entry taken the 11 of this instant appeareth[107]   nil

The 29 of September
[*372*] In the John of Kercaudye 30 tonns, William Williamson master,
to Kercaudy in Scotland

The same Williamson Scot merchant, with one tonn stronge beere		18d
	+8s	6d

The 12 of October
[*373*] In the Mary Katherin of Kercaudy 30 tonns, Andrewe
Messterton master, to Kercaudy in Scotland

The same Andrewe Scot marchant, with eight tonns stronge beere	12s	0d
	+£3 8s	0d

f. 14r
The 27 of October
[*374*] In the Barrbara of Lynn 30 tonns, Robert Hayes master, to
Amsterdam

The same Robert *ind'* merchant, with five lastes *di'* hempseed	55s	0d
Nyne hundred sheeps leather tawed	13s	4d
Thirty stone thistle downe – valued 6d *per* stone		9d

The 4 of November
[*375*] In the Henrie of Kercaudy 25 tonns, David Wilson master, to
Kercaudy in Scotland

The same Davide Scot marchant, with foure barrels stronge beere		12d
	+5s	4d

The 13 of November
[*376*] In the Tygar of Lynn 80 tonns, Vilett[108] Waynford master, into
the Straights of Gibralatair
Thomas Slaney[109] *ind'* marchant, with one hundred and tenn piggs

lead containing 13 foother and a half	£5	8s	0d
	+£13	10s	0d

The 14 of November
[*377*] In the Mary Katherin of Kercaudy 30 tonns, Andrew
Messterton master, to Kercaudy in Scotland

The same Andrewe Scot merchant, with foure tonns stronge beere	6s	0d
	+34s	0d

Eodem die
[*378*] In the Jacobe of Kercaudy 24 tonns, Thomas Cowey master,
to Kercaudy in Scotland

The same Thomas Scot marchant, with foure tonns stronge beere	6s	0d
	+34s	0d

The 24 of November
[*379*] In the Andrewe of Amstrother 24 tonns, William Richardson
master, to Amstrother in Scotland

William Simpson Scot marchant, with six tonns *di'* stronge beere	9s	9[d]
	+55s	3d
Five hundred waight barke valued at 20d *per cent*		5d

The 28 November
[*380*] In the White Swann of Enchuzan 80 tonn, Cornelius Evason
master, to Enchusan
Mathias Johnson alien merchant, with fourten lastes and sixten

combs rapseed and hempseed	£7	8s	0d
Strangers custom		37s	0d

Eodem die
[*381*] In the John of Kinghorne [?]25 tonns, John Tompson master,
to Kinghorne in Scotland
The same Tompson Scot merchant, with twoe tonns *di'* and twoe

barrells stronge beere	4s	3d
	+24s	1d

Eodem [*die*]
[*382*] In the White Swann of Enchusan *ut predict'*
Mathias Johnson *predict'* sufferd to passe with five lastes great bonnd tarr which hath
paid the duties and could not be sold in this port as *per* entry taken

of this instant last past [?second][110]	nil

f. 14v [*Blank*]
f. 15r
/ *Wells cum Burnham*
Outwarde/
The entries of all goods and marchandize shipped from the creeks and members of
this porte overseas for all which His Highnes duties of subsidy, custom and impost
have bene duely received in one wholle yere begonn at the feast of the Nativitye *alias*
the 25 of December 1611 and ended at the same feast next following *videlicet* 1612

The 27 daye of May
[*383*] In the Estrich of Camphire 20 tonns, Jacobe Bonis master,
to Camphire

The same Jacobe alien marchant, with twenty pound Englishe safferon	20s	0d
Strangers custom	5s	0d

The 18 November
[*384*] In the Estrich of Camphire 15 tonns, Jacobe Bonis master,
to Camphire

The same Jacobe alien, with twentie pounde Englishe safferon	20s	0d
Strangers custom	5s	0d

The 23 of December
[*385*] In the Estrich of Camphire 15 tonns, Jacobe Bonis master, to Camphire

The same Jacobe alien merchant, with eighteen English pounde safferon	20s	0d
Strangers custom	4s	6d

f. 15v [*Blank*]
f. 16r
Wyne
/ *Lynn Regis*/
The entries of all French and [?Reynish] wynes brought into this porte and members
thereof for all which the duties of subsidy, custome and imposts have bene duely
compounded for in one whole yere begonn at the feast of Sanct Michaell
th'Archangell *alias* the 29 of September *anno* 1611 and ended at the same feast next
following *videlicet* the 29 September *anno* 1612

The 29 of October 1611
[*386*] In the Pricila of Lynn 37 tonns, John Yongs master, from Burdeux in
Frannce[111]
Arnold Fiden alien marchant, with 36 tonns French wynes, and the shippmaster
abovesaid entred one tonn French wynes, whereof allowance to marchant and
shippmaster deducted. And more entred one hogshead two tierces
/ *Alien*/

The 25 of November
[*387*] In the Providence of Kercaudy 50 tonns, James Lawe master, from Burdeux in France[112]
William Atkin and Jervase Wharton English marchantes, with 50 tonns French wynes
And more entred by John Wallis *ind'*, one tierce
Prisage wynes and allowance deducted
/*Ind'*/

The 30 of December
[*388*] In the Cocke of Flushing 15 tonns, Garrard Nabbs master, from Flushing[113]
The same Garrard alien marchant, with three tonns French wynes
/*Alien*/

The 14 of Jannuary
[*389*] In the Fortune of Lynn 50 tonns, Robert Atkin master, from Burdeux in Frannce
William Atkin *ind'* marchant, with fortie seaven tonns two hogsheads
The shippmaster abovesaid *ind'* entred one tonn one hogshead, whereof prisage and allowannces deducted[114]
/*Ind'*/

The 20 of Jannuary
[*390*] In the Hope for Grace of Disert 64 tonns, Alexander Mancke master, from Burdeux[115]
Rowland Bradfford *ind'* marchant, with 62 tonns French wynes, and the shippmaster abovesaid entred one tonn two hogsheads French wynes, whereof prisage wynes and allowannces deducted
/*Ind'*/

The 30 of Jannuary
[*391*] In the Sheepe of Midlbrough 40 tonns, Joas Penn master, from Midlbrough[116]
The same Joas Penn alien brought in tenn tonns French wynes
/*Alien*/

f. 16v
The 19 of March
[*392*] In the Barrbara [? of Lynn] 30 tonns, Robert Hayes master, from Amsterdam[117]
The same Robert *ind'* brought in two tonns one hogshead French wynes
/*Ind'*/

The 16 of Aprill
[*393*] In the Cocke of Flushing 15 tonns, Garrard Nabbs master, from Flushing[118]
The same Garrard alien marchant, w[h]ich brought in one tonn two hogsheads
French wynes
/ *Alien* /

The 17 of Aprill
[*394*] In the Elzabeth of Barrowston[119] 70 tonns, George Gibb master, from
Burdeux in France[120]
Elias Errauld alien merchant entered 44 tonns French wyne
The same stranger enterd more the 22 of Aprill 7 tonns French wynes and more
two thirds of two tierces
Whereof allowances deducted
/ *Alien* /

The 17 of Aprill
[*395*] In the same shipp and master from Burdeux in Frannce
George Gibb Scotman, the shippmaster, entred 24 tonns
And more entered by the same George Gibb the 22 of Aprill one tonn, twoe
hogsheads, one third of two tierces
Whereof prisage wynes and allowannces deducted
/ *Ind'* /

The 23 of June
[*396*] In the Fortune of Amsterdam 40 tonns, Anthony Izerell master, from
Amsterdam[121]
Robert Hayes *ind'* brought in foure fatts French wynes containing two tonns
/ *Ind'* /

The 7 of September
[*397*] In the Margeret Alley of Lynn 20 tonns, John Gerdlston master, from
Amsterdam[122]
John Wallis *ind'* marchant entred three tonns one butt French wynes
/ *Ind'* /

French – *Ind'* – 195 *dol'* 2 hogsheads 1 ters'
           Alien – 102 *dol'* 1 hogshead

f. 17r
Wynes
/ *Wells cum Burnham* /
The entries of all French and Reynish [*wines*] brought into the creeks and
members of this porte for which the duties have been compounded in one whole

yere begonn at the feast of Sanct Michaell th'Archangell *anno* 1611 and ended at
the same feast *anno* 1612

The first of February *anno* 1611
[*398*] In the Swann of Flushing 40 tonns John Elders master, from Flushing[123]
Sir Henry Sidney knight entred two hogsheads French wynes
/*Ind'*/

The 10 of March
[*399*] In the John of Wells 30 tonns, John Curson master, from Amsterdam[124]
Henry Congham *ind'* marchant entred five tonns French wynes whereof
allowannce made to this marchant
/*Ind'*/

Eodem die
[*400*] In the Fortune of Amsterdam 60 tonns, Bernarde Albert master, from
Amsterdam[125]
The same Bernarde alien entred one tonn French wynes
/*Alien*/

The 21 of May
[*401*] In the Estrich of Camphire 20 tonns, Jacobe Bonis master, from
Camphire[126]
The same Jacobe alien, three tonns and three hogsheads French wynes
/*Alien*/

The thride of August
[*402*] In the Griffin of Amsterdam 40 tonns, Clawse Jacobson master, from
Amsterdam[127]
The same Clawse Jacobson alien entred one tonn twoe hogsheads French wynes
/*Alien*/

The 13 of August
[*403*] In the Adventer of Amsterdam 40 tonns, Freedricke Cornelison master,
from Amstredam[128]
Henry Congham *ind'* entred two awnes Reynish wynes
/*Ind'*/

French − *Ind'* − 7 *dol'* 2 hogsheads
       Alien − 6 *dol'* 1 hogshead

f. 17v [*Blank*]
f. 18r
Wynes
/*Lynn Regis*/
Enteries of Spaynish wynes brought into this porte from beyonde the seas and into the members thereof for one whole yere begonn the 29 of September 1611 and ended the 29 of September next following *videlicet* 1612

The 30 of January 1611
[*404*] In the Sheepe of Midlbrough 40 tonns, Joas Penn master, from Midlbrough[129]
The same Joas Penn alien, with twentie butts Spaynish wynes

The 19 of March 1611
[*405*] In the Barbara of Lynn 30 tonns, Robert Haies master, from Amsterdam[130]
The same Robert Hayes *ind'*, with two tonns Spaynish wynes

Sack	– Ind' –	2 dol'
	Alien –	10 dol'

/*Wells cum Burnham*/
Entries of all Spaynish wynes from beyonde the seas taken at the creeks and members of this porte in one whole yere ended the 29 of September *ut predict'* *anno* 1612

The 30 of December 1611
[*406*] In the Griffin of Amsterdam 50 tonns, Mynever Egbertson master, from Amsterdam[131]
Samuell Newgate *ind'* merchant for all other the goods in this shipp one hogshead and other smale runnletts esteam[ed] at *di'* hogshead muskadele

The 21 of May 1612
[*407*] In the Estrich of Camphire 20 tonns, Jacobe Bonis master, from Camphire[132]
The same Jacobe alien merchant, with foure butts sherrie sackes

Sacke	– Alien –	2 dol'
Muskadelles	– Ind' –	1 hogshead di'

f. 18v [*Blank*]

E190/434/1: Customer : Christmas 1612 – Christmas 1613

f. 1r
Lynn Regis
Entries of all goods and marc[h]andice brought into this porte in one
quarter begonn at the Nativity of Our Lorde Godd *anno* 1612

December 28 1612
[*408*] In the Margerett of Kercaudy 24 tonns, James Simpson master,
from Kercaudy in Scotland
The same James Scotsh marchant, with twenty six waighes white salte   34s   8d

December 29
[*409*] In the Angell of Kercaudie 35 tonns, Henry Reynoldson master,
from Kirrhen[133] in Scotland
The same Henry Scot merchant, with forty tonns Scot coales   13s   4d

December 30
[*410*] In the White Unicorne of Edam 120 tonns, Peter Clawson
master, from Ovis in Portingale[134]
The same Peter alien marchant, with thirty twoe waighes Spaynish salte   42s   8d
                                        Strangers custom   10s   8d

December *ult'*
[*411*] In the Barke Allen of Creile 45 tonns, John Dawsey master,
from Burdeux in Frannce[135]
William Atkin *ind'* merchant, with six puntchions prewnes containing
8 *C* 20 *pounds* *per* puncheon   24s   6½d
                                             +12s   3¼d
Twelve *di'* punchions containing 4 *C* 10 pounds net *per* puncheon   24s   6½d
                                             +12s   3¼d

Jannuarie 14
[*412*] In the Bruice of Kercaudie 30 tonns, William Collier master,
from Kercaudie in Scotland
The same William Scot merchant, with thirty six waighes white salte   48s   0d

Jannuarie 15
[*413*] In the same shipp and master from Kercaudy in Scotland
The same William with foure waighes salt *per* post entrie   5s   4d

Jannuarie 19
[*414*] In the Seahownd of Newhavon[136] 20 tonns, John Jacobson
master, from Delph havon[137]

The same John Jacobson alien marchant, with eight lastes white herringes full and shotten	40s	0d
Twoe hundred lynges	6s	8d
Strangers custom	11s	8d

f. 1v
Jannuarie [?]22
[*415*] In the Mary Katherin of Kercaudie 30 tonns, David Balfore
master, from Kercaudie in Scotland

The same David Scot merchant, with thirtie tonns Scot coales	10s	0d
Foure lastes white herringe	20s	0d
Half a hundred ells tiking	2s	0d
Twoo hundred waight Scot yarne	2s	6d
One hundred ells lynen cloth	3s	0d
More enterd the 29 of January *predict' per* the same merchant, [? half hundred] ells lynen cloth		18d

January *eod'*
[*416*] In the Mary Katherine *predict'* from Kercaudy in Scotland

David Boswell Scot marchant, with seaven hundred ells lynen cloth	20s	0d
Foure score pounds Scot yarne	2s	0d

January *eod'*
[*417*] In the Ann Charitee of Kingston *super* Hull 90 tonns, Sampson
Simpson master, from Burdeux in France[138]

Rowlande Bradforth *ind'* merchant, with twoe tonns French prewnes	20s	0d
	+10s	0d
One tonn *di'* vinagor	3s	6d
	+3s	6d
Half a tonn prewnes more entred for the shipmaster	5s	0d
	+2s	6d

January 26
[*418*] In the Angell of Abberdyn 52 tonns, John Hayton master, from
Abberdin in Scotland

William Donalson Scot merchant, with one hundred *di'* Norrway deales	7s	6d
Foure barrells herringes		20d
Three barrels smale band tarr		6d
Fifty yards flanell		22½d
Two hundred lynen cloth [*sic*] containing 1 *C* nynty twoe ells	5s	3½d

January *eod'*
[*419*] In the Isabell of Lynne 40 tonns, Thomas Ravens master,
from Enchuzan

Robert Thorey *ind'* marchant, with twentie waighes Spaynish salte	26s	4d
Two cables containing 1 thousand 3 hundred 43 pounds waight	8s	11½d
Foure coyles cordage waighing 2 *C* 12 pounds		17d
Tenn toppnetts figgs		15d
		+15d

January 28
[*420*] In the Ann Charitee of Hull *predict'*, Sampson Simpson master,
from Burdeux in France
The said shippmaster more two barrells containing one tonn

French prewnes	10s	0d
	+5s	0d

f. 2r
February [?]3[139]
[*421*] In the [?]Angelis of Hambrough [?]100 tonns, [?]Henry [*illegible*]
 master, from Hambrough

The said stranger [*remainder illegible*]		[?]£3	6s	8d
	Strangers custom	[?]16s	8d

February *eod'*
[*422*] In the Richarde of Scarrbrough 40 tonns, [? Os—s Humphrey]
master, from Rotterdam
Henry Congham *ind'* marchant, with [?]seaven lastes *di'* white

herringes	[*sum illegible*]	
One hundred bundles browne paper	[?]5s	0d
	+[?]5s	0d

February *eod'*
[*423*] In the Cocke of Flushing 16 tonns, Garrard Nabbs master,
from Flushing[140]

The same stranger with tenn waighes French salt	10s	0d
Twentie six earthen potts containing a gallon *per* pott *[?]saltie oyle*	2s	2d
	+2s	2d
Six hundred waight cheese	2s	0d
Strangers custom	3s	6½d

February [?]4
[*424*] In the Mary Katherin of Kercaudy 30 tonns, David Balfore
master, from Kercaudy in Scotland

The same David Scot merchant, one last white herrings p[ar]t rate   5s   0d

February 12
[425] In the Grace of God of Kercaudy 40 tonns, John Cuisen master,
from Kercaudy in Scotland
The same John Scot marchant, with fortie waighes white salte   53s   4d

February 13
[426] In the Paule of Amstrother 20 tonns, Henry Morris master,
from Amstrother
The same Morris Scot marchant, with seaven lastes tenn barrells
herrings   39s   2d
Tenn tonns seacoales   3s   4d

February 15
[427] In the George of Donndee 24 tonns, Andrewe Brand master,
from Donndee in Scotland
Robert Morris Scot marchant, fourten lastes white herrings   £3 10s   0d
One hundred waight Scot yarne   15d

f. 2v
February [?]18
[428] In the Oulde Henry of Kercaudy 20 tonns, David Wilson master,
from Kercaudy in Scotland
The same David Scot merchant, with twelve tonns seacoales   4s   0d
Five hundred waight Scot yarne   6s   6d
One hundred ells tiking [at] 6 score *per cent*   4s   0d

February [?]*eod'*
[429] In the Grace of Muntrosse 20 tonns, James Oglbey master,
from Mountrosse[141] in Scotland
John Beety Scot merchant, with five lastes nyne barrels herringes   28s   9d
Six barrells coddfishe   4s   0d
        +5s   0d
One last great bonnd tarr, one last great bonnd pitch   6s   8d
Two hundred Norrway deales   10s   0d
Three hundred waight Scot yarne   3s   9d
One hundred ells Scot lynen   3s   0d

February 19
[430] In the George of Kercaudy 30 tonns, George Balkreackewell
master, from Kercaudy in Scotland
The same George Scot marchant, with forty waighes white salt   54s   4d
And more two waighes white salt   2s   8d

February *eod'*
[*431*] In the Grace of Mountross *predict'* Robert Gryme Scot marchant,
with one hundred waight lynen yarne   15d

February *eod'*
[*432*] In the same shipp and master from Mountrosse in Scotland
James Oglbey Scot marchant, with [?]fifty score eleaven Norway deales   4s 7½d

February *eod'*
[*433*] In the William the William [*sic*] of Kercaudy 40 tonns, John More
master, from Kercaudy in Scotland
The same John More Scot merchant, with fifty six waighes white salt £3 14s 8d
Two lastes white herringes   9s 0d
One hundred yards tiking at 5 score *per cent*   3s 4d

February [?]22
[*434*] In the James of Dunndee 20 tonns, James Moncker master,
from Donndee in Scotland
The same James Scot marchant, with fiften waighes bay salt   15s 0d

f. 3r
February *eod'*
[*435*] In the Paradice of Amsterdam 40 tonns, William Cornelius
master, from Amsterdam
Robert Waters *ind'* marchant, with twenty five *waighes* bay salt   25s 0d
Three hundred waight cheese   12d
Two smale caske containing 2 *C* and a quarter white starch   2s 3d
                                                                     +15s 0d
Twenty two pounds net cloves   5s 6d
                                                                      +5s 6d
Two cables, one boat ropes [*sic*] and other smale tarrd ropes
containing 30 *C* waight   20s 0d
One hundred waight candleweeke   8d
                                                                      +8d
Two peeces Flannders *doble* serge containing 24 yards   4s 10d
                                                                      +4s 10d
Fifty bundles browne paper   2s 6d
                                                                      +2s 6d

February *eod'*
[*436*] In the Jonass[142] of Leith 18 tonns, William Hayden master, from
Donnbarr in Scotland
Thomas Smith Scot marchant, with tenn lastes white herrings   50s 0d

February 23
[*437*] In the William of Kercaudy 36 tonns, John Collier master,
from Kercaudy in Scotland
The same John Collier Scot marchant, with forty twoe waighes
white salte   56s   0d

February *eod'*
[*438*] In the Olde Henry of Kercaudy 20 tonns, David Willson master,
from Kercaudy in Scotland
The same David Scot merchant, *per* post entrie eight tonns Scotsh coales   2s   8d

February 24
[*439*] In the Grace of God of Kercaudy 25 tonns, James Browne master,
 from Kercaudy in Scotland
John Cuisen Scotsh marchant, *per* post entry two waighes whit salt   2s   8d

February 25
[*440*] In the James of Leith *predict'* William Hayden master from
Donnbarr in Scotland
Thomas Smith marchant, with two lastes white herrings *per* post entry   10s   0d

February *eod'*
[*441*] In the Paradice of Amsterdam 40 tonns, William Cornelius master,
from Amsterdam
Robert Thorey *ind'* merchant, with eight peeces legatures *alias* lome
worke vallued at 25s *per* peece   9s   0d
Foure half peec[e]s lawnes   4s   0d
                                                                 +4s   0d

f. 3v
February 26
[*442*] In the same shipp, master and marchant from Amsterdam
Two half peeces lawnes   2s   0d
                                                                 +2s   0d

February 27
[*443*] In the Griphen of Dort 40 tonns, Cornelius Clawson master,
from Dort
The same Cornelius alien, with twenty millstones   £3   6s   8d
                                                         +£3   6s   8d

Halfe a last of doggestones   3s   0d
One great hundred Luke coales   8s   0d
One hundred *di'* bundles browne paper   7s   6d
                                                                 +7s   6d
Two hundred coddfishe   4s   8d

                                    Strangers custom   22s   5½d

March [?]1
[*444*] In the Thomas of Disert 30 tonns, Cuthbert Robinson master,
from Disert in Scotland
Archball Creesty Scot marchant, with thirty five waighes white salte   46s   8d
More one waighe white salt   16d

March *eod'*
[*445*] In the [?]Swann of Yermoth 25 tonns, Robert Harris master,
from Rotterdam[143]
Robert Soame *ind'* marchant, with one hundred Spaynish salt
containing tenn waighes   13s   4d
Six barrels figgs containing net 3 *C di'*   2s   11d
    +2s   11d
One barrel reysons *solis* containing net 2 *C* waight   22d
    +22d
Six smole loaves white suger containing 30 pounds net   10d
    +15d
One sack Spaynish woll containing 2 *C di'*   7s   6d
    +2s   6d
Twenty two hundred waight cordage   14s   8d
Twenty five pound peper net   2s   1d
    +2s   1d

March 4
[*446*] In the James of Donndee, James Moncker *predict'* from Donndee
in Scotland
The same James with three waighes bay salt *per* post entry   3s   0d

March 6
[*447*] In the William of Kercaudy 40 tonns, John More master, from
Kercaudy in Scotland
The same John Scot marchant, with foure waighes more white salte
per post entry   5s   4d

March 9
[*448*] In the Guifft of God of Kercaudy 50 tonns, William Mellen
master, from Kercaudy in Scotland
The said William Scot merchant, with fifty tonns Scot coales and more
ten tonns Scot coales   20s   0d

March 12
[*449*] In the Angell of Kercaudy 40 tonns, John Tenant master, from
Kercaudie in Scotland
The same John Scot merchant, with forty waighes white salt   53s   4d

f. 4r
[Lynn Regis
Entries of all goods and marchandice shipped from this porte in this quarter
begunn at the Nativity of Our Lorde Godd *anno* 1612][144]

Jannuary [*illegible*] 1612
[*450*] In the Griphen of Dorte [?]50 tonns, [Cornelius Clawson]
master, to Dorte
The same Cornelius alien marchant, with eight thousand oil [?cakes]
[*remainder illegible*]   [*sum illegible*]
Three tonns stronge beere   [*sums illegible*]

Jannuary 5
[*451*] In the George of Dortt 30 tonns, [?]Hybert Johnson [master], to Dortt
The same Hybert alien, with two tonns beere   [?]1s   9d
                                                               [*2nd sum illegible*]

Jannuary 15
[*452*] In the [?]Barke Allen of Kercaudy 35 tonns, John [?]Darrsey
master, to Kercaudy in Scotland
The same John Scot marchant, with nyne barrells beere   2s   3d
                                                                 +12s   9d

February 1
[*453*] In the Angell of Abberdyn 50 tonns, John Hayton master,
to Abberdin in Scotland
William Donalson Scot merchant, with thirty five tonns beere   52s   6d
                                                            +£14 17s   6d

February 4
[*454*] In the Mary Katherin of Kercaudy 30 tonns, David Balfore
master, to Kercaudy in Scotland
The same David Scot marchant, with seaven tonns beere   10s   6d
                                                                 +59s   6d

February 9
[*455*] In the Angell of Abberdyn 50 tons, John Hayton master, to
Abberdyn in Scotland
William Donalson Scot merchant, with foure tonns beere   6s   0d
                                                                 +34s   0d

f. 4v

February 10

[456] In the [?]Greyhound of [?]Delphaven 13 tonns, John Jacobson
master, to Delphaven

The same John alien merchant, with twelve peeces [*illegible*]	8s	0d
Two [?]hundred waight [*illegible*] [145]	5s	4d
	+5s	0d
Three half peeces English fustians		18d
Two peeces of threed sackcloth		8d
Three great [?grosse] threed poynts		18d
One peece Englishe sea——- [*illegible*]		16d
[?]Six single peces narrowe mocadoes	4s	0d
Strangers custom	5s	7d

February 13

[457] In the Angell of Abberdyn 50 tonns, John Heyton master,
to Abberdyn in Scotland

Alexander Henry Scot marchant, with fiften Devonshire dosens sengle

whereof one for a wraper	23s	4d
Twenty goads cotton		9d
Eight half peeces fustians	4s	0d
Two more Devenshire dosens	3s	4d

February 16

[458] In the Cocke of Flushing 15 tonns, Garrard Nabbs master, to
Flushing

Roger Harrwicke *ind'*, with fourten peeces English seas [*sic*]	18s	8d
Fiften peeces English durances	10s	0d
Thirty two peeces sengle narrowe mocadoes	21s	4d

February *eod'*

[459] In the the [*sic*] same shipp and master to Flushing

Garrard Nabbs alien marchant, with foure lastes five combes hempseed	42s	6d
Strangers custom	10s	7½d

February 17

[460] In the Paule of Amstrother 20 tonns, Henry Morris master,
 to Amstrother in Scotland

The same Morris Scot marchant, with six tonns beere	9s	0d
	+51s	0d

February 23

[461] In the George of Donndee 20 tonn, Andrewe Brand master,
to Donndee in Scotland

Alexander Allibertson Scot merchant, eight tonns beere   12s 0d
                                                                    +£3 8s 0d

[462] In the Grace of God of Kercaudy 25 tons, James Browne
master, to Kercaudy
John Cuisen Scotsh merchant, with foure tonns *di'* beere   6s 9d
                                                                     +38s 3d

f. 5r
March 1
[463] In the Grace of God of Mountrosse 20 tonns, James Oglbey
master, to Mountrosse in Scotland
John Beety Scotsh marchant, with fourten tonns beere   21s 0d
                                                                    +£5 19s 0d

March *eod'*
[464] In the George of Donndee [?]20 tonns, Andrewe Brand master,
to Donndee in Scotland
Alexander [Allibertson] Scot merchant, with [?]2 tonns beere[146]   3s 0d
                                                                     +17s 0d

March 3
[465] In the George of Kercaudy 30 tonns, George Balcaukew[e]ll
master, to Kercaudy in Scotland
Andrew Leighton Scot merchant, with sixten grosse of cruell
gerdling containing 12 dosen *per* grosse   10s 8d

March 5
[466] In the Grace of Mountrosse 20 tonns, James Oglbey master, to
Mountrosse in Scotland
Robert Gryme Scotsh merchant, with eleaven yards browne coloured
kersye and eighten yards stamell coloureds accepted for half a short cloth 3s 4d

March 6
[467] In the Grace of Mountrosse 20 tonns, James Oglbey master,
to Mountrosse
John Beety Scotsh marchant, with three tonns beere   4s 6d
                                                                     +25s 6d

March 10
[468] In the James of Donndee 20 tonns, James Moncker master, to
Donndee in Scotland
The same James Scot, with three tonns *di'* beere   5s 3d
                                                                     +29s 9d

March 10

[*469*] In the Grace of Mountrosse 20 tonns, James Oglbey master,
to Mountrosse in Scotland

John Beety Scotsh marchant, with one dosen *di'* lyned hatts	3s	0d
Foure double peeces valures	8s	0d
One dosen *di'* rownd hatt bands valued at 15s		9d
Six half peeces English fustians	3s	0d
Three grosse eight dosen crewell gerdling	2s	5½d
One shortt broad cloth *di'* five yards	11s	4d
Three ounces gallown lace vallued at 6s 8d		4d

March 15

[*470*] In the Paradice of Amsterdam, William Cornelius master, from [*sic*] Amsterdam[147]

Nathaniell Maxey *ind'* allowed by speciell warrant by the fermers, 340 payre[148] short
worrstead stockens, 2 straights for wrappers, and more one hundred waight horse-
hayre and 5 *C* leather tawed
/ This was passed by store as will appeare by the booke of the farmors deputies/

f. 5v

Wells *cum* Burnham

Entries of all goods and marchandice brought into the creekes and members of this
porte for this quarter begonn at the Nativity of Our Lord God *anno* 1612

Jannuary 9 1612

[*471*] In the Estrich of Camphire 15 tonns, Jacobe Bonis master,
from Camphire[149]

The same Jacobe alien, with two [?]lastes oates	[?]3s	0d
Strangers custom		12d

February 22

[*472*] In the Fisher of Amsterdam 40 tonns, Hugh Hendrickson
master, from Amsterdam[150]

Henry Congham *ind'* merchant, with twenty two waighes Spaynish salt freed by speciall warrannt for his Island fishing		nil
Thirty barrells white herrings	12s	6d
Two thousand waight tarred cordage	13s	4d
One last smale tarr and one last *di'* smale pitch	5s	0d
Three hundred waight prewnes		18d
		+9d
One barrell containing foure peec[e]s great reasons	2s	0d
	+2s	0d
One hundred Norrway deales	10s[151]	0d

February 27
[*473*] In the Flying Hart of Rotterdam 40 tonns, John Engle master,
from Rotterdam

The same Engle alien, twenty six waighes Spaynish salt	34s	*8d*
One hundred *et di'* Holland cheese	6s	0d
Strangers custom	8s	9½d

March 8
[*474*] In the same ship and master from Rotterdam

The said John Engle alien, *per* post entrie one waighe Spaynish salte	20d

March 12
[*475*] In the Estrich of Camphire 15 tonns, Jacobe Bonis master,
from Camphire[152]

The same Jacobe alien marchant, 2 *C* waight cordage	16d
Foure hundred waight cheese	16d
Two barrells tarr	4d
Three cooper ketles vallued at 20s	12d
Strangers custom	12d

f. 6r
Wells *cum* Burnham
Entries of all goods and marchandice shipped from the creekes and members of
this porte for this quarter begon at the Nativity of Our Lord God *anno 1612*

February [?]12 1612
[*476*] In the Estrich of Camphire [15] tonns, Jacobe Bomis master
for Camphire

The same Jacobe alien entred two hundred waight [?]pewter	5s	4d
	+5s	0d
Strangers custom	5s	4d

March 12
[*477*] In the Mewne of Wells 80 tonns, Thomas Fasett master, for the
Isliond fishing
Henry Congham *ind'* entreth 22 waighes Spaynish salt for which the
custome was formerly allowed at the comeinge of the said salt inward
for this purpose as *per* entry inward taken the 22 of February last
appeareth[153]   nil

f. 6v
Lynn Regis
Entries of all goods and marchandice brought into this porte in this quarter begon at
the Annunciation of the Blessed Virgin *anno 1613*

March 26 1613
[*478*] In the Cocke of Flushing 15 tonns, Garrard Nabbs master,
from Flushing[154]

The same Garrard alien marchant, with five waighes *di'* bay salt	5s	6d
Tenn barrels Flemish onions		8d
Foure hundrend waight cheese		16d
Strangers custom		22½d

Aprill 7
[*479*] In the John of Kinghorne 25 tonns, John Tompson master, from
Kinghorne in Scotland

David Boswell Scotsh marchant with twenty five tonns Scot coales	8s	4d
[?]Foure hundred ells lynen cloth	12s	0d
One hundred waight Scot yarne		15d
Twenty yards tiking		8d

Aprill 7
[*480*] In the George of Kercaudy 40 tonns, George Balcauckwell master,
from Curras in Scotland

The same George Scot merchant, with forty twoe waighes white salt	56s	0d

Aprill *eod'*
[*481*] In the Jacobe of Kercaudy 24 tonns, John Cuisen master, from
Kercaudy in Scotland

The same John Scot marchant, with twentie five waighes white salt	33s	4d
Two hundred waight Scot yarne	2s	6d
One hundred ells lynen cloth	3s	0d
One hundred and quarter Scot tiking *yards* [*sic*]	5s	0d

Aprill 7
[*482*] In the Mary Katherin of Kercaudy 30 tonns, David Balfore master,
from Kercaudy in Scotland

The same David Scot marchant, with forty twoe waighes white salt	56s	0d
Six hundred waight yarne	7s	6d
Three [?]score yards Scot tiking	2s	0d

f.7r
Aprill [*illegible*]
[*483*] In the [Jacobe] of [Kercaudy] 24 tonns, John [Cuisen] master,
from Kercaudy in Scotland

The same John Cuisen Scot merchant, *per* post entry half a hundred ells lynen cloth	[?]18d

April 22
[*484*] In the [?]Judith of Lynn 40 tonns, Thomas Hillson master,
[from] Norwaie by distress of weather
John Corney *ind'* marchant, with twelve thousand [*illegible*] at 13s 4d
per thousand   8s   0d

Aprill *eod'*
[*485*] In the Barrbara of Lyn 30 tonns, Robert Hayes master,
from Amsterdam[155]
The said Robert *ind'*, with seaven hundred clapholt   5s   3d
Two lastes great band pitch, one last smale band pitch   8s   8d
One hundred bundles browne paper[156]   5s   0d
                                                                 +5s   0d

April 22
[*486*] In the Paradice of Amsterdam 40 tonns, William Cornelius
master, from Amsterdam
The same William alien marchant, with eleaven barrels great band
pitch, two lastes great band tarr, one last smale band tarr   11s   8½d
Three hundred smale sparrs and one hundred bomesparrs   4s   8d
Twenty foure cant sparrs   4½d
Forty five smale masts   7s   6d
One hundred Norway deales and *a* last great band pitch   8s   4d
                                          Strangers custom   8s   1½d

Aprill *eod'*
[*487*] In the same shipp and master from Amsterdam[157]
Robert Thorey *ind'* marchant, with half a last of great band pitch
and half a last great band tarr   2s   8d
Two hundred waight ropes   16d
Foure barrels reasens *solis* containing five hundred seaventy pound net   5s   1d
                                                                 +5s   1d
Five hundred waight gom arabecke   5s   0d
                                                                 +2s   6d
One hundred cane reeds   2d

f. 7v
Aprill *eod'*[158]
[*488*] In the Paradice of Amsterdam *predict'*
Nathaniell Maxye [?]*ind'* merchant, with half a last great band pitch   2s   8d
One puncheon prewnes containing net 4 *C* sixtie pounds[159]   2s   3½d
                                                                 +13¾d
One sacke [? currants containing net] one hundred five score two pounds   2s   10d
                                                                 +6s   4½d

One barrell powder suger containing [? 1 C] eight pounds net	3s	7d
	+2s	7¾d
One barrell [?]caster suger containing net 1 C 20 pounds	3s	11½d
	+5s	11d
One barrell reasons *solis* containing 1 C [?]48 pounds	[?]15½d	
	+15½d	

Six pounds [?]maces, [?24] pounds pepper, 4 pounds cloves, 6 pounds nuttmegs, six pounds sinamond, vallued at [?]£6 11s 1½d net 5 *per cent* allowed

	6s	6½d
	+6s	6½d

Aprill 29
[489] In the [?]Margarly Ann of Lynn 70 tonns, Thomas Drewery master from [?]Lesborne in Portingale
John Wallis, 69 wayes Spaynish salt
John Wallis *ind'* marchant, of that whereof this marchant was allowed forty five waighes for his Island fishing
The duties received for twenty foure waighes   32s   0d

May 26
[490] In the Margeret of Kercaudy 35 tonns, Andrew Messterton master, from Kercaudy in Scotland
The same Andrewe Scot merchant, with forty waighes white salt   53s   4d

May 29
[491] In the Emanuell of Lynne 100 tonns, John Bloy master, from [?]Krechin in Scotland
William Doughtie *ind'* merchant, with eightie five tonns Scotsh coales   28s   4d

June 2
[492] In the Cocke of Flushing 15 tonns, Garrard Nabbs master, from Flushing[160]
The said Garrard alien, entred five lastes French rye and more entred
the 5 of June next after by the said stranger, tenn combs French rye   13s   9d
Strangers custom   3s   5d

June *eod'*
[493] In the William of Kercaudy 16 tonns, Robert Donckan master, from Kircaudy in Scotland
The same Robert Scot merchant, twenty wayes whit salt   26s   8d

June 4
[494] In the same shipp and master from Kercaudy in Scotland
The said Robert Donckan *per* post entry one waye *di'* salt   2s   0d

f. 8r

June [*illegible*]

[*495*] In the [? Mary Katherine] of [?]Kercaudy 30 tonns, David
Balfore master, from Kercaudy [? in Scotland]

The same David [? Scot merchant], with forty twoe waighes of
white salt   56s   0d

June *eod'*

[*496*] In the Blessing of Curras [?]20 tonns, James Bawde master,
from Curras in Scotland

Patricke [?]Keyre Scot [?merchant], with twenty one waighes white salt   28s   0d

June *eod'*

[*497*] In the Michaell of [?]Barrowston 20 tonns, Alexander Gibb
master, from Barrowston in Scotland

The said Alexander Gibb Scot, with [?]eighteen [tonns] coales   6s   0d

June 21

[*498*] In the Paradice of Amsterdam 30 tonns, William Cornelius
master, from Amsterdam[161]

The same William alien merchant, with five hundred clapholt   3s   0d
Two hundred *di'* Norway deales   12s   6d
One last great band pitch   3s   4d
One hundred bome sparrs, one hundred smale sparrs and more
one hundred bome sparrs   4s   4d
                                         Strangers custom   5s   9½d

June *eod'*

[*499*] In the Paradice of Amsterdam *predict'*

William Doughtie *ind'* marchant, with two lastes great bonnd pitch and
three lasts smale band tarr   12s   8d
One barrell with powder suger containing five score net   2s 11d
                                                                      +2s   2d
*One barrel reysens *solis*[162] containing 2 *C* net [*sic*]   22d
                                                                        +22d*

June *eod'*

[*500*] In the Lion of Barrowston, James Gibbe master, from
Barrowston in Scotland

The same James Scot, with nynten tonns Scot coales   6s   4d

June *eod'*
[*501*] In the George of Kercaudy 40 tonns, Georg[*e*] Balcauckwell
master, from Kercaudy in Scotland

The said George Scot, with fortie two wayes whit salt	56s	0d
One hundred waight Scot yarne		15d

June 22
[*502*] In the Good Fortune of Kercaudy 30 tonns, John Hogg master,
from Kercaudy

Thomas Lambe Scot merchant, with forty wayes white salt	54s	4d

f. 8v
Lynn Regis
Entries of all goods and marchandice shipped from this porte for this quarter begon
at the Annunciation of the Blessed Virgin *anno* 1613

March 27 *anno* 1613
[*503*] In the Griphen of Dortt 40 tonns, Cornelius Clawson master,
for Doortt

The same Cornelius alien merchant, with two thousand oile cakes great and smale valued at £9	9s	0d
Three combs musterd seed containing [*illegible*] *C* waight		15d
Strangers custom	2s	7d
Twoe tonns *di'* stronge beere[163]	4s	8d
	+25s	0d

March 29
[*504*] In the Rose of Lynn 30 tonns, John Denmarke master, to Island

Erasmus Cootes alien marchant, with *di'* waigh Spaynish salt		8d
Two barrells *di'* wheate meale		6d
One hundred iron unwrought, one hundred iron wrought		14½d
Half hundred goads cotton at 6 score *per cent*	2s	0d
Two [?]runnletts aquavile containing quarter *et di'* hogshead		18d
Strangers custom		17½d
More fifty foure yardes kersies in remnants accepted for a short cloth	14s	6d
Five remnants penistones unfrized containing sixtie seaven yarde accepted for half a short cloth and 3 thirds [*sic*] of a peniston	8s	6d

Aprill 3
[*505*] In the Angell of Kercaudy 30 tonns, John Tenant master, to
Kercaudy in Scotland

Henry Reynoldson Scot, with one thousand oxe and cowe hornes	2s	6d
Two tonns stronge beere	3s	0d
	+17s	0d

Aprill [?]8
[506] In the Cocke of Flushing 15 tonns, Garrard Nabbs master, to
Flushing
The said Garrard alien, *one last* di' lynnseed   18s   9d

Aprill eod'
[507] In the same shipp and master to Flushing
Thomas Spicer ind', two dosen lynen capps and sixe payre worrstead
stockens   14½d

Aprill 15
[508] In the Jacobe of Kercaudy 24 tonns, John Cuisen master, to
Kercaudy in Scotland
The same John, with seaven tonns stronge beere   10s   6d
                                                                  +59s   6d

f. 9r
Aprill [?]17
[509] In the Jacobe of Kercaudy 24 tonns, John Cuisen master, to
Kercaudy [? in Scotland]
The same John Scotsh marchant, two tonns stronge beere[164]   [?]3s   0d
                                                                +[?]17s   0d

Aprill [?]21[165]
[510] In the Mary Katherin of Kercaudy 30 tonns, David Balfore
master, to Kercaudy in Scotland
The same David Scot, with six tonns stronge beere   9s   0d
                                                                  +51s   0d

Aprill 26
[511] In the Pleasure of Lynn 60 tonn, Edward Ackworth master, to
Elbing in the East Cuntrey
Thomas Snelling ind' marchant, with sixteen rowles gray conyskynes
seasoned containing 26 thousand   £4   6s   8d
And thirty eight thousand gray skynes stage   £3   3s   4d
Foure dryfitts, seaven trusses and a smale baskett containing foure
thousand black rabit skynes   30s   0d
Three hundred blacke cony skynes seasoned   8s   0d
Three hundred catt skynes   4s   0d
And thirten hundred sheeps leather tawed   19s   6d
More two thousand gray cony skynes tawed   13s   4d
And foure thousand untaw[e]d mortskynes   20s   0d
Twentie foure foxcaces[166]   10d
More packed in kipps sixten hundred sheeps leather tawed   24s   0d

Aprill 28

[*512*] In the same shipp and master to Elbing in th'East Cuntrey

Thomas March *ind'*, with six thousand gray cony skynes seasoned	20s	0d
Three thousand *di'* gray skynes stage	5s	10d
Three little trusses containing 15 *C* mort lambe skynes untawd	7s	6d
Fiften hundred white leather tawed	22s	6d
Twenty eight shortt broad cloathes in halves whereof two and a half for wrappers	£8 10s	0d

May 3

[*513*] In the George of Kercaudy 40 tonns, George Balcauckwell master, to Kercaudy in Scotland

The same George Scot marchant, with two tonns beere	3s	0d
	+17s	0d

May 4

[*514*] In the John of Kinghorne 20 tonns, John Tompson master, to Kinghorne in Scotland

David Boswell Scot marchant, with seaven tonns beere	10s	6d
	+59s	6d

f. 9v

May [?]*eod'*

[*515*] In the Dolphen of [? Lynn 50] tonns, Robart Constable[167] master, to Elbing

Thomas Snelling *ind*, with eight thousand sheeps leather tawd	£6 0s	0d
Two rowles gray conyskynes containing 4 thousand seasoned and four thousand stage	20s	0d
More foure hundred white leather tawd	6s	0d

May 7

[*516*] In the John of Kinghorne 20 tonns, John Tompson master, to Kinghorne in Scotland

David Boswell Scot merchant, with foure tonns beere[168]	6s	0d
	+34s	0d

May 8

[*517*] In the George of Kercaudy 40 tonns, George Balcauckwell master, to [?] Curras in Scotland

Sir George Bruice[169] *ind'* knight hath shipped in this porte by vertue of a speciall lycence bearing date the first of [?]May 1613 seaven *score* and seaven quarters pease and beanes, and hath paid duties for six score and seaven quarters	£8 9s	4d

May 13
[*518*] In the Paradice of Amsterdam 30 tonns, William Cornelius master,
to Amsterdam
Nathaniell Maxey *ind'* marchant, with six score payre shorte white
worrstead stockens   16s   0d

June 4
[*519*] In the Margeret of Kercaudy 30 tonns, Andrewe Messterton
master, to Curras in Scotland
Sir George Bruice *predict'* hath shipped in this porte by his said speciall
licence sixty quarters pease and beanes bare measure, and hath paid
duties for fifty quarters   £3   6s   8d
The shipp master above*said* hath paid duties and laden into this
shipp two tonns beere   3s   0d
                                                                   +17s   0d

June 19
[*520*] In the Mary Katherin of Kercaudy 30 tonns, David Balfore
master, to Kercaudie in Scotland
Sir George Bruice *predict'* hath shipped by his said speciall licence and
paid duties for fiften quarters pease and beanes   20s   0d
The shippmaster abovesaid hath shipped and paid duties for five
tonns beere   7s   6d
                                                                   +42s   6d

June 21
[*521*] In the same shipp and master to Kercaudy in Scotland
Sir George Bruice *predict'* hath shipped in this port by his said lycence
forty *two* quarters pease and beanes and hath paid duties for thirtie
six quarters   48s   0d

f. 10r[170]
Wells *cum* Burnham
Entries of all goods [and marchandice brought] into the creekes and [members
of this porte] in this quarter begon at [the Annunciation of] the Blessed Virgin
anno [1613]

March 25 1613
[*522*] In the Fortune of [?]Sneacke 30 tonns, Peter [?]Peterson master,
from Rotterdam[171]
Henry Congham master marchant [*sic*], twenty twoe waighes Spaynish salt
whereof he claymeth by order from the greene cloth[172] fiften waighes
for the furnishing his two shipps for Island, soe the duties paid for seaven
waighes Spaynish [salt]   [*sum illegible*]

Aprill 3
[*523*] In the Hope of Flushinge 10 tonns, Cornelius Verduse master,
from Flushing[173]
The said stranger, with two waighe[s] bay salt   [?]2s   6d

Aprill *eod'*
[*524*] In the Fortune of Amsterdam 40 tonns, Bernard Alberson
master, from Amsterdam[174]
Henry Congham *ind'* merchant, with twenty eight waighes
Spaynish salte   37s   4d
Three hundred smale sparrs, two hundred cant sparrs   6s   4d
Half a last smale band pitch and a last great band tarr   4s   4d
One cheest *et di'* white Normandy glasse   18d
Two hundred *di'* Norway deales   12s   6d

May 25
[*525*] In the Estrich of Camphire 15 tonns, Jacob Phillipson master
master [*sic*], from Camphire[175]
The said Jacobe alien, one last *et di'* French rye   4s   8d

June 22
[*526*] In the John of Kinghorne 25 tonns, John Tompson master,
from Kinghorne in Scotland
The said Tompson Scot marchant, with twenty five tonns Scotsh coales   8s   4d

f. 10v
Wells *cum* Burnham
Entries of all goods and marchandise shipped from the creekes and members of
this porte in this quarter begon at th'Anunciation of the Blessed Virgin *alias*
the 25 of March 1613

March 29
[*527*] In the Estrich of Camphire 15 tonns, Jacobe Bomis master,
for Camphire
The said Jacobe alien merchant, with twenty pounde English saffron   25s   0d

March *eod'*
[*528*] In the John of Wells 36 tonns, Eliza [*sic*] Kinge[176] master, for the
Island fishing
Henry Congham *ind'* entreth tenn waighes Spaynish salt which was
sufferd him to have free of custome for this vioag [*sic*] at the comeing
in of the said salt as *per* entry inward taken the 25 of March appeareth[177]   nil

March *eod'*
[529] In the Newyere of Wells 40 tonns, William Starking master,
for the Island fishing
Henry Congham *ind'* entreth five waighes Spaynishe salt which was
alloued unto *him* for this vioage at the brin[g]ing in of the said salt
as *per* entry thereof taken *ut supr' dict'*   nil

June 5
[530] In the Estrich of Camphire 15 tonns, Jacobe Phillipson master,
to Camphire
The said Jacope [*sic*] alien, with twenty pound English safferon   25s   0d

f. 11r
Lynn Regis
Entries of all goods and marchandice brought into this porte in this quarter
begonn at the feast of Sanct John Baptist *alias* middsomer *anno* 1613

June 26 1613
[531] In the Lion of Barrowston 20 tonns, John Gibb master, from
Barrowston in Scotlande
The same John Gibbe Scot marchant, *per* post entry nyne tonns
Scotsh coales   3s   0d

June *eod'*
[532] In the Michaell of Barrowston 20 tonns, Alexander Gibb
master, from Barrowston in Scotland
The said Alexander Scots marchant, *per* post entry twelve tonns
Scots coales   4s   0d

June 28
[533] In the Blessing of Curras 20 tons, James Bawde master, from
Curras in Scotland
Patricke Keyre Scots marchant, with six waighes white salt *per* post entry   8s   0d

June *eod'*
[534] In the Fortune of Enchuzan 7 score tonns, Bernard Isbrandson
master, from Romsdale in Norwaie
John Androws *ind'* marchant, with three hundred eightie foure peeces
of firr balkers containing 6 thousand 6 hundred eighten foote at
4d *per* foote   £5 10s   4d
Seaven hundred Norwaie deales   35s   0d

Jully 7

[535] In the Margert of Kercaudy 40 tonns, Andrewe Messterton
master, from Kercaudy in Scotland

The said Andrewe Scots merchant, with fortie tonns Scots coales	13s	4d
Half hundred ells lynen cloth		18d

Jully 7

[536] In the Margerett of Barrowston *alias* Kercaudie [*sic*] 40 tonns,
Andrewe Messterton master, from Kercaudy in Scotland

David Boswell Scots marchant, with eight hundred ells lynen cloth	24s	0d
And more foure hundred ells lynen cloth	12s	0d
Fiften score yards tiking	10s	0d
One hundred ells lynen cloth	3s	0d
Three quarters of the hundred Scotsh yarne		11d

f. 11v

Jully 9

[537] In the Dolphin of Lynn 50 tonns, Robert Constable master,
from Danske in th'East Cuntrey

Thomas Snelling *ind'*, with twenty and tenn lastes Dans[k]e rye freed of custome by speciall warrant		nil
Foure packes Spruce flax containing 34 *C* waight	25s	6d
One tonn, three quarters Spruce iron	12s	3d
Twentie two Spruce deales	2s	9d

Jully 10

[538] In the same shipp from Danske in the East Cuntrey

William Petis *ind'*, with sixten kaggs sturgeon[178]	5s	4d
	+5s	4d

July 14

[539] In the Providence of Kercaudy 50 tonns, James Lawe master,
from Kercaudy in Scotland

The same James Scots marchant, with fifty waighes white salt	£3	6s	8d

Jully 17

[540] In the Pleasure of Lynne 80 tonns, Edward Ackworth master,
from Danske

Thomas Snelling *ind'*, twenty six lastes rye freed by speciall warrannt			nil
Twelve packes flax containing nynty six hundred waight	£3	12s	0d
Two tonns Spruce iron		14s	0d
Foure hauckes *vocat'* tassells[179]		2s	8d
		+2s	8d
*Fifty *di'* cheests white Burgondy glasse		50s	0d*

Jully 19
[*541*] In the Blewhenn of Flyland 150 tonns, Lucas Jacobson master,
from Danske
John White *ind'* marchant,[180] with twenty lasts great band pitch and
tarr and more eight lastes great band pitch £4 13s 4d
Fourten lastes smale band pitch and 3 lastes smale tarr 34s 0d
Thirty six half cheests whit[*e*] Burgondy glasse 36s 0d
Twenty hundred clapholt 15s 0d
Half hundred waynscots 4s 0d
+4s 0d
Sixtie bundles Spruce flax containing 17 *C* 12s 9d
Tenn kaggs sturrgeon 3s 4d
+3s 4d
Seaven lastes Danske rye freed *per* speciall warrannt nil

Jully 19
[*542*] In the same shipp and master from Danske
Thomas March *ind'*, with 9 last great tarr, 9 last great pitch £3 0s 0d
Twenty waynscots, three kaggs sturrgeon[181] 2s 4d
+2s 4d

f. 12r
Jully 22
[*543*] In the Providence of Kercaudy 50 tonns, James Lawe master,
from Kercaudy in Scotland
The said James Scots merchant, six waighes white salt *per* post entry 8s 0d

Jully 23
[*544*] In the Mary Katherin of Kercaudy 30 tonn, David Balfore
master, from Kercaudy in Scotland
The same David Scots marchant, with forty twoe waighes white salt 56s 0d

Jully 26
[*545*] In the Jacobe of Kercaudy 25 tonns, John Cuisen master, from
Kercaudy in Scotland
The same John Cuisen Scots marchant, with foure thousand coddfishe
and forty lings £4 14s 5d

Jully *eod'*
[*546*] In the Clemence of Lynne 25 tonns, Deonis Olley master, from
Curras in Scotland
William Atkin *ind'*, with twenty foure waighes whit salt 32s 0d

Jully *ult'*
[547] In the same shipp and master from Curras in Scotland
William Atkin *ind', per* post entry foure waighes white salt   5s   4d

July *eod'*
[548] In the Jacobe of Kercaudy th'abovesaid John Cuisen master from
Kercaudy in Scotland
The said John Cuisen, *per* post entry one thousand three hundred
coddfish   30s   4d

August 16
[549] In the Fortune of Amsterdam 40 tonns, Anthony Iserell master,
from Amsterdam
Henry Robinson *ind'* merchant, with twenty one lasts Danske rye   52s   6d
Foure peec[e]s Holland[182] containing 30 ells *per* peece   8s   0d
   +8s   0d
Six barrels tarras   12d

August *eod'*
[550] In the same shipp and master from Amsterdam
Anthony Iserell master and mer*chant*, with one cheest one smale
barrel loaffe suger containing 2 *C* forty pounds net   8s   0d
   +12s   0d
Two waighes Reynish glasse   5s   0d
Six firkins Flemish soape   3s   0d
One smale caske containing 6 pounds maces[183]   2s   0d
   +2s   0d
    Strangers custom   4s   6d

f. 12v
August *eod'*
[551] In the Barrbara of Lynn 30 tonns, Robert Hayes master, from
Amsterdam
Henry Robinson *ind'*, with fiften lastes Danske rye   [?]37s   6d
Five hundredwaight cheese   20d

August 18
[552] In the Blacke Dogge of Delph 16 tonns, Roger Yearlove master,
from Memlicke[184]
The said Roger alien merchant, with five thousand bunches
Flemish onions   20s   10d
    Strangers custom   5s   2½d

August 19

[553] In the Barrbara of Lynne 30 t[onn]es, Robert Hayes master, from Amsterdam

The said Robert *ind'*, with one dry fatt containing 4 *C* waight suger	13s	4d
	+20s	0d
Foure hundred waight cordage	2s	8d
More one smale cable containing 6 *C* waight	[?]4s	0d

August 21

[554] In the Fortune of Amsterdam 40 tonns, Anthony Iserell master, from Amsterdam

Nathaniell Maxey[185] *ind'* marchant, with one sack containing thirty pounds West India ginger	12d	
	+12d	
One barrel containing 1 *C* fortie eight pounds net loaffe suger	4s	11d
	+7s	5d
One barrel containing 3 *C* 36 pounds net powder sugar	11s	2d
	+8s	4½d
One cheest containing fortie seaven pounds sinom[on]d net	7s	10d
	+7s	10d
One sack anniseeds containing three quarters of the hundred	15d	
	+9d	
One barrel containing 34 pounds net nuttmeggs	5s	1d
	+5s	1d

August 23

[555] In the Harry of Kercaudy 20 tonns, David Willson master, from Kercaudy in Scotland

The same David Scotsman, twentie foure tonns Scot coales	8s	0d

August 24

[556] In the George of Kercaudy 40 tonns, William Liele master, from Curras in Scotland

Sir George Bruice knight, with forty five waighes white salte	58s	8d
One hundred ells lynen cloth	3s	0d

August 28

[557] In the Grayhownd of Bolsworth[186] 140 t[onn]es Runnckey Grealtes master, from Danske

Thomas Snellinge[187] *ind'*, with 40 lasts smale pitch, twenty lasts *di'* great pitch, 12 lastes *di'* great tarr	£10	0s	0d
One hundred eighti[e] kaggs tarr at 12d *per* kagg		9s	0d
Six hundred *di'* ells hinderland linen cloth		8s	8d
		+4s	4d

Two hundred ells Slecia cloth	7s	4d
	+7s	4d
Thirty cheests containing 15 waighes Reynish glasse	37s	6d

f. 13r
September [?]2
[558] In the Grace of God of 40 tonns 40 tonns [*sic*], James Browne
master, from Kirrhon in Scotland

The said James Scotsman, with forty three tonns Scots coales	14s	4d

September 11
[559] In the Cocke of Flushing 15 tonns, Garrard Nabbs master,
from Flushing

Robert Sedgwicke *ind'*, with five lastes French rye	12s	6s

[560] In the same shippe the said Garrard alien merchant, with six

hundred bunches onions	3s	0d

September 20
[561] In the Bruice of Kercaudy [*no tonnage*], William Collier master,
from Kercaudy in Scotland

The said William marchant, with thirty eight waighes white salt	50s	8d
One last herrings	5s	0d
Six hundred ells lynen cloth	18s	0d

September *eod'*
[562] In the Margerett of Kercaudy 26 tonns, William Williamson
master, from Kercaudy in Scotland

The said Williamson Scotsman, with twenty six tonns Scots coales	8s	8d

f. 13v
Lynn Regis
Entries of all goods and marchandic[e] shipped from this porte in this quarter
begon at the feast of Sanct John Baptist *alias* midsomer *anno* 1613

June 25
[563] In the Blessing of Curras 20 tonns, James Bawd master, to Curras in
Scotland
Sir George Bruice knight hath shipped in this porte by vertue of his
speciall licence dated the first of May 1613 fifty two quarters
di' pease andbeanes and hath paid duties for forty eight quarters

pease and beanes	£3	4s	0d

June 26
[564] In the Clemence of Lynne 25 tonns, Deonis Olley master, to
Curras in Scotland
Sir George Bruice *predict'* hath shipp[ed] in this porte by vertue of
th'abovesaid licence seaven score and seaven quarters bare measure
pease and beanes and hath paid duties for six score and tenn
quarters pease and beanes   £8 13s   4d

June 28
[565] In the Blessinge of Curras *predict'*, James Bawde master, to Curras
Sir George Bruice hath shipped more in this porte by vertue of his
said licence twenty quarters of pease and beanes   26s   8d

June 30
[566] In the Michaell of Barrowston 18 tonns, Alexander Gibb
master, to Leith in Scotland
Sir George Bruice hath shipped more in this porte by the aforesaid
licence foure score quarters pease and beanes and hath paid
duties for three score and twelve quarters pease and beanes £4 16s   0d

[567] In the said shipp for James Bawde two tonns beere   3s   0d
                                                               +17s   0d

/ *Videlicet in the Blessing last abovesaid* /[188]

Jully 7
[568] In the Good Fortune of Kercaudy 30 tonns, John Hogg master,
to Kercaudy in Scotland
John Greene *ind'* hath shipped in *this* porte by vertue of
another speciall licence *dat'* 10 May *1613* [*illegible*] [?]quarters
pease and beanes   £4   4s   0d
/ *Greens licence* /

f. 14r
Jully 14
[569] In the Paradice of Amsterdam 40 tonns, William Cornelius
master, to Amsterdam
The said William alien, with fourten hundred oile cakes great and
smale vallued at 9s *per cent*   6s   4d
One last of lynnseed   10s   0d
                                        Strangers custom   4s   1d

July *eod'*
[570] In the [*same*] shipp and master to Amsterdam
Nathaniell Maxey *ind'*, with eight score and five payre of shortt
worstead stockens   22s   0d

Jully 17
[571] In the Margerett of Kercaudy 35 tonns, Andrew Messterton
master, to Kercaudy in Scotland
John Greene *ind'* hath shipped in this porte by speciall licence dated
ut predict' thirty quarters of pease and beanes   40s   0d
/ Greens licence dated 10 of May 1613/

Jully *eod'*
[572] In the same shipp and master to Kercaudy in Scotland for
Sir George Bruice by his foresaid speciall licence, shipped twenty two
quarters pease and beanes and hath paid duties for twenty quarters   26s   8d

July 19
[573] In the George of Kercaudy 40 tonns, George Balcauckwell
master, to Curras in Scotland
Sir George Bruice knight hath shipped in this port by speciall
warrannt eight score quarters pease and beanes and hath paid
duties for seven score and two quarters *et di'* quarter   £9 10s   0d

Jully 20
[574] In the same shipp and master to Curras in Scotland
Sir George Bruice hath *shipped* in this porte by speciall lycence
twentie two quarters pease and beanes and hath paid duties for
twenty quarters[189]   26s   8d

Jully 29
[575] In the Mary Katherin of Kercaudy 30 tonns, David Balfore
master, to Kercaudy in Scotland
Sir George Bruice by speciall licence *ut predict'* hath shipped and
paid duties for 6 score quarters pease and beanes   £8   0s   0d

f. 14v
Jully *ult'*
[576] In the Jacobe of Kercaudy 25 tonns, John Cuisen master, to
Kercaudy in Scotland
John Greene *ind'* hath shipped more by speciall lycence thirty quarters
pease and beanes   40s   0d

Jully *eod'*
[*577*] In the Jacobe of Kercaudy *predict'*, John Cuisen master, to
Kercaudy in Scotland
The said John Cuisen Scots, two tonns beere   3s   0d
                                                              +17s   0d

August 4
[*578*] In the same shipp and master to Kercaudy
John Cuisen *predict'*, with one tonn *et di'* beere[190]   2s   3d
                                                              +12s   9d

August 9
[*579*] In the Mary Katherin of Kercaudy, David Balfore master,
to Kercaudy in Scotland
The same David Scotsman, with three tonns beere   4s   6d
                                                              +25s   6d

August 14
[*580*] In the Alice of Lynne 30 tonns, John Taylior master, to
Leith in Scotland
David Boswell Scotsh marchant, twelve tonns beere   18s   0d
                                                            +£5   2s   0d

August 21
[*581*] In the same shipp and master to Leith in Scotland
David Boswell *predict'*, with six tonns beere[191]   9s   0d
                                                              +51s   0d

August 27
[*582*] In the Fortune of Amsterdam 40 tonns, Anthonie Iserell master,
to Amsterdam
Nathaniell Maxey *ind'* merchant, with eight score and eighten payre
shortt worrstead stockens   23s   9d

August 28
[*583*] In the Harry of Kercaudie 25 tonns, David Wilson master,
to Kercaudy in Scotland
The same David Scotsman, with five tonns beere   7s   6d
                                                              +42s   6d

September 11
[*584*] In the Grace of God of Kircaudie 40 tonns, James Browne
master, to Kercaudy in Scotland
The same James Browne Scotsman, with six tonns *di'* beere   9s   9d
                                                               +5s   3d

September 16
[585] In the Pleasure of Lynne 60 tonns, Edward Ackworth master, to
Elbing in th'East Cuntrey
Thomas Snelling *ind'* marchant, with foure thousand sheeps
leather tawed   £3   0s   0d
One trusse containing fiften hundred blacke rabett skynes   11s   3d

*[586] In the Harry *predict'*, David Wilson master and merchant,
the third of September, one tonn *di'* stronge beere[192]   2s   3d
                                                                    +12s   9d*

f. 15r
September 17
[587] In the same shipp and master to Elbing, *videlicet* the Pleasure
predict'
Thomas Snelling *ind'* merchant, with two thousand sheeps leather
tawed and more *di'* thousand[193]   37s   6d

September *eod'*
[588] In the Pleasure of Lynne aforesaid, Edward Ackworth master,
to Elbing
Thomas Slaney *ind'* merchant, with twenty seaven northerne kersies
for which the duties have bene paid at the porte of London as by
certificate thereof there dated the 10 of August 1613   nil

September *eod'*
[589] In the same shipp and master to Elbing in th'East Cuntrey
Thomas Snelling *ind'*, with five dosen of wollen stockens and six dosen
woollen stockens for children   13s   5d

September *eod'*
[590] In the Amey of Lynn 60 tonns, Robert Waters master, to
Leisborne in Portingale
Thomas Slaney *ind'* merchant, with twelve hundred pipe staves at
6 score *per cent*   4s   0d
Two hundred oiled sheeps leather   5s   4d
Tenn dozen oild calves skynes   6s   0d

September 27
[591] In the Bruice of Kircaudy 30 tonns, William Collier master,
to Amstrother in Scotland
The said William Scots merchant, with eight tonns stronge beere   12s   0d
                                                                    +£3   8s   0d

f. 15v
Wells *cum* Burnham
Entries of all goods and marchandice brought into the creekes and members of
this porte in this quarter ended at the feast of Sanct Michaell th'Archangell *anno*
1613

Jully 7
[592] In the Estrich of Camphire 15 tons, Jacobe Bonis master, from
Camphire
The same Jacobe alien brought in foure lastes French rye[194]   12s   6d

August 5
[593] In the Suzan of Wells 50 tons, Thomas Browne master, from Island
Henry Buckston *ind'* merchant, with foure hauckes *vocat'* jerfalkons[195]   6s   0d
                                                                        +6s   0d
Twoe hundred and a quarter lings   7s   6d
One barrell trayne oyle   12d
Two smale trusses and three barrels waddmole wattlings and
waddmole stockens valued at £10   10s   0d

August 7
[594] In the Meane of Wells 80 tons, Thomas Fasset master, from Island
John Webbster *ind'*, with seaven hauckes called jerfalkons and seaven
hauckes called tercells[196]   15s   2d
                                                                       +15s   2d
Six merlions valued at 40s   2s   0d

Eod' [*sic*]
[595] In the same shipp and master from Island
William Artson alien merchant, with six haucks *vocat'* jerfalkons and
nyne haucks called tassells[197]   15s   0d
                                                                       +15s   0d
                                              Strangers custom   3s   9d

Eod'
[596] In the same shipp and master from Island
Robert Coulte *ind'* merchant, with 12 score yards Island wadmole   9s   0d
Six hauckes called merlians valued at 20s   12d

August 20
[597] In the Estrich of Camphire 15 tons, Jacobe Bonis master,
from Camphire
The said Jacobe alien merchant, with twoe lasts French rye[198]   5s   3d

August 30
[*598*] In the Robert of Wells 20 tons, Simon Capps master, from Leith
in Scotland

John Yates *ind'* merchant, with sixten wayes whit salt	21s	3d
Three score ells Scots lynen cloth	3s	0d

f. 16r
Wells *cum* Burnham
Entries of all goods and marchandice shipped from the creekes and members of
this porte in this quarter ended at Michaelmas *ut predict'* anno 1613

July 27
[*599*] In the Estrich of Camphire 15 tons, Jacobe Bomis master,
to Camphire
The said Jacobe alien master [*sic*], with foure fothers and a

quarter of lead[199]	34s	0d
	+£4 5s	0d
Strangers custom	8s	6d

September 4
[*600*] In the Estrich of Camphire *predict'*, Jacobe Bomis master,
to Camphire

The said Jacobe alien merchant, with two tonns and half trayne oyle	20s	0d
Strangers custom	5s	0d

f. 16v
Lynn Regis
Entries of all goods and marchandice brought into this porte this quarter ended at
the Nativity of Our Lord *anno 1613*

September *ulti'*
[*601*] In the Tegar of Lynne 80 tonns, Violett Waynfforth master,
from Leizborne in Portingale

John Spence *ind'* merchant, with fifty waighes Spaynish salte	£3	6s	8d

September *eod'*
[*602*] In the same shipp and master from Leyzborne in Portingale
Thomas Slany *ind'* merchant, with three cheestes white sugar

containing seaven hundred waight	23s	4d
	+35s	0d
Two cernes licorise containing two hundred waight		12d
		+12d

October 1
[*603*] In the same shipp and master from Leizborne in Portingale
Thomas Slany *predict'* merchant, with two hundred three quarters
sugar *per* post entrie

9s 2d
+13s 9d

October 6
[*604*] In the Fortune of Amsterdam 40 tonns, Maltha' Garta master,
from Amsterdam
Nathaniell Maxey *ind'* marchant, with one hogshead two barrels and
one firkin containing one hundred three quarters powder suger

5s 10d
+4s 4½d

Two hundred waight loaffe sugar which perished in the haven in the
landing thereof

nil

Ten pounds cloves, twelve pounds maces

6s 6d
+6s 6d

Half hundred anniseeds

10½d
+6d

October *eod'*
[*605*] In the same shipp and master from Amsterdam
Robert Thorey *ind'* merchant, with two lastes Danske rye

5s 0d

Six hundred Norway deales

30s 0d

Two hundred bundles browne paper

10s 0d
+10s 0d

Two cables and other smale ropes containing 14 *C* waight

9s 4d

Fortie pounde net loaffe sugar

14½d
+21½d

October 11
[*606*] In the Margerett of Kircaudy 24 tonns, Davide Andreson
master, from Kircaudie in Scotland
The same David Scots merchant, with twenty six waighes white salt

34s 8d

Two barrels white herrings

10d

Three score ells linen cloth

18d

October 13
[*607*] In the Alice of Lynn 30 tonns, John Taylior master, from
Kinghorne in Scotland
The said John *ind'* merchant, with twentie six tonns Scots coales

8s 8d

f. 17r

October 20

[*608*] In the Margeret of [?Len]kell[200] 26 tonns, William Gray master, from Anverkeden[201] in Scotland
The said William Gray Scots merchant, with twentie six waighes
white salt   34s   8d

October *eod'*

[*609*] In the Margeret of Kircaudy 45 tonns, Alexander Lawe master, from Curras in Scotland
The said Alexander Scots marchant, with fortie five waighes
white salt   £3   0s   0d

October 21

[*610*] In the Marie Katherin of Kircaudie 30 tonns, David Balfore master, from Kircaudy in Scotland
The said Davide Scots merchant, with fortie two waighes white salte   56s   0d

October *eod'*

[*611*] In the Harry of Kircaudy 25 tonns, David Wilson master, from Kircaudy in Scotland
The same David Scots merchant, with twentie five waighes white salte   32s   0d

October *eod'*

[*612*] In the Angell of Creyle 20 tonns, William Cade master, from Creyle in Scotland
John Smith Scots merchant, with nyne lasts white herrings   45s   0d

October 25

[*613*] In the John of Kinghorne 25 tonns, John Tompson master, from Kinghorne in Scotland
The said John Scots merchant, with twenty five tons coales   8s   4d

October *eod'*

[*614*] In the George of Kircaudy 25 tonns, George Balkauckwell
The said George Scots marchant,[202] with fortie twoe waighes white salt   56s   0d
Twoe lastes white herrings   10s   0d

October *eod'*

[*615*] In the Margeret of Lenkell 25 tonns, William Gray master,
<to> *from* Lenkell in Scotland
The said William Scotsh merchant, with two waighes white salt by
post entrie   2s   8d

October *eod'*
[*616*] In the Margeret of Kircaudy 45 tonns, Alexander Lawe master,
from Kircaudy in Scotland
The said Alexander Scots merchant, with one waighe white salte *per*
post entrie   16d

f. 17v

October 27
[*617*] In the Margeret of Kircaudy 24 tonns, William Williamson
master, from Kircaudy in Scotland
The said William Scots merchant, with twenty six waighes white salt   34s   8d

October *eod'*
[*618*] In the John of Kinghorne 30 tonns, John Tompson master,
from Kinghorne in Scotland
The said John Scots merchant *per* post entrie, nyne tonns Scot coales   3s   0d

October 29
[*619*] In the Mergery of Amstrother 10 tonns, Robert Mellin master,
from Amstrother in Scotland
The said Robert Scots merchant, with eight lastes white herrings   40s   0d

October *eod'*
[*620*] In the Andrewe of Dondee 15 tonns, Alexander Kircaudy master,
from Dondee in Scotland
Andrewe Gray Scots merchant, with fiften chalder seacoales   10s   0d
One hundred ells lynen cloth   3s   0d

November 15
[*621*] In the Pleasure of Lynn 80 tonns, Edward Ackworth master,
from Danske in th'East Cuntrey
Thomas Snelling *ind'* marchant, with thirty seaven lasts Danske rye
and foure lastes Danske wheate freed of the duties by speciall licence   nil
Six hundred *di'* waight candleweeke   4s   4d
                                                                           +4s   4d
                                                                            8d
One hauke *vocat'* a tessell   +8d

November [?]15
[*622*] In the Orrengtree of Amsterdam 40 tonns, Peter Messell master,
from Amsterdam
Jervase Wharton *ind'* merchant, with nynten lasts Danske rye freed by
speciall warrannt *ut superius dicte*   nil
Two hundred three quarters Norway deales   13s   9d
Two hundred and quarter smale sparrs   2s   3d
One trusse Spruce canvas containing 12 boults   8s   0d

November 17

[623] In the Fortune of Amsterdam 80 tonns, Andrewe Johnson
master, from Amsterdam

Jervase Wharton *ind'* merchant, with twelve lastes *di'* wheate freed by speciall licence *ut supra*		nil
Five hundred sparrs smale, two hundred bomsparrs and seaven hundred Norwey deales	43s	4d
Two thousand waight cordage	13s	4d
Half hundred waight frying panns		6d
		+6d
Three hundred waight cheese		12d
Half the great hundred Luke coales	4s	0d

f. 18r

November *eod'*

[624] In the Andrewe of Donndee 20 tonns, Alexander Kircaudy
master, from Donndee in Scotland

Andrewe Gray Scots marchant, with two barrels salmon	4s	0d

November 19

[625] In the [?]Jane of Sanct Andrewes 20 tonns, Andrewe Forrett
master, from Sanct Andrewes in Scotland

The said Andrewe Scots merchant, with six lastes white herringes	30s	0d
One hundred ells Scots lynen	3s	0d

November 26

[626] In the Goulden Ilande of Emden 40 tonns, Nicholas Henrickson
master, from Emden

The said Nicholas alien marchant, with thirten lastes Danske rye	32s	6d
Six lastes of beanes valued as pease	12s	0d
Strangers custom	11s	1½d

December 8

[627] In the Dolphen of Lynne 55 tonns, Robert Constable master,
from Burdeux in France[203]

William Wharton *ind'* free merchant, with eight half punchions French prewnes containing 5 *C per* peece	20s	0d
		+10s	0d

December 11

[628] In the Elaphant of London 4 score tonns, Gabriell Robinson
master, from Kales[204] in Spayne

The said Gabriell *ind'* marchant, with fortie waighes Spaynish salt	53s	4d

December *eod'*
[*629*] In the Margeret of Kircaudy 24 tonns, David Anderson master, from Kircaudy in Scotland

The said Davide Scots merchant, with twenty six wayes white salt	34s	8d
Half hundred ells lynen cloth		18d

December 13
[*630*] In the Joye of Amster [*sic*] 11 tonns, John Smith master, from Amstrother in Scotlande

The said John Smith Scots merchant, with fowre lastes *et di'* white herrings	22s	6d
Sixe waighes *di'* white salt	8s	8d

December 15
[*631*] In the Good Fortune of Kircaudy 36 tonns, John Hogg master, from Kircaudie in Scotland

The said John Hogg Scots merchant, with fortie waighes white salt	53s	4d

f. 18v
[*632*] In the Elaphant of London 80 tonns, Gabriell Robinson master, from Kales in Spayne

The said Gabriell *ind'* merchant, with eighten waighes Spaynishe salt *per* post entrie	24s	0d

December 22
[*633*] In the Mary Katherin of Kircaudy 30 tonns, David Balfore master, from Kircawdie in Scotland

The said Davide Scots merchant, with fortie two waighes white salte	56s	0d

December 24
[*634*] In the Margeret of Kircaudy 20 tonns, William Williamson master, from Kircaudy in Scotland

The said William Williamson Scots merchant, with twenty five waighes white salte	33s	4d

f. 19r
Lynn Regis
Entries of all goods and marchandice shipped from this porte in this quarter ended at the Nativity of Our Lord *anno* 1613

September 30
[*635*] In the Margeret of Kercaudy 25 tonns, William Williamson master, to Kircaudy in Scotland

The said William Scots merchant, with twoe tonns *di'* stronge beere	3s	0d
	+21s	3d

October 13
[636] In the Barrbara of Lynn 25 tonn, Robert Hayes master, to
Amsterdam
Thomas Slaney *ind'* marchant, with seaven thousand sheeps
leather tawed   £5   5s   0d
Twentie hundred waight musterd seed   5s   0d
Two thousand oyle cakes valued at 9s *per cent*   9s   0d
Six kersies and one northern dosen sengle   16s[?]8d

October 16
[637] In the same shipp and master to Amsterdam
Nathaniell Maxey *ind'* marchant, with nyne score and five payre shorte
worsteed stockens   24s   4d

October 23
[638] In the Angell of Creyle 20 tonns, William Cade master, to
Donndee in Scotland
John Smithe Scots marchant, with tenn tonns stronge beere[205]   15s   0d
                                                                 +£4   5s   0d
Three loads oken barke valued at 30s *per* loade[206]   4s   6d

October 26
[639] In the Ann of Lynn 60 tonns, Nicholas Tubbin master, to
Burdeux in France
William Wharton *ind'* free marchant, with two thousand clapholt   15s   0d
Two dosen of oares   14d

Eod'
[640] In the Olde Harry of Kircaudy 18 tonns, David Wilson master,
to Kircaudy in Scotland
Davide Balfore Scots merchant, with seaven tonns stronge beere   10s   6d
                                                                      +49s   6d
Five baggs English hopps containing 8 *C* waight   8s   0d

October 30
[641] In the Mary Katherin of Kircaudy 40 tonns, David Balfore
master, to Kircaudy in Scotland
The saide David Scots merchant, with seaven tonns stronge beere   10s   6d
                                                                      +49s   6d
Eight hundred waight Englishe hopps   8s   0d

October *eod'*
[*642*] In the Margeret of Lenkell 24 tonns, William Gray master,
to Lenkell in Scotland

The said William Gray Scots, with eight tonns stronge beere | 12s | 0d

+£3 8s 0d

Twentie foure hundred waight oken barke being part of three
loads for which the duties were paid in the Angell of Creyle as *per*
entrie taken the 23 of this instant[207] | nil

f. 19v
October *eod'*
[*643*] In the Margeret of Kircaudy 40 tonns, Alexander Law master,
to Kircaudy in Scotland

The said Alexander Scots marchant, with five tonns stronge beere | 7s | 6d

+42s 6d

November 6
[*644*] In the Mergery of Amstrother 10 tonns [*word illegible*], Robert
Mellen master, to Amstrother in Scotland

The said Robert Scots merchant, with six tonns stronge beere | 9s | 0d

+51s 0d

November *eod'*
[*645*] In the Andrew of Donndee 15 tonns, Alexander Kircaudy
master, to Donndee in Scotland
Andrew Graye Scots marchant, with thirten tonns stronge beere
whereof the duties were formerly paid for one tonn laden in the
Angell of Creyle, one William Cade master, as by entrie taken the
23 of October last appearth,[208] so sub[*sidy*] [*and*] impo[*st*] received
for twelve tonns stronge beere | 18s | 0d

+£5 2s 0d

November 8
[*646*] In the John of Kinghorne 30 tonns, John Tompson master, to
Kinghorne in Scotland

The said John Scots marchant, with three tonns stronge beere | 4s | 6d

+25s 6d

December 1
[*647*] In the Orrengtree of Amsterdam 40 tonns, Peter Mussell
master, to Amsterdam

Robert Thorey *ind'* merchant, with twelve pound English safferon | 12s | 0d

December 2

[*648*] In the Jane of Sanct Andrewes 15 tonns, Andrewe Forrett
master, to Sanct Andrewes in Scotland

David Ramsey Scots merchant, with tenn tonns stronge beere   15s 0d

+£4 5s 0d

December *eod'*

[*649*] In the Jonas of Lynn 50 tonns, Violet Waynfforth master,
to Emden

Thomas Slaney *ind'* merchant, with 6 score payre short worsteed
stockens   16s 0d
Twenty hundred waight musterdseed   5s 0d
Eight hundred white sheeps leather tawed   12s 0d
Twenty dosen calves skynes tawed in oyle   5s 8d
One thousand decayed oyle cakes valued at 6s *per cent*   3s 0d

December 3

[*650*] In the Golden Iland of Emden 40 tonns, Nicholas Henrickson
master, to Emden

The same Nicholas alien merchant, with fowre hundred greate oyle
cakes valued at 9s *per cent* accounting five for one   21½d
Strangers custom   5½d

December 22

[*651*] In the Joy of Amstrother 11 tonns, John Smith master, to
Amstrother in Scotland

The said John Scots marchant, with seaven tonns stronge beere   10s 6d

+49s 6d

f. 20r

Wells *cum* Burnham

Entries of all goodes and marchandice brought into the creeks and members of
this porte this quarter ended at the Nativity of Our Lord *anno* 1613

October 11

[*652*] In the Estrich of Camphire 15 tonns, Jacobe Bomis master,
from Camphire[209]

The said Jacobe alien merchant, with three lasts French rye   [?]7s 6d
Foure hundred waight Flemish hopps   4s 0d
+2s 0d
Six barrells seasticks[210] white herrings   20d
Strangers custom and newe ympost   3s 4½d
+ 6d impost

Wells *cum* Burnham
Entries of all goods and marchandice shipped from the creeks and members of
this porte this quarter ended at the Nativity of Our Lord *anno* 1613

November 3
[*653*] In the Estrich of Camphire 15 tonns, Jacobe Bomis master,
to Camphire

The said Jacobe alien marchant, with tenn pounds safferon	10s	0d
One chalder of seacoales	[?]7d	
	+5s ympost	
Strangers custom and newe ympost	2s	8d
	+15d	

November 18
[*654*] In the John of Wells 24 tonns, Eliza Kinge master, to Rotterdam
Henry Congham *ind'* merchant, with nyne foother of lead in

72 piggs	£3	16s	0d
	+[?]£19	0s	0d
Fortie pounds English safferon		40s	0d

December 11
[*655*] In the same shipp and master to Rotterdam

Henry Congham *predict' per* post entrie, twenty pounds English saffron	20s	0d

f. 20v [*Blank*]
f. 21r
Lynn Regis
Entries of all French and Reynish wynes brought into this porte in one whole yere
and a quarter begonne at the feast of Sanct Micheall *anno* 1612 and ended at the
Nativity of Our Lorde *anno* 1613

November 25 1612
[*656*] In the Dolphen of Lynne 55 tonns, Robert Constable master, from Burdeux
in Frannce[211]
William Atkin *ind'* marchant brought in fifty one tonns
And more brought by the same merchant, entred the seconnd October, two tonns
Out of all which allowance was geven
All French wynes

December *ulti'*
[*657*] In the Barke Allen of Creyle in Scotland 45 tonns, John Darrsy master, from
Burdeux[212]
William Atkin *ind' predict'* brought forty tonns, and more entred by the same

marchant the fift[h] of Jannuary three hogsheads
Out of all which allowance was geven
All French wynes

January 22
[658] In the Ann Charitee of Kingston *super* Hull 90 tonns, Sampson Simpson
master, from Burdeux[213]
Rowland Bradforth *ind'* marchant brought in eighty six tonns
And more entred by the shippmaster abovesaid three hogsheads
Out of all which allowance was geven
All French wynes

February 3
[659] In the Cocke of Flushing 15 tonns, Garrard Nabbs master, from Flushing
The said Garrard alien brought in three tonns French wynes[214]

March 1
[660] In the Swan of Yermoth 25 tonns, Robert [?]Harrise master, from
Rotterdam
Robert Soame *ind'* brought in three tonns and more entred the daie *predict* by
the same marchant three tonns French wynes[215]

March 30 *anno* 1613
[661] In the Cocke of Flushing 15 tonns, Garrard Nabbs master, from Flushing
The said Garrard alien brought in seaven tonns French wynes[216]

Aprill [?]22
[662] In the Barrbara of Lynn, Robert Hayes master, from Amsterdam in Holland
The said Robert *ind'* brought in three tonns French wynes[217]

June 2
[663] In the Cocke of Flushing 15 tonns, Garrard Nabbs master, from Flushing
The said Garrard alien brought in fowre tonns French wynes[218]

December 8
[664] In the Dolphen of Lynne 55 tonns, Robert Constable master, from Burdeux
William Wharton *ind'* brought in fiftie fowre tonns French wynes and by the same
marchant entred the 18 December one hogshead two tierces French wynes[219]
Out of all which allowance was geven

French − English − 243 tons   3 hogsheads   2 terces
              Aliens   −   14 ton

f. 21v
Wells *cum* Burnham
Entries of all French and Reynish wynes brought into the creeks and members of
this porte in one whole yere and a quarter begonn at the feast of Sanct Micheall
anno 1612 and ended at the Nativity of Our Lorde *anno* 1613

November 10 1612
[665] In the Estrich of Camphire 15 tonns, Jacobe Bomis master, from Camphire
The said Jacobe alien brought in fowre tonns two hogsheads French wynes[220]

December 14
[666] In the Estrich of Camphire 15 tonns, Jacobe Bomis master, from Camphire
The said Jacobe alien brought in three tonns French wynes[221]

Jannuarie 19
[667] In the Estrich of Camphire 15 tonns, Jacobe Bomis master, from Camphire
John Greene *ind'* marchant brought in fowre tonns French wynes[222]

January *eod'*
[668] In the Estrich of Camphire 15 tonns, Jacobe Bomis master, from Camphire
The said Jacobe alien brought in one tonn French wynes[223]

February 22
[669] In the Fisher of Amsterdam 40 tonns, Hugh Henderickson master, from
Amsterdam
Henry Congham *ind'* merchant brought in two tonns French wynes[224]

March 12
[670] In the Estrich of Camphire 15 tonns, Jacobe Bomis master, from Camphire
The said Jacobe alien brought in eight tonns two hogsheads French wynes,[225]
out of which there was allowance geven

March 25 1613
[671] In the Fortune of Sneake 30 tonns, Peter Peterson master, from Rotterdam
Henry Congham *ind'* merchant brought two tonns three hogsheads French
wynes[226]

Aprill 3
[672] In the Hope of Flushing [*blank*] tonns, Cornelius Verduse master, from
Flushing
The said Cornelius alien brought in two tonns two hogsheads French wynes[227]

Aprill *eod'*
[*673*] In the Fortune of Amsterdam [*blank*] tonns, Bernard Albertson master, from Amsterdam
Henry Congham *ind'* merchant brought in one tonn French wynes[228]

May 25
[*674*] In the Estrich of Camphire 15 tonns, Jacobe Phillippson master, from Camphire
The said Jacobe alien brought in fowre tonns one hogshead French wynes[229]

Jully 7
[*675*] In the Estrich of Camphire 15 tonns, Jacobe Bomis master, from Camphire
The said Jacobe alien brought in two tonns French wynes[230]

August 20
[*676*] In the Estrich of Camphire 15 tonns, Jacobe Bomis master, from Camphire
The said alien Jacobe Bomis brought in three tonns three hogsheads French wynes[231]

October 11
[*677*] In the Estrich of Camphire 15 tonns, Jacobe Bomis master, from Camphire
The said Jacobe alien brought in two tonns of French wynes, and more by post entrie taken the 21 October *predict'* two hogsheads French wynes[232]

French − English − 9 ton   3 hogsheads
          Aliens − 32 ton[233]

f. 22r
Lynn Regis
Entries of all Spaynish wynes brought into this porte in one whole yere and a quarter begonn at the feast of Sanct Micheall *anno* 1612 and ended at the Nativity of Our Lord *anno* 1613

December 7 1612
[*678*] In the Barrbara of Lynn 30 tonns, Robert Hayes master, from Amsterdam
The said Robert *ind'* marchant brought in one butt sack[234]

March 1
[*679*] In the Swan of Yermoth 25 tonns, Robert Harvice master, from Amsterdam
Robert Soame *ind'* merchant brought in seaven butts sacks[235]

Aprill 22 1613
[*680*] In the Paradice of Amsterdam 40 tonns, William Cornelius master, from Amsterdam
Robert Thorey *ind'* merchant bought in three butts sacks[236]

June 2
[*681*] In the Paradice of Amsterdam 40 tonns, William Cornelius master, from Amsterdam
Robert Thorey *ind'* merchant brought in fowre butts sacks[237]

Sack – English – 15 buttes

Wells *cum* Burnham
Entries of all Spaynish wynes brought into the creeks and members of this porte in one whole yere and quarter begonn at the feast of Sanct Micheall *anno* 1612 and ended at the Nativity of Our Lord *anno* 1613

Januarie 19 1612
[*682*] In the Estrich of Camphire 15 tonns, Jacobe Bomis master, from Camphire
The said Jacobe alien brought in two butts sacks[238]

March 12
[*683*] In the Estrich of Camphire 15 tonns, Jacobe Bomis master, from Camphire
The said Jacobe alien brought in twoe butts sacks[239]

March 25 1613
[*684*] In the Estrich of Camphire 15 tonns, Jacobe Phillippsonn master, from Camphire
The said Jacobe alien brought in two butts sacks and one butt muskadell[240]

Sack – Alien – 6 butts
Muscadell – Alien – 1 butt

E190/434/2: Collector of New Impositions 1613[241]

f. 1r
The 22 of Aprill
[*685*] In *le* Paradice of Amsterdam *predict'*
Robert Thorey, 5 *C* 70 poundes raisons *solis* and 5 *C* weight gum arabecke[242]   7s 7d
Nathaniell Maxey, 4 *C* 60 pounds proins[243]   8s 11¾d
Robart Hayes, 1 *C* bundles brown paper[244]   5s 0d

The 21 of June
[*686*] In *le* Paradice of Amsterdam *predict'*
William Doughty, 3 *C* weight raisons of the sonn[245]   1s 10d
/1 – 3– 4/[246]

The 10 of July
[*687*] In *le* Dolphin of Lynn *predict'*
William Pettes, 16 cagges of sturgeon[247]   5s   4d

The [?]17 day
[*688*] In *le* Pleasure of Lynn *predict'*
Thomas Snelling, 4 tassells[248]   2s   8d

The 19 day
[*689*] In *le* Blew Henn *predict'*
John White, *di'* 1 *C* wainscottes, 10 cagge sturgeon[249]   8s   4d
Thomas March, 20 wainscottes, [?10] cagges sturgeon[250]   2s   4d

The 16 August
[*690*] In *le* Fortune of Amsterdam *predict'*
Henery Robinson, 4 pieces Holland[251]   8s   0d
Anthony Izeraell, 6 pounds of mace[252]   2s   0d

The 21 day
[*691*] In *le* Fortune *predict'*
Nathanyell Maxey, 47 *li'* synom[*on*], 34 *li'* of nuttmegge, with other
petty grocery[253]   14s   8d

[*No date*]
[*692*] In *le* Greyhounde *predict'*
Thomas Snelling, 6 *C* [? *& di'*] hinderlandes [*illegible*] and 2 *C* elles
Slecia cloth[254]   11s   8d
/2 – 14 – 0/

f. 1v
Burnham
The 7 of August 1613
[*693*] In *le* Suzan of Welles *predict'*
Henery Buckestone, 4 jerfalkons[255]   6s   0d

The same day
[*694*] In *le* Meane of Welles *predict'*
John Webster, 7 jerfalkons, 7 tasselles and six marlians[256] 15s   2d
William Artson, 6 jerfalkons and 9 tasselles[257]   15s   0d

The 27 of July
[*695*] In the Eastridge of Camphere *predict'*
Jacobe Bonis, 4 tonns one quarter of leade[258]   £4   5s   0d
/6 – 1 – 2/Ex' £6   1s   2d paid[259]

E190/434/3: Controller : Christmas 1613 – Christmas 1614

f. 2r [sic]

Lynn Regis

Entries of all goods and marchandize brought into this porte from the partes beyonde the seas in one whole yeare begune at the Nativity of Our Lord God 1613 and ended at the same feast *anno* 1614

December 29 1613

[696] In *le* Grace of God of Kercawdy 40 tonns, David Wise master, from Kercawdy, the said David Scot merchant with[260]

Forty wayes white salte	£2	13s	4d
Three barrells of white herringe			15d

Eadem die

[697] In *le* Margreat of Kercawdy 40 tonns, James Collier master, from Kercawdy, the saide James Scot merchant with

Forty sixe wayes of white salte	£3	1s	4d

January 3

[698] In *le* Cocke *de* Flusshinge 15 tonnes, Garrard Nabbes master, from Flushing, the said Garrard alien merchant with[261]

Three lastes *di'* Fleemish wheate	11s	8d
One last of French rye	2s	6d
Strangers custom	3s	6½d

Eadem die

[699] In *le* Angell of Creylle 10 tonnes, William Cadde master, from Creile, Thomas Clayhills Scot marchant with

One laste fower barrels white herringes	6s	8d
One laste *di'* smale bond tarr	3s	0d
One truse containing two hunderd waight Scot lynnen yearne	2s	6d
One cheste of Scot lynnen cloth containing 3 *C* ells	9s	0d
Three feather [bedds][262]	4s	0d
One trusse containing [*number missing*] hunderd waight Scot feathers		12d

[Jan]uary 12

[700] In *le* St John *de* Duncarke 80 t[ons] [?La]wrance Johnsonne master, from Duncarke, Thomas [?M]arche *ind'* marchant with

Forty lastes of rye freed *per* speciall warrant		nil
Two sackes Fleemish hoops containing five hund*red* waight	5s	0d
	+2s	6d

January 17
[*701*] In *le* Blessinge *de* Disearte 20 tonns, Robert [*illegible*] master, from
Mountrosse, John Garden Scot merchant with

Theirtene tonns of great Scot coales	4s	4d
One laste of white herringe	5s	0d
Fower barrells of middle bond pitch		13½d
Three hunderd waight of Scot yearne	4s	4½d
Fower barre[ls] [*missing*] bond tarr		13½d
Two hunderd [*missing*] Scot lynnen clothe	6s	0d

f. 2v
January 19 1613
[*702*] In *le* Margreat of Amstrother 16 tonnes, William Burntside master,
from Amstrother, George Andersone Scot merchant with

Nyne lastes of white herringes	45s	0d

January 20
[*703*] In *le* Orrengtree of Amsterdam 50 tonnes, Peter Musslere master,
  from Flushinge, Thomas Slaney *ind'* merchant with

Sixteene lastes of Fleemish oates	32s	0d
Tenn waies of French salte which was freed to this marchant for his Island fiesshinge this yere		nil

January 21
[*704*] In *le* Anne *de* Lynn 60 tonnes, Nicholas Tubbin master, from
Burdux in France, William Wharton *ind'* marchant with[263]
Twenty halfe peaces of French prewnes containing five hunderd

waight *per* peece	50s	0d
	+25s	0d
Forty cakes of rozen containing fower thousand waight	10s	0d

January 24
[*705*] In *le* Mary of Lynn 80 tonnes, John Ravenes master, from Curras
in Scotland, William Wolman *ind'* marchant with

Fower score tonnes of great Scot coales	26s	8d

January 25
[*706*] In *le* Grace of God of Kercawdy 30 tonnes, Henry Raynoldsone
master, from Curras in Scotland, John Forgasson Scot marchant with

Therrtty [*sic*] five wayes of white salte	46s	8d
Two hunderd elles of Scot lynnen cloth	6s	0d
Three score yeardes of Scot tykinge	2s	0d
Three hunderd waight of Scot yearne	3s	9d

Eadem die
[*707*] In *le* Joye *de* Amstrother 16 tonnes, John Smythe [master, from]
Amstrother in Scotland, the same John Smith [Scot merchant] with
Eight lastes of white herringe[*s*]   40s   0d

Eadem die
[*708*] In *le* Oulde Harry *de* Kercawdy 20 tonns, David Wilson master,
from Kercawdy in Scotland, John Lambe Scot marchant with
Twenty five wayes of white salte   33s   4d
One hunderd yeardes of Scot tyking at 6 score *per centum*   4s   0d
Halfe an hundred waight of Scot yearne   7½d

January 29
[*709*] In *le* Jonas *de* Lynn 50 tonnes, Violet Waynford master, from
Flushing, Garvise Wharton *ind'* marchant with
Seaven lastes of Danske rye freed *per* spetiall warrant *ut predict'*   nil

Eadem die
[*710*] In *le* same shipp and master from Flushinge *predict'*, Thomas
Slayney *ind'* with
Seaven lastes of Danske rye   17s   6d
Fower peaces of great raysones   2s   0d
                            +2s   0d
One barrell of rayson great containing one *C* waight   11d
                            +11d

f. 3r
The laste day of January 1613
[*711*] In *le* Goulden Iland of Emden 50 tonnes, Nicholas Henrickson
master, from Emden, the said Nicholas alien marchant with
Fowertene lastes of Danske rye   35s   0d
                    Strangers custom   8s   9d

Eadem die
[*712*] In *le* Hope *de* Amsterdam 40 tonnes, Peter Muslare master,
from Amsterdam, Nathaniell Maxey *ind'* marchant with
One hundred waight of white suger net   3s   4d
                              +5s   0d
Eight topnetts figgs net   12d
                             +12d
Halfe an hunderd waight West India ginger net   20d
                             +20d
Twelve pownde of peper net   12d
                             +12d

Halfe an hunderd waight reysons *solis* net		5½d
		+5½d
Two peeces great raysones		12d
		+12d
Fower pownds of mace net		16d
		+16d
Fower powndes of cloves *net*		12d
		+12d
Twelve pownds of nutemeggs net		21½d
		+21½d

Eadem die
[713] In *le* same shipp and master from Amsterdam *predict'*,
Jonas Tompson *ind'* merchant with[264]

Fowertene lastes of Danske rye	35s	0d

Eadem die
[714] In *le* same shipp and master from Amsterdam *predict'*, Robert
Thory *ind'* merchant with[265]

Tenn lastes of Danske rye	25s	0d
Five hunderd waight of white starche	5s	0d
	+33s	4d
Theirty topnetts of figgs	3s	9d
	+3s	9d

February 3
[715] In *le* Grace of Dundee 15 tonnes, William Duncan master,
from Curras in Scotland, the same William Scot marchant with

Fiftene tonnes of great Scot coales	5s	0d
Halfe an hund[erd] Scot lynnen clothe		18d

Eadem die
[716] In *le* Grace of God *de* Kerc[awdy] [*tonnage missing*], David Wise
master, from Curras in Scotland, the [same D]avid Scot merchant with

Forty wayes of white salte	53s	4d
Two hunderd waight of Scot yearne	2s	6d

Eadem die
[717] In *le* Margreat *de* Kercawdy 24 tonns, David Andersone master,
from Kercawdy in Scotland, the same David Scot merchant with

Twenty sixe wayes of white salte	34s	8d

Februarye 4
[*718*] In *le* Goulden Iland *de* Emden *predicte*, Nicholas Henricksone
master, from Emden, John Wallys *ind'* merchant with
Seaven lastes of Danske rye   17s   6d

Eadem die
[*719*] In *le* Josua of Berghen 140 tonns, John Johnsone master, from
Berghen in Norway bound for Rochell in France and by tempest of
weather forsed one [*sic*] shore with the members of this porte, the
said John alien marchant with
Eightene hunderd Norway deales entred at 5 score *per centum*   £3 15s   0d
Fowertene barrels of salmon   28s   0d
Fower lastes of great band tarr   13s   4d
Fower score Norway hides valued at 3s 4s *per* [?peace]   13s   4d
                              Strangers custom allowed

f. 3v
Februarie 11 1613
[*720*] In *le* Goulden Fleece *de* Lynn 1 *C* tonns, Thomas Drewry master,
from Carrickfargus in Ireland, John Masone *ind'* merchant with
Seaventene thousand pipe staves   56s   8d
Twenty fower hogsheades of Iresh beiffe whereof fower hogsheades
allowed for packinge   £3   0s   0d
Fower hogsheades of porke vallued at 40s the hogsheade   8s   0d
Eight smale caske tallow containing 10 *C* waight   8s   4d

February 16
[*721*] In *le* Grace of God of Barrowstone 30 tonnes, David Hardye
master, from Barrowstone, John Glenn Scot marchant with
Theirty wayes of white salte   40s   0d

February 26
[*722*] In *le* Margreat *de* Kercawdy 40 tonnes, James Collier master,
from Kercawdy in Scotland, the saide James Scot merchant with
Forty sixe wayes of white salte   £3   1s   4d

Eadem die
[*723*] In *le* Jacob *de* Kercawdy 20 tonns, John Daviesone master,
from Curras in Scotland, the said John Davisone Scot merchant with
Twenty eight wayes of white salte   37s   4d

March 1
[*724*] In *le* Blessinge *de* Diseart 20 tonnes, Robert Williamsone master,
from Diseart in Scotland, the said Robert Scot marchant with
Fowertene lastes of oates   28s   0d

Eadem die
[*725*] In *le* Cocke *de* Flushinge 15 tonnes, Garrard Nabbes master,
from Flushinge, the said Garrard alien merchant with[266]

Sixe lastes of Fleemish whe[at]	20s	0d
Str[angers] custom	5s	0d

March 2
[*726*] In *le* Drake *de* Emden 30 tonnes, Steven St[evenes maste]r,
from Emden, the said Steven Stevenes [alie]n with

Theirtene lastes of Danske rye	32s	6d
Three lastes of beanes rated as pease	6s	0d
Strangers custom	9s	7½d

Eadem die
[*727*] In *le* Neptune *de* Dorte 34 tonnes, Andrew Blome master, from
Dorte, John Wallis *ind'* marchant with[267]

Twenty lastes of Fleemish oates	40s	0d
One laste of white herringes	5s	0d
Three hunderd bundles of browne paper	15s	0d
	+15s	0d
One paier of millstones	6s	8d
	+6s	8d

Eadem die
[*728*] In *le* William *de* Barrowstone 20 tonnes, James Gibbes master,
from Mountrosse in Scotland, the said James Scot merchant with

Twelve lastes of Scot oates	24s	0d

f. 4r
March 3 1613
[*729*] In *le* Elizabeth *de* Lynn 60 tonns, Andrew Page master, from
Burdux in France, the said Page *ind'* merchant with[268]

One tonne of viniger	2s	4d
	+2s	4d
Two baggs feathers containing three hunderd waight	6s	0d
	+6s	0d
Fower bales of coppi[e] paper containing one hunderd and twenty eight reames	13s	0d
	+6s	5d
Sixe peeces of French canvis containing 20 ells *per* the peace	4s	0d
	+2s	0d

March 5

[730] In le Hoape de Enchuzen 40 tonnes, [?]Garbrant Garardson
master, from Enchuzen, Christopher Newgate ind' with

Twenty five lastes of Fleemish oates	50s	0d
Five lastes of Fleemish wheate	16[s]	8d

March 10

[731] In le Griffen de Amsterdam 40 tonns, Claues Jacobson master,
from Amsterdam, Henry Robinsone ind' marchant with

Twenty lastes of Fleemish wheate	£3	6s	8d
Sixe lastes of Danske rye		15s	0d

March 11

[732] In le same shipp and master from Amsterdam predicte, William
Doughty ind' marchant with

Two cables, one hawcer containing 20 C waight	13s	4d

March 22

[733] In le Marye Keatherne de Kercawdy 40 tonnes, John Law
master, from Kercawdy in Scotland, the said John Scot merchant with

Forty two wayes of white salte	56s	0d

[Ea]dem die

[734] In le Jonas de Kercawdy in Sco[tland], [A]lexander Law master,
from Kercawdy in Sco[tland], [the said] Alexander Scot merchant with

Twenty to[ns] [g]reat Scot coales	6s	8d

Aprill 7

[735] In le Grace of God de Kercawdy 30 tonnes, David Wise master,
from Kercawdy in Scotland, the said David Scot merchant with

Forty wayes of white salte	[?]63s	4d

Aprill 12

[736] In le Margreat de Kercawdy 40 tonns, James Collier master,
from Kercawdy in Scotland, the said James Scot merchant with

Forty sixe wayes of white salte	[?]£3	1s	3d

Eadem die

[737] In le Gedion de Harlinge 80 tonnes, Dericke Adrianson master,
from [?]Soundwater[269] in Norway, the said Derick allien [with]

Ten score eight balkes at five foote per balk valued at 4d per the foote	17s	4d
Forty smale mastes for boates	6s	8d
Eight great balkes at eight foote per balke [? vallued ut predict']		12¾d

Five score cant spares		16¾d
Three hunderd *di'* Norway deales	[?]22s	0d
Fower hunderd and a quarter [?]bome sparres		[*illegible*]
Twenty sixe hunderd *di'* smale sparres		[*illegible*]
Two hunderd more of bome sparres	[?]1s	4d
One hundred *di'* smale [?]balkes at [*remainder illegible*]	5s	0d
Strangers [custom]	[?]15s	5½d

f. 4v

Aprill 12 1614

[*738*] In *le* Margreate *de* Kercawdy, James Collier master,
from Kercawdy in Scotland *predict'*, George Walker Scot merchant with

Sixe hunderd waight of Scot yarne	7s	6d
One hunderd yeardes of Scot tyking	4s	0d
Forty elles of Scot lynnen cloth		12d

Aprill 13

[*739*] In *le* Grace of God *de* Kercawdy 24 tonns, Henry Raynallsone
master, from Curras in Scotland, the saide Henry Scot marchant with

Theirty three wayes of white salte	44s	0d

Aprill 21

[*740*] In *le* Hope *de* Amsterdam 70 tonnes, Peter Musslere master,
from Barghan in Norway, Thomas Flory *ind'* with

Nynetene hunderd of Norway deales	£4 15s	0d

Aprill 27

[*741*] In *le* Goulden Fleece *de* Lynn 1 *C* tonnes, Robeat Hayes master,
from Kerhen in Scotland, John Masone *ind'* merchant with

Fower score tonnes of great Scot coales	26s	8d

May 3

[*742*] In *le* Hope *de* Enchuzen 30 tonnes, Garbrant Garrardson master,
from Norway, Bartholomew Wormell *ind'* merchant with

Five hunderd Norway deales	25s	0d
Halfe an hunderd fir baulkes containing 48 foote vallued *ut predict'*	8s	0d
More entred in the same shipp and master from Norway upon the		
11 of Maye, forty square sparres containing 80 foote vallued *ut predict'*		16d
Three quarters of the hunderd [?Norway] deales	3s	9d

May 5
[*743*] In *le* Jonas *de* Kercawdy 20 tonnes, Alex[ander] [*missing*] master, from
Kercawdy in Scotland, the saide Ale[xander] [*missing*] [mercha]nt with
Twenty tonnes of great Sco[t ?coal]es   6s   8d
One hunderd waight of Scot lynnen yearne   15d

Eadem die
[*744*] In *le* Mary Keatherne *de* Kercawdy 30 tonnes, David Balforde
master, from Kercawdy, the said David Scot merchant with
Forty two wayes of white salte   56s   0d
Halfe an hunderd ells of Scot lynnen cloth   18d

May 7
[*745*] In *le* White Bucke *de* Enchuzen 80 tonnes, Love Peterson master,
from Danske, John Wallis *ind'* merchant with
Fifty lastes of Danske rye   £6   5s   0d

May 13
[*746*] In *le* Willian [*sic*] *de* Kercawdy 50 tonnes, John More master,
from Rochell in France, the said John More Scot merchant with
Forty five wayes of bay salte   45s   0d

f. 5r
May [?]15 1614
[*747*] In *le* Rose *de* Emden 24 tonnes, [*illegible*] [?]Meakes[270] master,
 from Emden, the saide [? Meakes alien merchant] with
Twelve [?lasts] of Danske rye   30s   0d
One last of wheate   3s   4d
                                     Stranger custom   8s   4d

Eadem die
[*748*] In *le* Redd Lyon of Emden 16 tonnes, John Eurens master,
from Emden, the said John alien merchant with
Seaven lastes of Danske rye   17s   6d
One laste of wheate   3s   4d
                                     Stranger custom   5s   2½d

Eadem die
[*749*] In *le* Drake *de* Emden 30 tonnes, Steven Stevenes master, from
Emden, the said Steven Stevens alien merchant with
Fowertene lastes Danske rye   35s   0d
One laste of Fleemish wheate   3s   4d
                                     Stranger custom   9s   4d

May 17
[*750*] In *le* William *de* Kercawdy, John More master, from Rochell *predicte*,
the said John Scot merchant with
Sixe wayes of bay salte *per* post entry   6s   0d

Eadem die
[*751*] In *le* Drake *de* Emden *predicte*, Steven Stevens master, from Emden,
the said Steven alien merchant with
One laste of Fleemish wheate *per* post entry   4s   2d

May 19
[*752*] In *le* [?]Garebonaventur *de* Lynn 70 tonnes, John Boy master,
from Barghan in Norway, T[*hole in document*] Thomas Perkyn *ind'*
merchant with
Twenty hund[erd — N]orway deales[271]   £5   0s   0d

[M]aye 26
[*753*] In *le* Marye *de* Lynn 80 to[ns, W]illiam Hudsone master, from
Diseart in Scotland, William [?Par]kyn *ind'* merchant with
Fower score tonnes of great Scot coales   26s   8d

Maye 28
[*754*] In *le* Elaphant *de* London 70 tonnes, Gabrill Robinson master,
from Danske, Frannces Goodwinn *ind'* marchant with
Forty lastes of Danske rye   [?]£5   0s   0d

Maye 30
[*755*] In *le* John *de* Kercawdy 30 tonnes, William Williamsone master,
 from Kerhene in Scotland, the said William Scot merchant with
Theirty tonnes of great Scot coales   10s   0d

Maye *eadem die*
[*756*] In *le* Neptune of Lynn 30 tonnes, John Masone master, from
Amsterdam, John Leade *ind'* merchant with
Two hunderd and theirty bundles of browne paper[272]   12s [?]6d
                                                           +[?]12s [?]6d

f. 5v
May 30 1614
[*757*] In *le* Elizabeth of Lynn 30 tonnes, Thomas Skinner master, from
Amsterdam, Thomas Snelling *ind'* marchant with
Seaventene lastes of Danske rye, five lastes *di'* Fleemish wheate   £3   10s   0d

Eadem die

[*758*] In *le* Boare *de* Amsterdam 40 tonnes, Huch [*sic*] Henricksone
master, from Amsterdam, William Doughty *ind'* merchant with

Eleaven lastes Danske rye	27s	6d
Fower lastes *di'* wheate	15s	0d
Two hunderd of clapholt		18d
Three hunderd Norwaye deale		[*no sum*]
Two hawcers containing nyne hunderd waight	6s	0d
Three hunderd bundles of browne paper[273]	15s	0d
	+15s	0d
One smale barrell containing halfe an hunderd waight of white suger		20d
	+2s	0d

May 31

[*759*] In *le* Joane *de* Lynn 40 tonnes, Edward Fuller master, from
Amsterdam, Robert Thory *ind'* marchant with[274]

Three lastes of wheate	10s	0d
Forty Norway deales		20d

Eadem die

[*760*] In *le* same shipp and master from Amsterdam in Holland *predicte*
John Leade *ind'* marchant with[275]

Eleaven lastes of Danske rye	27s	6d

June 3

[*761*] In *le* Jonas *de* Barghen burden 55 tonnes, Mynor Lynn master,
from Berghen in Norway, Edmond Gilman *ind'* with

One thousand one hunderd and theirty Norway deales	£2 16s	6d
Two hunderd of baulkes containing one thousand foote vallued at 4d th[*hole in document*]	16s	8d
Theirty smale sparres & 3 [?]can[*hole in document*]		3d

June 7

[*762*] In *le* Gedeon of Harlinge 70 tonnes, Dericke [*hole in document*]son
master, from Copperwicke[276] in Norway, Garvise Wharton *ind'* with

Twenty five hunderd Norway deales	£6 5s	0d
Theirty middle mastes, theirty smale maste[*s*] and one great maste	21s	0d
Three hunderd *di'* smale sparres	3s	6d
Theirty sixe baulkes containing fifty foote		10d
Twelve long baulkes at 13 foote *per* peece	2s	4½d
Sixe great tymber loggs containing 15 foote *per* peece		18d

Eadem die
[*763*] In *le* Gifte of God of Kercawdy 30 tonnes, Henry Raynallsone
master, from Kercawdy in Scotland, the said Henry Scot merchant with
Theirty tonnes of great Scot coales   10s   0d

June 10
[*764*] In *le* John *de* Meechinge 25 tonnes, John Hudsone master, from
[?]Rone in France, Henry Buckhenham *ind'* merchant with
Twelve French milstones[277]   40s   0d
                                                                       +40s   0d

One mounte of playster of Paris   12d

f. 6r
June 10 1614
[*765*] In *le* Scowte *de* Eckronford[278] 40 tonnes, Peter Schroder master,
from Eckronford, Erasmus Cootes allien merchant with
Ten lastes of Danske rye   25s   0d
                                           Strangers custom   6s   3d

June 11
[*766*] In *le* Jonas *de* Kercawdy 20 tonnes, Alexander Law master, from
Kercawdy, the saide Alexander Scot merchant with
Twenty tonnes of great Scot coales   6s   8d
Fower barrells barrelled fiesh   2s   8d
                                                                        +3s   4d

June 15
[*767*] In *le* Goulden Hounde *de* Emden 30 tonnes, Poppe Johnsone
master, from Emden, the saide Johnsone alien marchant with
Eight lastes of Danske rye   20s   0d
                                           Stranger custom   5s   0d

Eadem die
[*768*] In *le* Unicorne *de* Emden 24 tonnes, Garrard Henrickson master,
from Emden, the saide Garrard alien merchant with
Eightene lastes of Fleemish maulte   45s   0d
                                           Stranger custom   11s   3d

Eadem die
[*769*] In *le* Unicorne *de* Emden 30 tonnes, Wyard Poppe master, from
Emden, Rollfe Camault alien marchant with
Fiftene lastes of Danske rye   37s   6d
                                           Stranger custom   9s   4½d

Eadem die
[*770*] In *le* Redd Lyon of Stavearne 180[279] tonnes, Martyne Oates
master, from Danske, Thomas Snelling *ind'* merchant with
Eighty five lastes of Danske rye   £10 12s   6d

June 21
[*771*] In *le* Goulden Hauke of [?]N[or]den[280] 36 tonnes, Bartholomew
Rymattes master, from [?Norden], the said Rimattes alien with
Twenty la[sts of] Fleemish maulte   £2 10s   0d
                                        Strangers custom   12s   6d

[*Ea*]*dem die*
[*772*] In *le* Violet *de* Lynn 40 tonn[es], Morrice Miles master, from
Amsterdam, Thomas Marche *ind'* merchant with
Twenty lastes of Danske rye   £2 10s   0d
Fower score bundles of browne paper[281]   4s   0d
                                                             +4s   0d

Eadem die
[*773*] In *le* Boare *de* Amsterdam 40 tonnes, Hugh Henrickson master,
from Amsterdam, William Doughty *ind'* with
Twenty fower lastes of Danske rye   £3   0s   0d

June 25
[*774*] In *le* Anne *de* Lynn 60 tonnes, Nicholas Tubbin master, from
Rochell in Frannce, John Percivall *ind'* merchant with[282]
Forty wayes of bay salte   40s   0d
One tonne of viniger   2s   4d
                                                           +[?2s   4d]

f. 6v
June 25 1614
[*775*] In *le* Weypen of Henlopp in Freezland[283] 120 tonnes, Jacob Symones
master, from Danske, Thomas Slayney *ind' ind'* [*sic*] merchant with
Theirty lastes of Danske rye   £3 15s   0d
Eight halfe chestes of white Burgadyne glasse   8s   0d
More fortye Sprewce deales of the shipmaster being beinge [*sic*]
an alien   6s   3d

Eadem die
[*776*] In *le* Richarde *de* Lynn 40 tonnes, Robeart Skynner master,
from Amsterdam, Thomas Marche *ind'* marchant with
Twenty lastes of Danske rye   £2 10s   0d

Eadem die
[*777*] In *le* Weypen *de* Henlopp *predicte*, Jacobe Symons master, from Danske,
Thomas Brewster *ind'* marchant with
Theirty lastes of Danske rye   £3 15s   0d

June 30
[*778*] In *le* Amye *de* Lynn 60 tonnes, Robert Waters master, from
Danske in the Easte Country, Thomas Slayney *ind'* merchant with
Forty fower lastes of Danske rye   £5 10s   0d
More for the shipp master five caggs of sturgion[284]   20[*d*]
                                                              +20d
Nyne keggs Sprewce elles containing one barrell   2s   0d

July 2
[*779*] In *le* Redd Lyon *de* Staverne 180 tonnes, Martyne Oates master,
from Danske, Thomas Snellinge *ind' per* post entrye
Five lastes of Danske rye   12s   6d
Twelve kaggs of sturgion[285]   4s   0d
                                                          +4s   0d

Eadem die
[*780*] In *le* Weypen *de* Henlopp *predicte*, Jacob Symones master, from
Danske, Thomas Slayney *ind' et* Thomas Brewster[286] *ind' per* post entry,
Ten lastes of Danske rye   25s   0d

Eadem die
[*781*] In *le* Anne *de* Lynn, Nicholas Tubbin master, from [?Rochelle]
predicte,[287] Gervise Wharton and Bryan Luptonn *in[d'* mercha]nts,
allowed for their fieshing provition f[*hole in document*] year in to Island,
fiftene wayes of Fr[en]ch salte   nil

July 4
[*782*] In *le* Margreat *de* Kercawdy 40 tonnes, William Collier master,
from Curras in Scotland, Sir George Brewse knight with
Forty five wayes of white salte   £3   0s   0d

July 5
[*783*] In *le* White Bucke *de* Enchuzen 100 tonnes, Loue Petersone
master, from Danske, John Wallis *in[d]'* marchant with
Fiftye lastes of Danske rye   £6   5s   0d

July 5
[*784*] In *le* Dolphen *de* Lynn 50 tonnes, Robert Cunstable master, from

Elbinge in the East Cuntry, Thomas Snelling *ind'* merchant with

Twenty eight lastes of Danske rye	£3	10s	0d
Fower tonnes of Sprewce iron		28s	0d

f. 7r

July 7 1614

[785] In *le* Grace of God *de* Kercawdy 40 tonnes, David Wise master, from Kercawdy, the said David Scot merchant with

Forty tonnes of great Scot coales   13s   4d

Eadem die

[786] In *le* Gifte of God *de* Kercawdy 30 tonnes, Henry Raynallson master, from Kercawdy, the saide Henry Scot merchant with

Theirty tonnes of great Scot coales   10s   0d

July 8

[787] In *le* John *de* Kercawdy 30 tonnes, William Williamsone master, from Kercawdy in Scotland, the said Henry [*sic*] Scot merchant with

Theirty tonnes of great Scot coales   10s   0d

Eadem die

[788] In *le* same shipp and master from Kercawdy *predicte*
George Walker Scot merchant with

One hunderd waight of Scot yearne		15d
One hunderd elles Scot lynnen cloth	3s	0d
Halfe an hunderd yeardes of Scot tykinge	2s	0d
One hunderd elles of Scot hurden[288] lynnen cloth	3s	0d

July 13

[789] In *le* Harry *de* Kercawdy 24 tonnes, David Wilsone master, from Kerkyaudy [*sic*], the said David Scot marchant with

Twenty fower tonnes of greate Scot coales   £8   0s   0d

July 14

[790] In *le* Gifte of God of Kercawdy, Henry Raynallsone master, from Kercawdy, the said Henry Scot marchant with

Fower tonnes of Scot coales *per* post entry   16d

Eadem die

[791] In *le* Jonas *de* Kercawdy 20 tonnes, Alexander Law master, from Kercawdy in Scotland, t[he sai]d Law Scot marchant with

Twenty [?tonnes] of great Scot coales   6s   8d

[July] 16
[792] In *le* Sanct Michaell *de* Hem[289] 16 [tonn]es, Cornelius Jacobsone
master, from Danske, Thomas Slayney *ind'* marchant with
Forty laste[s] of Danske rye   £5   0s   0d

Eadem die
[793] In *le* same shipp and master from Danske *predicte*
Bartholmew Wormell *ind'* marchant with
Theirty lastes of pitch and tarr great bond   £5   0s   0d
Ten hunderd waight of Sprewce flaxe unwrought   7s   6d
Fower hunderd of clapholte   3s   0d
Theirty halfe chestes of Renish glasse   37s   6d

July 18
[794] In *le* Neptune *de* Lynn 30 tonnes, John Bloy master, from
Amsterdam in Holland, John Masone *ind'* marchant with
Nyne lastes of Danske rye   22s   6d
Five lastes of wheate   16s   4d

f. 7v
July 18 1614
[795] In *le* Boare *de* Amsterdam 30 tonnes, Hugh Henricksone master,
from Amsterdam, Thomas Baker *ind'* merchant with
Twenty five wayes of Spannish and bay salte   29s   2d
Three hunderd of Norway deales   15s   0d
One laste of great bond tarr   3s   4d
Three lastes greate bond pitche   10s   0d

July 19
[796] In *le* Redd Lyon *de* Emden 15 tonnes, John Ewrins master, from
Emden, the said John alien marchant with
Eight lastes of Danske rye   25s   0d
A quarter of a laste of wheate   12½d
More entred the 29 of July by the said merchant
One laste of rye and fower combes wheate   3s   11½d

Eadem die
[797] In *le* Joane *de* Lynn 40 tonnes, Robert Thory master, from
Amsterdam in Hollande, John Leade *ind'* marchant with
Fiftene lastes of Danske rye   33s   6d
Halfe an hunderd waight of corke   5d

Eadem die
[*798*] In *le* same shipp and master from Amsterdam *predicte*
Robert Thory *ind'* marchant with

Eleaven lastes of Danske rye	27s	6d
One hunderd of clapholte		9d
Twenty dozan smale treakle barrells estimated at halfe a barrel in a caske		12d
One barrell of drinkeing glasses vallued at 30s		18d

July 20
[*799*] In *le* Redd Lyon of Amsterdam 80 tonnes, Aurus Sibells master,
from Amsterdam, Thomas Marche and John Leade *ind'* with

Forty lastes of Danske rye	£5	0s	0d

Eadem die
[*800*] In *le* Rose *de* Emden 24 tonnes, Meane [*hole in document*]es[290]
master, from Emden, the saide Meane ali[en merc]hant with

Eleaven lastes of rye	27s	6d
One laste wheate	3s	4d
More entred the 29 of July, one laste rye	2s	6d
Strainger custom	8s	4d

July 21
[*801*] In *le* Drake *de* Emden 30 tonnes, Steven Stevenes master, from
Emden, the saide Steven alien with

Theirtene lastes *et di'* Danske rye	32s	9d
Two lastes of wheate	6s	8d
Strainger custom	10s	1¼d

July 23
[*802*] In *le* William *de* Kercawdy 24 tonnes, James Burrell master, from
Kercawdy, John Tenant Scot merchant with

Twenty seaven wayes of white salte	36s	0d

f. 8r
July 23 1614
[*803*] In *le* Goulden Hawke *de* Norden 30 tonnes, Bartholomew
Rymattes master, from Norden, Thomas Marche *ind'* with

Fowertene lastes of Danske rye	35s	0d

Eadem die
[*804*] In *le* same shipp and master from Norden *predicte*
The said Bartholomew Rymattes alien merchant with

Three lastes of Danske rye	9s	4½d

Eadem die

[*805*] In *le* Redd Lyon *de* Enchuzen 150 tonnes, Melchar Seabrandsone
master, from Danske, Edward Jones *ind'* merchant with hawkes [*sic*]

Nyne faulcons and twelve tarcelles[291]	20s	0d
	+20s	0d

July 26

[*806*] In *le* Goulden Hownde *de* Emden 30 tonnes, Poppe Johnsone
master, from Emden, the saide Poppe alien marchant with

Sixtene lastes of Danske rye	£2	0s	0d
Straingers custom		10s	0d

Eadem die

[*807*] In *le* Redd Lyon *de* Enchuzen, Melchar Seabrandsone master,
from Danske *predicte*, Thomas Snellinge marchant with

Eighty five lastes of Danske rye	£10	12s	6d
Forty halfe chestes Renish glasse	£2	10s	0d
More forty wayneskottes for the master being an alien[292]		3s	4d
		+3s	4d

July 27

[*808*] In *le* Eliphant *de* London 80 tonnes, Gabrill Robinsone master, from
Danske in the East Country, Thomas Snellinge *ind'* merchant with

Forty lastes of Danske rye	£5	0s	0d

July 29

[*809*] In *le* Margreat *de* Kercawdy 30 tonnes, James Sympsone master,
from Kerheine, the [said] James Scot merchant with

Theirty *sixe* ton[nes] of great Scot coales	12s	0d

Eadem die

[*810*] In *le* Fortune *de* Emden 50 tonnes, Lubeart Poppe master, from
Emden, John Wallis *ind'* marchant with

Twenty lastes of Danske rye	£2	10s	0d

Eadem die

[*811*] In *le* same shipp and master from Emden *predicte*, the saide
master Lubeart Poppe alien marchant with

Sixe lastes of Danske rye	18s	9d

Eadem die

[*812*] In *le* Sollamon *de* Newcastle 60 tonnes, William Carr master,
from Danske, Thomas Chapman *ind'* merchant with

Theirty lastes of Danske rye	£3	15s	0d
Ten hunderd waight r[o]ughe hempe for the master		6s	8d

f. 8v

August 2 1614

[*813*] In *le* Grace of God of Kercawdy 36 tonnes, John Masterton
master, from Curras in Scotland, Richard Christy Scot merchant with

Theirty sixe wayes of white salte	£2	8s	0d
Three trusses containing 4 *C* waight Scot yearne		5s	0d
More entred upon the 6 of August by the said merchant			
Two hunderd waight of Scot yearne		2s	6d
One waye *di'* white salte		2s	0d

August 6

[*814*] In *le* Margreat *de* Kercawdy 40 tonnes, James Collier master,
from Kercawdy in Scotland, the saide James Scot merchant with

Forty sixe wayes of white salte	£3	1s	4d
Eight quarters of wheate		2s	8d

August 9

[*815*] In *le* Mary Keatherne *de* Kercawdy 30 tonnes, Andrew Masterton
master, from Kercawdy, the said Andrew Scot merchant with

Twenty tonnes of great Scot coales	6s	8d
Fower lastes of wheate	13s	4d
Twenty yeardes of twill vallued as lynnen cloth		6d

Eadem die

[*816*] In *le* Grace of God *de* Kercawdy 40 tonnes, David Wise master,
from Kercawdy, the said David Scot marchant with

Forty tonnes of great Scot coales	13s	4d

August 10

[*817*] In *le* Besse *de* Lynn 30 tonnes, Thomas Guntrope master,
from Island, John [?]Wabstber *ind'* marchant with *hawkes*[293]

Ten jarfalcons and sixe tercells	19s	0d
	+19s	0d

Eadem die

[*818*] In *le* Neptune *de* Lynn 30 tonnes, Robert Dix[*hole in document*] master,
from Amsterdam in Holland, John Mason *in*[*d*]' [merch]ant with

Fowertene lastes of Fleemish wheate	£2	6s	8d

August 11

[*819*] In *le* Jonas *de* Berghen 50 tonnes, Jochyn Croger master, from
Berghen in Norway, the said Jochyn alien merchant with

Twenty two hunderd Norway deales	£5	10s	0d
One laste of great bond tarr		3s	4d
Strainger costom		28s	4d

August 15
[*820*] In *le* John *de* Kercawdy 30 tonnes, William Williamsone master,
from Kercawdy in Scotland, the said William Scot merchant with
Theirty tonnes of great Scot coales   10s 0d

Eadem die
[*821*] In *le* Besse of Lynn *predicte*, Thomas Guntrope master, from
Island, Henry Ellis alien marchant with
Two barrels of trayne oyle   2s   6d
More in the same shipp of the goodes of Robert Hally *ind'*, two barrels
of trayne oyle   2s   0d

f. 9r
[?] August 19 1614
[*822*] In *le* Jonas *de* Kercawdy 20 tonnes, Alexander Law master, from
Kercawdy in Scotland, the said Alexander Scot merchant with
Twenty tonnes of great Scot coales   6s   8d

August 22
[*823*] In *le* Fortune *de* Amsterdam, Meltha Garrardsone master, from
Amsterdam, William Doughty *ind'* merchant with[294]
Seaven lastes of smale bond pitch   14s 0d
Two lastes of greate bond pitche   6s   8d
Nyne lastes of wheate   30s 0d
Fower lasstes of maulte   10s 0d
One hunderd of clapholte   9d

Eadem die
[*824*] In *le* David *de* Deepe 17 tonnes, David Mersive master, from Deepe
in France, Sylvester Rochyre *ind'* [*sic*] with
Fower tonnes of viniger[295]   9s   4d
                                                                      +9s   4d
Sixtene cases of white Normandy glasse   16s 0d
Seavenscore dossen of earthen bottles covered with wicker   11s 8d

August 27
[*825*] In *le* Fortune *de* Kercawdy 40 tonns, Robert White master,
from Curras, George Walker Scot marchant with
Fower hunderde ells Scot lynnen cloth   12s 0d
Forty yeardes of tykinge   16d

Eadem die
[*826*] In *le* same shipp and master from Curras *predicte* the said master
Robearte White Scot marchant with

Forty seaven wayes of white salte   £3   2s   0d
More entred the same daye in the same shipp and master of the
goodes of Henry Clarke
Sixe score ells of Scot lynnen cloth   3s   0d
Twenty Scot cussions vallued at 13s 4d   8d

Eadem die
[*827*] In *le* same Fortune of Kercawdy *predicte,* the said Robert master,
from Curras, John Stamporte *ind'* merchant with
Two hunderd waight Scot feathers[296]   4s   0d
                                                                   +4s   0d

One hunderd elles of Scot lynnen cloth   3s   0d

August 29
[*828*] In *le* George *de* Memlique 120 tonnes, Minis Cornelisone
master, from Danske, Thomas Snellinge *ind'* merchant with
Fiftene lastes of great bond tarr   £2 10s   0d
Sixtene lastes of great bond pitche   £2 13s   4d
Eightene hunderd of clapholte   13s   6d
Two hunderd of Sprewce deales   30s   0d
Fyfty halfe chestes of Renish glasse   £3 15s   0d
One thousande treenayles vallued at 12s *per centum*   [?]6s   0d
Forty keegs of girkins vallued at 16d *per* keage   2s [?]8d

f. 9v
August 29 1614
[*829*] In *le* Good Fortune *de* Kercawdy 36 tonnes, John Hogg master,
from Kercawdy in Scotland, the said John Scot merchant with
Forty wayes of white salte   £2 13s   4d

August 30
[*830*] In *le* Fortune of Kercawdy *predicte,* Robert White master, from Curras,
Georg[e] Walker Scot merchant *per* post entry with
Three hunderd ells Scot lynnen cloth   9s   0d

Eadem die
[*831*] In *le* Jacob *de* Kercawdy 2<0>4 tonnes, Michel Shankes master,
from Kercawdy, the said Michell Scot merchant with
Twenty tonnes of great Scot coales   6s   8d

August 31
[*832*] In *le* Margreat *de* Kercawdy 25 tonnes, William Williamsone
master, from Kercawdy, David Balford Scot marchant with
Twenty sixe wayes of white salte   34s   8d

One hunderd ells of Scot lynnen cloth	3s	0d
Five combes of wheate		10d

September 1
[*833*] In *le* Mary Keatherne *de* Kercawdy 30 tonnes, Andrew Masterton
master, from Kercawdy, the said Andrew Scot merchant with

Two lastes of wheate	6s	8d
Twenty five tonnes of great Scot coales	8s	4d
Three combes of otmelle vallued at 16s the combe	2s	5d

Eadem die
[*834*] In *le* Margreat *de* Kercawdy 40 tonnes, James Collier master,
from Kercawdy, the said James Scot marchant with

Forty sixe wayes of white salte	£3	1s	4d
One laste of wheate		3s	4d

September 2
[*835*] In *le* Swane *de* Lynn 40 tonnes, Phillip Ewers master, from
Amsterdam in Hollande, William Doughty *ind'* marchant with

Twenty lastes of Danske rye	£2	10s	0d
Three hunderd bundles of browne paper[297]		15s	0d
		+15s	0d

Eadem die
[*836*] In *le* George Bonaventer *de* Lynn 60 tonnes, Robert Hayes master,
from Amsterdam, the saide Robert *ind'* marchant with[298]

Sixe lastes of great bond pitche	20s	0d
Five lastes of smale bond pitche	10s	0d
Three hunderd Norway deales	15s	0d
Two hunderd of clapholte		18d
Two lastes of great bond tarr	6s	8d

Eadem die
[*837*] In *le* same shipp and master from Amsterdam *predicte*, William
Doughty *ind'* marchant with

Twelve lastes of Danske rye	30s	0d

f. 10r
September 5 1614
[*838*] In *le* Margreat *de* Kercawdy 40 tonnes, James Sympson
master, from Curras, the said James Scot merchant with

Forty wayes of white salte	£2	13s	4d

Eadem die

[*839*] In *le* Clemance *de* Lynn 20 tonnes, Steven Selly master, from
Ortna[299] in Scotland, William Atkyn *ind'* marchant with

Three thousand codfiesh	£3	10s	0d
Two hunderd of lyngs		6s	8d

Eadem die

[*840*] In *le* Gifte *de* Lynn 40 tonnes, Robert Braddy master, from
Amsterdam in Holland, Thomas Marche *ind'* merchant with

Theirtene lastes of Danske rye	32s	6d
Seaven lastes of smale bond pitche	14s	0d
One laste of smale bonde tarr	2s	0d
One laste of greate bond pitch	3s	4d
Fower pockets of Fleemish hoops containing 10 *C* waight[300]	10s	0d
	+5s	0d
Five wayes of bay salte	5s	0d

Eadem die

[*841*] In *le* George *de* Kercawdy 40 tonnes, John More master, from
Kercawdy in Scotland, Patricke Keare Scot merchant with

Twenty five wayes of white salte	33s	4d
Three lastes of Scot wheate	10s	0d
More entred the 28 or the 29 of September, two wayes of white salte	2s	8d

September 6

[*842*] In *le* same shipp and master from Kercawdy in Scotland, the
fore saide Patricke Keare Scot merchant with

One laste of wheat *per* post entry	3s	4d

September 7

[*843*] In *le* Mary Keatherne *de* Kercawdy and master from Kercawdy
predicte [*sic*], the said Andrew Masterton Scot merchant with

Five tonnes of Scot coales	20d

September 8

[*844*] In *le* George *de* Memliqua *predicte*, Minis Cornelius master, from
Danske in the E[a]st Cuntry, Thomas Snelling *ind'* merchant with

Halfe an hunderd of Sprewce deales	7s	6d
Two hunderd clapholte		18d
One last greate bond tarr *per* post entry	3s	4d

September 17

[*845*] In *le* John *de* Kercawdy 30 tonnes, David Williamsone master,
from Kercawdy, the said David Scot merchant with

Theirty tonnes of great Scot coales	10s	0d

f. 10v

September 20 1614

[*846*] In *le* Griffen *de* Berghen 45 tonnes, Antony Antonisone master,
from Berghen, the said Antonisone alien merchant with

Eightene hunderd Norway deales	£4	10s	0d
Stranger costom		22s	6d

September 23

[*847*] In *le* Goulden Angell *de* Amsterdam 70 *tonns*, Harmon Williamsone
master, from Amsterdam, John Masson *ind'* marchant with

Theirty fower lastes of Danske rye	£4	5s	0d
Syxe baggs of hopps containing 16 *C* waight[301]		16s	0d
		+8s	0d

Eadem die

[*848*] In *le* Neptune *de* Lynn <20> *30* tonnes, Robert Dixsone master,
from Amsterdam, John Masson *ind'* merchant with

Fiftene lastes of maulte		37s	6d

Eadem die

[*849*] In *le* [?]Teane *de* Amsterdam 40 tonnes, Claus Dericksone master,
from Amsterdam, Henry Robinsone *ind'* merchant with

Twenty fower lastes of Danske rye	£3	0s	0d

September 24

[*850*] In *le* Pleasure *de* Lynn 80 tonnes, Edward Acworth master, from
Danske, Thomas Snellinge *ind'* merchant with

Theirtie sixe lastes of Poulish wheate	£6	0s	0d
One last great bond pitch		3s	4d
Halfe a last great bond tarr			20d

September 26

[*851*] In *le* Loue *de* Harlinge 60 tonnes, Vigor Elwortes master, from
Amsterdam, the said Vigor alien with

Twenty five lastes of Danske rye /[?] *hetherto examined*/	£3	2s	6d
Stranger costom		15s	7½d

October 3

[*852*] In *le* Goulden Fleece *de* Lynn 1 *C* tonnes, Deonis Ollye master,
from Lysburne, John Sendall *ind'* merchant with

Fower score wayes of Spannish salte whereof there is allowed unto the merchants[302] that brought in this salte at their adventure fiftene wayes to be imployed at their adventure in this saide shipp for the Island fieshinge the next yeare *anno* 1614	£4	6s	8d

Eadem die

[*853*] In *le* Gedeion of Harlinge 80 tonnes, Dericke Adriansone master, from Tyngwell[303] in Norway, Garvice Wharton *ind'* with

Twenty five hunderd Norwaye deales	£6	5s	0d
Three hunderd halfe Norway deales		7s	6d
Theirty fower baulkes containing 650 foote[304] fir timber vallued at 4d *per* foote		11s	4d

f. 11r

October 4 1614

[*854*] In *le* Precilla *de* Lynn 35 tonnes, John Younges master, from Amsterdam, Thomas Snellinge *ind'* merchant with

Eightene lastes of Danske rye	£2	5s	0d

October 5

[*855*] In *le* Blessinge *de* Kercawdy 35 tonnes, George Hayes master, from Kercawdy, the saide George Scot merchant with

Theirty five tonnes of great Scot coales	11s	8d
One barrell of salmon girldes[305]	*[blank]*	

Eadem die

[*856*] In *le* Margreat *de* Kercawdy 24 tonnes, David Andersone master, from Kercawdy, the saide David Scot marchant with

Twenty sixe wayes of white salte	34s	8d

October 8

[*857*] In *le* Fortune *de* Amsterdam 30 tonnes, Meltha Garrardsone master, from Amsterdam, William Doughty *ind'* merchant with

Tenn lastes of wheate	33s	4d
Sixe lastes of rye	15s	0d

October 10

[*858*] In *le* Eliphant *de* London 80 tonnes, Gabrill Robinsone master, from Danske, Thomas Chapman *ind'* marchant with

Forty lastes of Danske rye	£5	0s	0d

October 11

[*859*] In *le* Hoape *de* Flushinge 16 tonnes, Cornelius Collyns[306] master, from Flushinge, the saide Cornelius alien merchant with

Two bagges of Fleemish hopps containing 3 *C* waight	3s	0d
	+18d	
One barrell containing a quarter of an hunderd waight of pepper	2s	4d
	+2s	4d

One smale barrell of nutmeggs containing net halfe an hunderd waight   8s   5d
                                                                         +8s   5d
                                                  Strainger custom   3s   5d
                                                                         +6s   1d

Eadem die
[*860*] In *le* Jacob *de* Kercawdy 24 tonnes, John Davisone master, from
Kercawdy in Scotland, the said John Scot merchant with
Twenty fower wayes of white salte   32s   0d

October 17
[*861*] In *le* Goulden Hound *de* Emden 30 tonnes, Poppe Johnsone
master, from Emden, the saide Poppe alien merchant with
Fiftene lastes of Danske rye   [?]35s   0d
Whereof one laste freed of custome
                                                  Strainger costom   9s [?]4½d

October 22
[*862*] In *le* Goulden Fleece *de* Lynn *predict'*, Denis Ollye master, from
Portingall, John Sendall *ind'* merchant *per* post entry with
Twenty wayes of Spannish salte   26s   8d

f. 11v
[?] November 5 1614
[*863*] In *le* Margreat *de* Kercawdy 40 tonnes, James Sympsonne master,
from Kercawdy, the said James Scot marchant with
Forty wayes of white salte   £2 13s   4d

Eadem die
[*864*] In *le* Mary Keatherne *de* Kercawdy 30 tonnes, David Balforde
master, from Kercawdy, the said David Scot marchant with
Forty two wayes of white salte   £2 16s   0d

Eadem die
[*865*] In *le* John *de* Kercawdy 30 tonnes, David Williamsonne master,
from Kercawdy in Scotland, the saide David Scot merchant with
Theirty tonnes of great Scot coales   10s   0d

Eadem die
[*866*] In *le* Margreat *de* Kercawdy 24 tonnes, William Williamsonne master,
from Kercawdy in Scotland, the said William Scot merchant with
Twenty sixe wayes of white salte   34s   8d

Eadem die
[*867*] In *le* Good Fortune *de* Kercawdy 40 tonnes, Jerimy Lytster master,
from Kercawdy, the said Jerimy Letster Scot merchant with
Forty wayes of white salte   £2 13s   4d

November 7
[*868*] In *le* Gifte of God *de* Kercawdy 40 tonnes, Robert Duncan master,
from Kercawdy in Scotland, the saide Robert Scot merchant with
Theirty tonnes of Scot coales   10s0d

November 11
[*869*] In *le* same shipp and master from Kercawdy *predicte*, the said
Robert Scot marchant *per* post entry with
Tenn tonnes of Scot great coales   3s   4d

November 14
[*870*] In *le* Hary and Thomas *de* Lynn 40 tonnes, Henry Johnsone master,
from Amsterdam, Robert Thory *ind'* merchant with[307]
Five lastes of Danske rye   12s   6d
Three cables, three warpes and three coyles tarred ropes containing
32 *C* waight   21s   4d
Three score bundles browne paper   3s   0d
                                                                     +3s   0d
Fower hunderd of clapholte   3s   0d
Eight peeces dubble sayes   24s   0d
                                                                    +24s   0d

/ [Marginal entry illegible] /
Two peeces canvis tufted with silke   20d
                                                                         +20d

Eadem die
[*871*] In *le* same shipp and master *predicte* from Amsterdam, Thomas
March *ind'* with
Nyne lastes *di'* Danske rye   23s   9d
Five lastes *di'* white herringe   27s   6d
One laste of barrell fiesh   8s   0d
                                                                    +10s   0d
One hunderd of Hulland lyngs   3s   4d
One hunderd of clapholte   9d
Five cables, one hawcer and three coyles containing five thowsand
waight   33s   4d
One smale fatt of brasse kettles containing five hunderd waight   15s   0d
                                                                    +15s   0d

More entred the [?]second of December [? by the abovesaid]

Three hunderd waight of brasse kettles	9s	0d
	+9s	0d

f.12r [308]

November 14

[*872*] In *le* Harry and Thomas *de* Lynn *predict'* and master from
Amsterdam, Nathaniell Maxei *ind'* merchant with

One barrell and three smale baggs containing net one hunderd three quarters of whit suger	5s	10d
	+8s	9d
Eleaven pownde of nutmeggs		20d
		+20d
Five pownd of cloves		15d
		+15d
Five pownd of sinamon		10d
		+10d

November 25

[*873*] In *le* Weypen *de* Henlopp 120 tonnes, Jacob Symons master,
from Danske, Thomas Chapman *ind'* merchant with

Three score lastes of Danske rye	£7	10s	0d
Nyne wayes of Renish glasse		22s	6d

December 1

[*874*] In *le* Clemance *de* Lynn 24 tonnes, Denis Ollye master, from
Flushinge, Thomas Slayney *ind'* marchant with[309]

Seaven lastes of white herringe	35s	0d
Seaventy five bundles browne paper	3s	9d
	+3s	9d
Two hunderd of stone pottes covered		16d
Five peeces great raysons	2s	6d
	+2s	6d
Ten topnettes of figgs		15d
		+15d
Five hunderd waight of Holland cheese		20d

December 10

[*875*] In *le* Elizabeth of Lynne 40 tonnes, Thomas Skynner master,
from Amsterdam, Nathaniell Maxey *ind'* marchant with

One barrell and one bagge containing neete [*sic*] eighteene topnets figgs	2s	3d
	+2s	3d
Eight pownde synamon		16d
		+16d

Five pownde cloves   15d
                                                                                15d
Five pownde of nutmegs   9d
                                                                                +9d

Eadem die
[*876*] In *le* Weypen of Henlopp 140 [*sic*] tonnes, Jacob Symons master,
from Danske, Thomas Chapman *ind'* merchant with *per* post entry
Fower lastes of Danske rye   10s   0d

December 12
[*877*] In *le* Clemance of Lynn 24 tonnes, Deonis Olly master, from
Flushinge, Thomas Slayny *ind'* merchant *per* post entry with
One laste of white herringe   5s   0d
Twelve pownde of cloves   3s   0d
                                                                  +3s   0d

December 13
[*878*] In *le* Elizabeth of Lynn 40 tonnes, Thomas Skynner master,
to Amsterdam,[310] John Percivall *ind'* merchant with
Three thousand waight of cordage   20s   0d
Eight lastes of white herringe   £2   0s   0d
One thousand waight of cheese   3s   4d
Fower boultes of Sprewce canvis   2s   8d
Five score bundles of browne paper   5s   0d
                                                                +[?]5s   0d

Eadem die
[*879*] In *le* same shipp and master from Amsterdam *predict'*, William
Doughty *ind'* with
Tenn wayes of Spannish salte   [?]13s   4d
Fower thousand waight of cordage   26s   8d
Nyne boultes Sprewce canvis   6s   0d
Six peeces of great raysones   [?]3s   0d
                                                                  +3s   0d

f. 12v
December 17 1614
[*880*] In *le* [*blank*] Margreat[311] of Kercawdy 40 tonnes, James Collier
master, from Kercawdy in Scotland, the said James Scot merchant with
Forty sixe wayes of white salte   £3   1s   4d
One laste of white herringe   5s   0d

December 21
[*881*] In *le* same shipp and master from Kercawdy, the saide James Scot
merchant with *per* post entry
One last *di'* white herrings   7s   6d

Eadem die
[*882*] In *le* Mary Keatherne of Kercawdy <20> *30* tonnes, David
Balford master, from Kercawdy in Scotland, the said David Scot
merchant with
Twenty sixe tonnes of greate Scot coles   8s   8d
Syxe lastes of white herringe   30s 0d

Eadem die
[*883*] In *le* Margreat of Kercawdy 24 tonnes, James Benn
master, from Kercawdy, the said James Scot merchant with
Twenty fower tonnes of great Scot coales   8s   0d

Eadem die
[*884*] In *le* John of Kercawdy 30 tonnes, David Williamsone master,
from Kercawdy in Scotland, the saide David Scot merchant with
Theirty tonnes of great Scot coles   10s 0d
Eight barrells of white herrings   3s   4d

December 22
[*885*] In *le* Harry of Kercawdy 24 tonnes, John Law master, from
Kercawdy in Scotland, the said John Scot merchant with
Twenty fower tonnes of Scot coales   8s   0d
Fower barrells of white herringe   20d

December 23
[*886*] In *le* Margreate of Kercawdy 24 tonnes, David Andersone master,
from Kercawdy in Scotland, the saide David Scot merchant with
Twenty sixe wayes of white salte   34s 8d

December 24
[*887*] In *le* Dolphen of Lynn 50 tonnes, Robert Cunstable master, from
Burdeux in France, John Percivall *ind'* marchant with[312]
Twelve halfes [*sic*] peeces of French prewnes containing nete fifty
fower hunderd waight   27s 0d
                                                 +13s 6d
Tenn hunderd waight of rozen   2s   6d

Eadem die
[*888*] In *le* William of Kercawdy 28 tonnes, John Boswell master, from
Kercawdy in Scotland, Thomas Hutchyn Scot marchant with
Twenty eight wayes of white salte   37s   4d

Eadem die
[*889*] In *le* Swann of Kercawdy 24 tonnes, Alexander Law master,
from Kercawdy in Scotland, William Garden Scot merchant with
Fyfteene lastes of great bonde tarr   £2   10s   0d

Somma totalis [*blank*]
John Greene: Comptroller

f. 13r [*blank*]
f. 13v [*blank*]
f. 14r
Lynn Regis
Entryes of all goodes and marchandiz[e] shipped from this porte into the partes
beyond the seas in one whole yeare begune at the Nativitie of Our Lord 1613 and
ended at the same feast 1614

January 4 1613
[*890*] In *le* Grace of God of Kercawdy 30 tonnes, David Wise master,
to Kercawdy, the said David Scot merchant with
Sixe tonnes of strong beare   Subsidy   9s   0d
                                                    Impost   £2 11s   0d

January 8
[*891*] In *le* Margeat [*sic*] *de* Kercawdy 40 tonnes, James Collier master,
to Kercawdy in Scotland, the saide James Scot merchant with
Fower tonnes of stronge beare[313]   6s   0d
                                                                 34s   0d

January 10
[*892*] In *le* Angell *de* Creyll 16 tonnes, William Cadde master, to
Creyll in Scotland, Thomas Clayhills Scot merchant with
Eight tonnes of stronge beare   12s   0d
                                                           £3   8s   0d

January 14
[*893*] In *le* Redd Hearte *de* Harllinge 80 tonnes, Seith Johnson master,
to Leith in Scotland, Allexander Law Scot merchant with
Fowertene tonnes of stronge beare   16s   0d
                                                           £5   19s   0d

January 15
[*894*] In *le* Mary Keatherne *de* Kercawdy 30 tonnes, David Balforde
master, to Kercawdy, the said David Scot merchant with
Seaven tonnes of stronge beare

        10s 6d
 £2 19s 6d

January 27
[*895*] In *le* Cocke *de* Flushinge 15 tonnes, Garrard Nabbes master, to
Flushing, the said Garrard alien merchant with
Fyve lastes of hempeseede, with strangers custom   £3 2s 6d

January 18
[*896*] In *le* Good Fortune *de* Kercawdy 30 tonnes, John Hogge master,
to Kercawdy, the said John Scot merchant with
Five tonnes of stronge beare

        7s 6d
 £2 2s 6d

Eadem die
[*897*] In the Cocke *de* Flushinge *predicte* and master to Flushing, the said
master Garrard Nabbes alien merchant *per* post entry with
One laste of hempe seede, with strangers custom   12s 6d

January 20
[*898*] In *le* Mary Keatherne *de* Kercawdy *predicte*, the said master
David Balford Scot merchant *per* post entry with
Eighte barrelles strong beare

      2s 0d
    11s 4d

f. 14v
January 24 1613
[*899*] In *le* Margreat *de* Kercawdy 24 tonnes, William Williamsone
master, to Kercawdy, the said William Scot merchant with
Three tonnes *di* of stronge beare

      5s 3d
    29s 9d

January 27
[*900*] In the same shipp and master to Kercawdy in Scotland, the said
master with
One tonne of strong beare *per* post entry

        18d
    8s 2d

Eadem die
[*901*] In *le* Blessinge *de* Disearte 24 tonnes, Robert Williamsone master,
to Mountrose in Scotland, John Garden Scot merchant with
Theirteene tonnes of stronge beare

     19s 6d
 £5 10s 6d

Fower hunderd waight of welde   2s 0d

January 31
[*902*] In the Margery *de* Amstrother 10 tonnes, Georg[*e*] Andersone
master to Amstrother in Scotland, William Burnesaide Scot
merchant with

Syx tonnes of stronge beare	9s	0d
	£2 11s	0d

February 3
[*903*] In *le* Joye *de* Amstrother 15 tonnes, John Smith master, to
Amstrother in Scotland, the saide John Smyth Scot merchant with

Syxe tonnes of strong beare	9s	0d
	£2 11s	0d

February 11
[*904*] In the Grace of God *de* Dundee 15 tonnes, William Duncan
master, to Dundee in Scotland, the said William Scot merchant with

Nyne tonnes of strong beare	13s	6d
	£3 11s	6d

Febrewary 12
[*905*] In *le* Grace of God *de* Kercawdy 30 tonns, David Wise master,
to Kercawdy in Scotland, the said David Scot merchant with

Five tonnes of stronge beare	7s	6d
	42s	6d

February 17
[*906*] In *le* Margreat *de* Kercawdy 20 tonnes, David Andersone master,
to Kercawdy in Scotland, the said David Scot merchant with

Tenn tonnes of strong beare	15s	0d
	£4 5s	0d

February 18
[*907*] In *le* Oulde Harry *de* Kercawdy 24 tonnes, David Wilsone
master, to Leith in Scotland, John Lambe Scot marchant with

Nyne tonnes of stronge beare	13s	6d
	£3 16s	6d

Febreuary [*sic*] 19
[*908*] In *le* Grace of God *de* Kercawdy 20 tonnes, Henry Raynallsone
master, to Kercawdy, Andrew Leighton Scot merchant with

Three tonnes of stronge beare	4s	6d
	25s	6d
Seaventene grosse of crewell gerdling at twelve dossen to every groce	11s	4d

February 22
[*909*] In *le* Hoape *de* Amsterdam 40 tonnes, Peter Petersone master,
to Norway, Thomas Flory and Thomas Parkyn *ind'* merchantes with

Eight tonnes of strong beare	12s	0d
	£3 8s	0d
Sixtene kerseyes accounted for five shorte cloth and 1 kersey	35s	6d
Ten northan dossens single and two double	£2 6s	8d
Eightene paier of shorte worsteed stockings	2s	5d
One barrell of English soape	2s	8d

f. 15r
[*Date illegible*]
[*910*] In *le* Oulde Harry *de* Kercawdy *predicte*, David Wilsone master, to
Leight [*sic*] in Scotland, John Lambe Scot mercharnt [*sic*] *per* post
entry with

One tonne of stronge beare		18d
	13s	6d

March 1
[*911*] In *le* Grace of God of Barrowstone 30 tonn, David Hardy master,
to Barrowstone in Scotland, John Glenn Scot merchant with

Fower tonnes of stronge beare	6s	0d
	34s	0d

March 2
[*912*] In *le* Clemance *de* Lynn 20 tonnes, Deonis Olly master, to Orkney
in Scotland, the said Deonis Ollye Scot merchant with
Tenn tonnes of stronge beare besides drinking beare for his

fieshing vioage	15s	0d
	£4 5s	0d

March 11
[*913*] In *le* Cocke *de* Flushinge 15 tonnes, Garrard Nabbes master, to
Flushinge, Roger Harwicke *ind'* marchant with

Fyve peeces of dornexe		20d
Theirty smale beddes of tyking, 6 yeardes to a bedd, vallued at 8d *per*		
the yearde	6s	0d
Twelve peeces narrow mocadoes	8s	0d
Nyne English made sayes at 24 yeardes *per* peece	12s	0d

March 18
[*914*] In *le* George Bonaventure *de* Lynn 60 tonnes, John Bloye master,
to Berghen in Norway, Edmond Gilman *ind'* with

Three northan dossens sengle	10s	0d
Two northan playnes	3s	4d

Marche 21
[*915*] In *le* Hoape *de* Enchuzen 40 tonnes, [?]Isbrand Garrardsone
master, to Romsdall in Norway, Barthollomew Worlmell *ind'* with
Two tonnes of stronge beare   3s   0d
                                                                17s   0d

Marche 28
[*916*] In *le* Besse *de* Lynn 40 tonnes, Thomas Guntrope master, to
Island, William Hauser *ind'* entred, which were freed *per* spetiall
warrant from the farmars,
Three remnants of collered broad cloth accepted for a cloth and a halfe   [*blank*]
More sixe yeardes three quarters broad cloth   [*blank*]
Fifty fower yeardes narrow reddes vallued at £6 6s   [*blank*]
Fower score fower yeardes of collered cotten accepted for halfe a
hunderd goades cotten   [*blank*]

Aprill 5
[*917*] In *le* Mary Keatherne *de* Kercawdy 30 tonnes, John Law master,
to Kercawdy in Scotland, the said John Scot merchant with
One tonne of stronge beare   18d
                                                                     8s   6d

f. 15v
[*Date illegible*]
[*918*] In *le* Dolphen de Lynn 50 tonnes, Robert Cunstable master, to
Elbing in the East Cuntry, Thomas Snellinge *ind'* marchant with
Two halfe roules containing two thousand seasoned gray conny
skynnes and two thousand stage gray conny skynes   10s   0d
Two trusses containing forty five northan kerseyes whereof fower
allowed for wrappers   £4 11s   2d
One drye fatt containing three thousand blacke rabbette skynnes
<vall> vallued at fiftene shillinges *per cente'*   22s   6d
One thousand tawed morte lambe skynes   8s   4d
One packe containing eightene hunderd untawed morte lambskyns   9s   0d
Two trusses containing 16 *C* white sheepes leather tawed   24s   0d
Tenn thousand more of white sheepes lether tawed in kypps   £7 10s   0d

Aprill 16
[*919*] In *le* Amye *de* Lynn 80 tonnes, Robert Waters master, to
Hambrough, Thomas Slayney *ind'* marchant with
Three rolls and one smale packe gray conny skynes containing
seaven thousand seasoned and eighte thousand stagge   36s   8d
Three smale trusses morte lamskynes untawed containing sixtene
hunderd   8s   0d

Two rolles more gray conny skynes containing fower thousand
seassoned and five thousand of stage   21s   8d
Three smale trusses morte lamskyns untawed containing eightene
hunderd   9s   0d
Ten thousand of white sheepes leather tawed   £7 10s   0d
Twenty northan kerseys whereof two for wrappers allowed   £2   0s   0d

Aprill 18
[*920*] In *le* same shipp and master to Hambrough *predict'*, the said
Thomas Slayney *ind'* with
One trusse containing ten kersies whereof two for wrappers alowed
and five shorte broade clothes in the trusse part[314]   £2 11s   1½d
One thowsand morte lamskyns untawed   5s   0d
One thowsande white sheepes leather tawed   15s   0d

Aprill 20
[*921*] In *le* Dolphen *de* Lynn *predict'*, Robert Cunstable master, to Elbinge
in the East Cuntrye, Thomas Snellinge *ind'* merchant *predict'* with[315]
Three smale trusses containing two thousande morte lambskynnes
untawed   10s   0d
One hunderd of white sheepes leather tawed   18d
One trusse containing 3 *C* seasoned blacke conny skynes   8s   0d

Aprill 23
[*922*] In *le* Gedeon *de* Harllinge 80 tonnes, Dericke Adriansone master,
to Sound Water,[316] the said Dericke alien marchant with
Sixe northan dossens sengle   £2   3s   6d

Aprill 27
[*923*] In *le* Elizabeth *de* Lynn 40 tonnes, Robert Skynner master, to
Emden in the East Cuntry, Thomas Snellinge *ind'* merchant with
Forty five dozan of calves leather   26s   6d
Fower thousand white sheepes leather tawed in kypps   £3   0s   0d

f. 16r
[*No date*]
[*924*] In *le* Amye *de* Lynn 80 tonnes, Robert Waters master,
[? *to Hambrough*], Thomas Slayney *in*[*d*]' merchant with *predict'* [*sic*][317]
Two trusses of morte lamskyns untawed containing twelve hunderd   6s   0d
Fiftene hunderd white sheeps leather tawed   22s   6d
One shorte broade clothe   6s   8d
More the same day of the goods of Steven Layghton
Two trusses of morte lamskyns containing 12 *C* untawed   6s   0d

Eadem die
[*925*] In *le* Grace of God *de* Kercawdy 24 tonnes, Henry Raynallsone
master, to Kercawdy in Scotland, the said Henry Scot merchant with
Three tonnes of stronge beare   4s   6d
                                                                                       25s   6d

Aprill 30
[*926*] In *le* Joane *de* Lynn 50 tonnes, Edmond Fuller master, to
Amsterdam in Hollande, John Leade *ind'* marchant with
Theirty kerseyes and five shorte broade clothes whereof three kerseyes
allowed for wrappers   £4 13s   4d
Two thousand two hunderd white sheepes leather tawed   33s   0d

May 3
[*927*] In *le* Dolphen *de* Lynn *predict'* and master to Elbinge,
Thomas Snelling *ind'*
Two trusses of morte lamskyns untawed containing eleaven hunderd[318]   5s   6d

Eadem die
[*928*] In *le* Amye *de* Lynn 80 tonnes, Robert Waters master, to
Hambrough *predict'*, Thomas Slayney *ind'* merchant with
One thousand of white sheepes leather tawed[319]   15s   0d

May 4
[*929*] In *le* Joane *de* Lynn *predict'*, Edmund Fuller master, to
Amsterdam in Holland, Robert Thory *ind'* merchant with
Sixtene hunder[d] waight of musterd seede   4s   0d

Eadem die
[*930*] In *le* Pleasure *de* Lynn 80 tonnes, Edward Acworth master, to
Ryegate[320], John Wormell *in[d]'* marchant with
Twelve hunderd of white sheepes leather tawed and more for the
master t[w]o hunderd sheeps leather   21s   0d

May 14
[*931*] In *le* Mary Keatherne *de* Kercawdy 30 tonnes, John Law master,
to Berghen in Norway, the said John Scot merchant with
Two tonnes *di'* stronge beare   3s   9d
                                                                           21s   3d

Maye 19
[*932*] In *le* same shipp and master to Berghen *predict'*, the said merchant with
Halfe a tonne of stronge beare *per* post entry   9d
                                                                            4s   3d

f. 16v

[?] May 24

[*933*] In *le* White Buck *de* [?]Enchuzen [*tonnage illegible*], Lo[ue] Petersone
master, to Enchuzen, the said [?]Loue alien merchant with

Three thousand of white sheepes leather tawed	£2	5s	0d
Stranger custom		11s	3d

June 3

[*934*] In *le* Eliphant *de* London 80 tonnes, Gabrill Robinsone master,
to Elbinge in the East Cuntry, Thomas Snellinge *ind'* marchant with

Seaven trusses of untawed morte lambe skyns containing seaven thousande	35s	0d
One trusse containing five hunderd gray connye skynes seasoned and five hunderd stage gray conny skynes	2s	4d
Three hunderd white sheepes leather tawed in kyppes	4s	6d

June 16

[*935*] In *le* Joane *de* Lynn 40 tonnes, Robeart Thorye master, to
Amsterdam in Holland, Nathaniell Maxei *ind'* marchant with

Syxe score and tenn paier of shorte white worsteede stockyns	17s	4d

Eadem die

[*936*] In *le* Gifte of God *de* Kercawdy 25 tonnes, Henry Raynallsone
master, to Kercawdy in Scotland, the said Henry
Scot marchant with

One tonne *di'* stronge beare	2s	3d
	12s	9d

July 2

[*937*] In *le* Red Lyon *de* Staverne 180 tonnes, Marten Oates master,
to Elsonoure,[321] Thomas Snellinge *ind'* marchant with

One dry fatt containing two thousand blacke rabet skyns tawed vallued at 15s *per centum*		15s	0d
Five hunderd tawed morte lambe skyns		4s	2d
Three trusses containing three thousand white sheepes leather tawed	£2	5s	0d
Seaven hunderd white sheepes leather tawed in kypps		10s	6d
One smale trusse containing five hunderd gray conny skyns tawed		3s	4d
One smale trusse containing 6 *C* morte lambe skynes		3s	0d
More two hunderd morte lambe skyns of James Riches *ind'* being the pylott of the shipp			12d

July 16
[*938*] In *le* Gifte of God of Kercawdy 30 tonnes, Henry Raynallsone
master, to Kercawdy in Scotland, the saide Henry Scot merchant with
One tonne *di'* stronge beare   2s   3d
                                                                                 12s   9d
Two tonne waight of oken barke vallued at 30s the tonne[322]   3s   0d

July 23
[*939*] In *le* Pleasure *de* Lynn 70 tonnes, Edward Acworth master, to
Hambrough, John Wormell *ind'* marchant with
Two thousand sheepes leather tawed   30s   0d
More for the master *ind'* five hunderd sheepes lether tawed   7s   6d

July 26
[*940*] In *le* same shipp and master to Hambrough *predict'*, Thomas
Snelling *ind'* with
Two hunderd mort lambe skynes   12d
Two trusses containing sixe hunderd gray cony skyns tawed   4s   0d

f. 17r
[*Date illegible*]
[*941*] In *le* Margreat *de* Kercawdy 36 tonnes, James [?]Sympsone master,
to Kercawdy in Scotland, the said James Scot merchant with
One tonne *di'* of stronge beare   18d
                                                                                 8s   6d

August 25
[*942*] In *le* Neptune *de* Lynn 20 tonnes, Robert Dixsone master,
to Amsterdam in Holland, Nathaniell Maxei *ind'* marchant with
Five score and twelve paier white short worsteede stockyns   14s   11d

September 5
[*943*] In *le* Fortune *de* Kercawdye 40 tonnes, Robert White master, to
Kercawdy in Scotland, the saide Robert White Scot marchant with
Twenty five hunderd waight oken barke vallued 18d the hunderd
whereof five hunderd paide custome as appeareth by entry taken the
16 of July last in a shipp called the Gifte of God[323]   18d

September 9
[*944*] In *le* David *de* Deepe bur[*then*] 17 tonnes, David Mersire master,
to Deepe in France, Silvester Rocheire *ind'* marchant with
One thousand *di'* shanke boanes   6d
Twelve barrels of <g> broken glasse vallued 20d the barrel   12d

Three hunderd rambes hornes   4d
Two hunderd oxe hornes   6d
Halfe an hunderd dozan paier oulde shooes   12d

September 12
[*945*] In *le* Margreat *de* Kercawdy 24 tonnes, William Williamsone
master, to Kercawdy, David Balforde Scot merchant with
Two tonnes *di'* stronge beare   3s   9d
                                                                 21s   3d

September 17
[*946*] In *le* George *de* Memliqua 120 tonnes, Minis Cornelius master,
to Danske in the East Cuntry, Thomas Slayney *ind'* merchant with
Three thousand white sheepes leather tawed   £2   5s   0d
Five hunderd gray conny skyns tawed   3s   4d

September 24
[*947*] In *le* Amye *de* Lynn 070 [*sic*] tonnes, Robert Waters master, to
Calles in Spayne, John Percivall *in*[*d*]' marchant with
Seaven hogsheades, one barrell and one pipe containing 25
hunderd wa[*igh*]t of English waxe   £5   0s   0d
More entred the 28 of September of the goods of the saide
merchantes[324] in the caske afore saide, one hunderd waight of
English waxe   4s   0d

October 12
[*948*] In *le* Margreat *de* Kercawdy 24 tonnes, David Andersone master,
to Kercawdy in Scotland, the saide David Scot marchant with
Two tonnes of stronge beare   3s   9d
                                                                21s   3d
Three baggs English hopps containing sixe hunderd wa[*igh*]t   6s   0d

Eadem die
[*949*] In *le* Blessinge *de* Kercawdy 30 tonnes, George Hayes master, to
Kercawdy in Scotland, the saide George Scot merchant with
Two tonnes of stronge beare   3s   0d
                                                                17s   0d

f. 17v
[*Date illegible*]
[*950*] In *le* Jacobe *de* [?]Kercawdy, [*name illegible*][325] master, to
Kercawdy, the said John [?]Scot marchant with
Five tonnes of stronge beare   7s   6d
                                                        £2   2s   6d

October 22

[951] In *le* Clemence *de* Lynn <40> *20* tonnes, Denis Olly master,
to Duncarke in Flonders, Thomas Slayney *ind'* merchant with

Fiftene quarters of rape seede	15s	0d
Five quarters of lynn seede	5s	0d
Forty hunderdwaight of musterde seede	10s	0d
One hunderd of white sheepes leather tawed		18d

More in the same shipp three shorte broade clothes which formerly
paide the custome as may appeare *per* entry taken the 18 of Aprill last in
the Amy *de* Lynn[326] affermed to be trew *per* an officer, Nathaniell Maxey[327]   nil

October 24

[952] In *le* Blessinge *de* Kercawdy *predict'* George Hayes master to
Kercawdy in Scotland, James Forret Scot merchant *per* post entry with

Fowertene baggs and three endes English hopps containing theirty three hunderd and *di'* waight	32s	6d
Halfe a tonne of stronge beare		9d
	4s	3d

Eadem die

[953] In *le* Margreat *de* Kercawdy *predict'* David Andersone master to
Kercawdy in Scotland, the said David Scot marchant with *per* post entry[328]

Two baggs of English hopps containing 4 *C* waight	4s	0d
Halfe a tonne of stronge beare		9d
	4s	3s

Eadem die

[954] In *le* Jacob *de* Kercawdy *predicte,* John Davisone master, to
Kercawdy in Scotland, the said John Scot merchant *per* post entry with

Fower tonnes of stronge beare	6s	0d
	34s	0d

November 11

[955] In *le* Margreat *de* Kercawdy 40 tonnes, James Sympsone master,
to Kercawdy in Scotland, the saide James Scot merchant with

Five tonnes of stronge beare	7s	6d
	£2 2s	6d

November 12

[956] In *le* Gifte of God *de* Kercawdy 40 tonnes, Robert Duncan
master, to Amstrother in Scotland, the saide Robert Scot marchant with

One tonne *di'* stronge beare	2s	3d
	12s	9d

Eadem die

[*957*] In *le* Mary Keatherne *de* Kercawdy 30 tonnes, David Balford master, to
[*blank*]³²⁹ in Scotland, the saide David Scot merchant with

Five tonnes of stronge beare	7s	6d
	£2 2s	6d

November15

[*958*] In *le* Elizabeth *de* Lynn 30 tonnes, Thomas Skynner master, to
Amsterdam in Holland, Nathaniell Maxei <*ind'*> *ind'* merchant with

Five score and sixetene paier of white shorte worsteede stockyns	15s	6d
Three dozen of shorte worsteede stockens collered	4s	9d

Eadem die

[*959*] In *le* Mary Keatherne *de* Kercawdy *predict'* David Balford master to
Anstrother in Scotland, the said David Scot merchant with *per* post entry

Three smale baggs of English hopps containing 6 *C* wa[*igh*]t	6s	0d

f. 18r

[*Date illegible*]

[*960*] In *le* Hoape *de* Flushinge 16 tonnes, Cornelius Collyns master,
to Flushinge, the saide Cornelius alien marchant with

One chalder *di'* sea coales Lynn measure		12d
	+5s	0d
Stranger custom'		3d

December 12

[*961*] In *le* Neptune *de* Lynn [?]30 tonnes, Robert Dixsone master,
to Midlebrugh, John Mason *in*[*d*]' marchant with

Six thousand of smale oyle cakes vallued 15d the hunderd	3s	9d
Eight score paier of white shorte worstede stockings	21s	4d
Fower barrells of allablaster dust vallued at 30s		18d
Fower smale barrells allablaster wrought vallued at two powndes tenn shillings	2s	6d
Fower chalders of sea coles Lynn measure		16d
	+13s	4d

December 13

[*962*] In *le* Mary and Josepth [*sic*] of Lynn 16 tonnes, Samuell Morgan
master, to Leight in Scotland, Roger Bungey *ind'* merchant with

Syxe tonnes of stronge beare	9s	0d
	£2 11s	0d

Somma totalis   [*blank*]
John Greene, Comptroller

Lynn Regis *et* Welles *cum* Burnham
Entryes of all Spannish, French and Renish wines brought in to this porte from the partes beyond the seas in one whole yeare begun *at* the Nativitie of Our Lord 1613 and ended at the same feast 1614

January 3 1613
[963] In *le* Cocke of Flushinge burden 15 tonnes, Garrard Nabes master, from Flushinge, the saide Nabes alien' merchant with[330]
Syxe buttes of shery sacke

January 21
[964] In *le* Ann of Lynn 60 tonnes, Nicholas Tubbinge master, from Burdux in France, William Wharton *ind'* merchant with[331]
Fyfty two tonnes of French wines whereof the two tonnes is freed for
His Majesties butler, and more entred of the foresaid merchant upon the
29 of January three hogsheades of French wine
More three hoghsheades entred [? for the master]

January the laste
[965] In *le* Hoape *de* Amsterdam 60 tonnes, Peter Mousleare master, from Amsterdam, Jonas Tompsone *ind'* merchantes [*sic*] with[332]
Two buttes of sherry sacke
Two tonnes French wines

Eadem die
[966] In the same shipp and master from Amsterdam *predict'* Robert Thory *ind'* merchant with[333]
One tonne of French wines
Fower butes of sherry sacke

*March the first[334]
[967] In *le* Cocke of Flushing, Garrard Nabes alien master, [?]which [*remainder illegible*]*[335]

*March the [*illegible*]
[968] In *le* Neptune of Dorte, Andrew Blome master, from Dorte, John Wallis [*remainder illegible*]*[336]

f. 18v
[?] March 3
[969] In *le* Elizabeth of Lynn [*tonnage illegible*], [?]Andrew Page master, from Burdux in France, Rowland Bradforde *ind'* with[337]
Fyfty sixe tonnes of French wines whereof two tonnes freed of impost for His Majesties butler, and more for the shippmaster one butt of Spannish wine

May 30
[*970*] In *le* Joane of Lynn 40 tonnes, Edmond Fuller master, from Amsterdam,
Robert Thory *in*[*d*]' marchant with[338]
Three tonnes of French wines

June 25
[*971*] In *le* Ann of Lynn 80 tonnes, Nicholas Tubbing master, from Rochell in
France, John Percivall *ind'* merchant with[339]
Eight tonnes *di'* French wines in pipes

August 22
[*972*] In *le* Fortune of Amsterdam 40 tonnes, Meltha Garrardsone master, from
Amsterdam, John Mason *ind'* marchant with
Fyve hogsheades of French wine[340]

September 2
[*973*] In *le* George Bonaventer of Lynn 60 tonnes, Robert Hayes master, from
Amsterdam, the saide Robert *ind'* merchant with[341]
Two tonnes of French wines and one pipe of Maliga sacke

October 11
[*974*] In *le* Hoape of Flushinge 16 tonnes, Cornelius Collins master, from
Flushinge, the saide Cornelius alien merchant with[342]
Nyne buttes two hogsheades of Malliga sacke

November 14
[*975*] In *le* Harry and Thomas of Lynn 40 tonnes, Henry Johnsone master, from
Amsterdam, Robert Thory *ind'* merchant with[343]
One tonne of oulde French wine

November 21
[*976*] In *le* Hoape of Flushinge 16 tonnes, Cornelius Collyns master, from
Flushing, Frances Fyan subject unto the French kinge
Sixe tonnes of French wine and more entred the 23 of November one hogshead of
French wine, and more of the saide master alien fower pipes of Malliga sacke[344]

December the firste
[*977*] In *le* Clemance of Lynn 24 tonnes, Deonis Olley master, from Flushinge,
Thomas Slayney *ind'* marchant with[345]
One tonne *di'* French wines

December 13
[*978*] In *le* Elizabeth of Lynn 40 tonnes, Thomas Skynner master, from

Amsterdam, John Percivall *ind'* merchant with[236]
Fower tonnes of French wines

December 24
[*979*] In *le* Dolphen of Lynn 50 tonnes, Robert Cunstable master, from
[?]Burdeux in France, John Percivall *ind'* merchant with[347]
Fyfty two tonnes of French wines whereof the two tonnes is freed for
His Majesties butler

John Greene, Comptroller

f. 19r
Welles *cum* Burneham
Entryes of all goodes and marchandize brought from the partes beyond the seas
into the creekes of Wells and Burneham, members of the porte of Lynn, in one
whole yeare begun at the Nativitie of Our Lorde 1613 and ended at the same
feast *anno* 1614

January 29
[*980*] In *le* John *de* Welles 34 tonnes, Thomas Fawset master, from
Rotterdam in Holland, Henry Congham *ind'* marchant with

Three lastes of white herringe full packed	15s	0d
Three lastes of Danske rye	7s	6d
Two hunderd and *di'* Luke coales	20s	0d
Twelve quearne stones vallued at 20s		12d
Fifty bundles of browne paper	2s	6d
	+2s	6d

March 1
[*981*] In *le* Elaphant *de* Amsterdam 40 tonnes, Claus Cornelius
master, from Amsterdam, Henry Congham *ind'* merchant with

Fower hunderd of Norwaye deales	20s	0d
Twenty smale baulkes vallued at 40s	2s	0d
One last of white herringe	5s	0d
One laste of great bond tarr	3s	4d
Ten hunderd waight of tarred cordage	6s	8d
Two hunderd of smale sparres	2s	0d

Theirty wayes of Spannish salte allowed unto this marchant for the
furnishinge of his shipps this yeare for Island, *videlicet* twenty *two* wayes
for the Meane of Wells, whereof Robert Leeche master, for Island
fieshinge, and more eight wayes for the John *de* Wells, Eliza King master,
for Island *predicte*   nil

Eadem die

[*982*] In *le* Blacke Horse *de* Roterdam 40 tonnes, [?]Rakes Dericksone master, from Rotherdam [*sic*] in Holland, Robert Money *ind'* merchant with

One hunderd an[d] a halfe Luke coales	12s	0d
Ten hunderd waight of tarred ropes	6s	8d
One thousand paving tyles		12d

Theirty wayes of Spannish salte alowed unto this merchant for the furnishinge of his shipps for Island, *videlicet* into the Sara of Wells, Steven Leake master, for Island fieshing, aleaven wayes and more nyne wayes into the God Grace of Wells, Nicholas Dey master, for Island, and more into the Robert *de* Wells tenn wayes, whereof one John Tompsone master, for the Island fieshinge   nil

f. 19v

July [?]18

[*983*] In *le* George *de* Harlinge 20 tonnes, William Henrickson *ind'* from Harlinge, Henry Congham *in*[d]' merchant with

Fower hunderd Meabrogh[348] deales	16s	0d
Three score baulkes vallued at £4 10s	4s	6d
Two hunderd of smale sparres	2s	0d

Eadem die

[*984*] In *le* Love of Harlinge 40 tonnes, Weazer Ellis master, from Amsterdam in Holland, Henry Congham *in*[d]' merchant with

Eight hunderd Norway deales	£2	0s	0d
Three hunderd of clapholte		2s	6d
One hunderd of cant sparres			20d

August 26 1614

[*985*] In *le* Lambe of Harlinge 40 tonnes, Henrick Cornelisone master, from Rone in France, Stephen Housgoe *ind'* merchant with

Nyneteene milstones[349]	£3	3s	4d
	+£3	3s	4d

John Greene: Comptroller

f. 20r

Entryes of all goodes and marchandice shipped from the creaks of Wells *cum* Burnham, members of the porte of Lynn Reges, into the partes beyond the seas in one whole yeare begune at the Nativitie of Our Lord *anno* 1613 and ended at the same feast *anno* 1614

December 10
[986] In le John of Wells 34 tonnes, Thomas Fawsett master, to
Rotterdam in Holland, Henry Congham ind' merchant with
Three score pownds waight of safforne   £3 0s 0d

John Greene: Comptroller

E190/434/4: Collector of New Impositions 1614[350]

f. 2r
Inwardes
The 30 of May 1612 [*sic*]
[987] In *le* Neptune of Lynn from Amsterdam
John Lead, 2 *C* bundles browne paper[351]   12s 6d

[988] In *le* Bore of Amsterdam
William Doughtie, thre[e] hunderd bundles browne paper[352]   15s 0d

The 10 of June
[989] In *le* John *de* Mechinge from Roan
Henry Bokenham, 12 milstones[353]   £2 0s 0d

The 21 June
[990] In *le* Vyolett *predict'*
Thomas Marche, 80 bundles browne paper[354]   4s 0d
/3 – 11 – 6/

The 25 of June 1614
[991] In *le* Anne of Lynn from Rochell
Nicholas Tubbin, 1 tonn vineger[355]   2s 4d

30 June
[992] In *le* Amey of Lynn from Danske
Thomas Slanye, 5 kagges sturgeon[356]   1s 8s

2 of July
[993] In *le* Redlion of Staverne from Danske
Thomas Snelling, 12 kagges sturgeon[357]   4s 0d

23 July
[994] In *le* Red Lyon of Enchusan from Danske
Edward Jones, 9 falcons, 12 tercelles[358]   £1 0s 0d

26 day
[*995*] Thomas Snelling, 40 wainscottes[359]   2s   8d

10 August
[*996*] In *le* Beese of Lynn from Island
John Webster, 11 jerfalcons, 6 tercelles[360]   19s   0d
/2 – 9 – 8/

f. 2v
The 22 of August 1614
[*997*] In *le* David of Deepe *a predict'*
Silvester Rochier, 4 tonnes vineger[361]   9s   4d

27 August
[*998*] In *le* Fortune of Kercaudy *a p[redict']* Curras
John Stanford, 2 *C* weight feathers[362]   4s   0d

2 of September
[*999*] In *le* Swann of Lynn from Amsterdam
William Doughtie, 3 *C* bundles browne paper[363]   15s   0d

5 September
[*1000*] In *le* Guifte of Lynn from Amsterdam
Thomas March, 10 *C* weight Flemish hopps[364]   5s   0d

23 of September
[*1001*] In *le* Goulden Angell of Amsterdam *a predict'*
John Mason, 16 *C* weight Flemish hopps[365]   8s   0d
/2 – 1 – 4/   *Ex'* [366]   £2   1s   4d

f. 3r
Wells *cum* Burnham
Inwardes
The 26 of August 1614
[*1002*] In *le* Lambe of Harling *a* Roane
Stephen Howsegoe, 19 French milstons[367]   £3   3s   4d
/3 – 3 – 4/

*Hunc librum continentem octo folia quorum primum et secundum partim scribuntur reliqua abiit
liberauit hic predictus collector super sacramentum suum*[368]

NOTES TO THE TEXT

1 Kirkcaldy, Scotland.
2 Now Vlissingen, Netherlands.
3 Snettisham, Norfolk.
4 This merchant is described here as alien even though the name looks very English. He may have been living abroad, even temporarily, which would make him 'alien' for the purposes of trade and customs – cf. Hinton, *Boston*, p xxiv. In such a case he would have had to pay the additional 25% levy.
5 Heacham, Norfolk.
6 Blakeney, Norfolk.
7 Dordrecht, Netherlands.
8 Unidentified home-port.
9 Pittenweem, Scotland.
10 Crail, Scotland.
11 This apparent 'post entry' has a date, quite clearly and unequivocally stated, which is *before* the date of the entry itself, for which it is difficult to find an explanation, unless the peas actually were somehow recorded in the custom house before the rest of the shipment. Alternatively, the clerk may have meant either '22 February' or '12 March' when making up his book.
12 Anstruther, Scotland.
13 An unidentified, probably Scottish, port. It might conceivably refer to Culross in Fife, but that port is repeatedly rendered as Curras or Currus (see Index to the Text), so the identification remains suspect. The name only appears twice as the home-port of the ship *Blessing* (see also entry *100*) so it could be an inland place. The transcription might also be Coucra' and later (in entry *100*) Courac or even Courar. I am grateful to members of the staff of the National Archives of Scotland for their advice in trying to resolve this issue, along with others to which attention is drawn elsewhere.
14 The Dutch port of Veere, in Zealand.
15 This merchant, although an alien for customs purposes, became a Lynn resident and died in the town. His will was proved in the Prerogative Court of Canterbury (81 Hele, 1626; TNA PRO PROB 11/149/196).
16 The abbreviation in this particular context could indicate 'dozen' but it remains unclear.
17 Presumably meaning 'red', a variety of cloth.
18 Bremen, following Hinton, *Boston*, p. 329
19 A fustian made at Ulm in Germany.
20 Raw or unseasoned skins.
21 The handwriting in this book changes notably at this point and continues in the new hand to the end of the section, at entry number *94*. Thereafter the original hand is resumed until part way through entry number *151*, when the new hand reappears and continues to the end of the document. This suggests that the book was made up for each half-year separately.
22 This merchant is invariably recorded as alien, but the clerk on this occasion appears to have made a mistake.
23 In spite of the wording employed here, this is the first reference to this merchant.
24 Vlieland, Netherlands
25 Hamburg, Germany.
26 Enkhuizen, Netherlands.
27 Dordrecht, Netherlands.
28 Malaga, in Spain. And see entry *315* for confirmation of the unit of weight for the raisins as 'pieces' rather than 'pockets' or any of the other possible alternatives.

29 As for note 13 above – the reference is to the homeport of the same ship.

30 A frequent reference to coal from Liege, Spanish Netherlands.

31 Roofing tiles.

32 A vague reference to Caithness, Scotland?

33 Not an abbreviation for Amsterdam, but see entries *42* and *44* for some confusion over the home port.

34 The usual reference to the Iceland fishing.

35 Nun's or fine sewing thread.

36 A roughly squared beam of timber; sometimes used technically to designate Baltic timber, roughly dressed before shipment.

37 Probably the same thing as the 'capravins' recorded in the early-seventeenth century Boston Port Books – see Hinton, *Boston*, p. 332. Capravens were prepared or semi-prepared timbers intended for use as ships' spars – see N. Cox and K. Dannehl, *Dictionary of Traded Goods and Commodities 1550–1820* (University of Wolverhampton, 2007), accessed via *British History Online*, at URL: http://www.british-history.ac.uk/source.aspx?pubid=739 on 28 November 2008.

    The word might also be a variant of 'chevron' meaning a beam or rafter. 'Cheverons' of pine were being used in Lynn for the construction of pontoon bridges in 1303 – D. M. Owen, ed., *The Making of King's Lynn* (1984), p. 434. I am grateful to Susan Maddock for steering me towards this last reference.

38 Akersloot, Netherlands.

39 The change of hand occurs with the duty amount shown on the right and relating to the preceding details of the various items of timber.

40 Kinghorn, Scotland.

41 This could refer to either Stavern, near Larvik, in Norway or Stavoren, south of Hindeloopen, in the Netherlands. The cargo items given here suggest the former, and the name crops up again as a ship's homeport in entries *770, 779, 937* and *993* in connection with other Baltic shipments, both imports and exports. Stavern was apparently better known as Fredriksvern in the eighteenth and nineteenth centuries and developed as a naval base. Earlier it had been a fishing harbour and so may well have been a more general small port as well.

42 Unidentified. The home port is referred to again in entry *178*, but with a rather fuller ship-name.

43 It is not clear why this entry appears to repeat part of entry *181*, other than the possibility that it was simply a clerical error.

44 Written in the more conventional or 'modern' formulation of roman numerals, Cxxvij, and so more safely transcribed as 127.

45 Possibly referring to cloth from Silesia?

46 And see entry number *386*, from a different book, for the associated wine details for this shipment. The further entry also tells us that the whole shipment came from Bordeaux in a ship of which John Young was the master, and that some of the wine was entered in the name of a certain Arnold Fiden.

47 See entry number *336* for the ultimate destination of some of the honey, which was apparently sold to another merchant in Lynn. See entry number *387* for wine details. Note also that the wine, from Bordeaux, presumably along with the other items, was entered in the joint names of William Atkin and his brother-in-law Gervase Wharton, with further wine for the Lynn merchant John Wallis.

48 See entry number *388* for the associated wine items. The whole cargo was probably from Flushing.

49 The second sum given here, following the + sign, actually appears alongside the first in a second column, but to save space on the printed page all such additional sums have been included underneath and indicated with +.

50 Culross, Fife.

51 Dyzart, Scotland.

52 See entry *390* for the wine items, the whole shipment probably from Bordeaux.

53 Middelburg, Netherlands.

54 See entries *391* and *404* for wine items, separate sections for French/Rhenish and Spanish wines.

55 Prestonpans.

56 See *341* for the re-export of this and subsequent items.

57 See *392* and *405* for wine items.

58 See *393* for wine items.

59 Saardam, later Zaandam, in the seventeenth century a shipbuilding centre just north of Amsterdam, where, later in the century, Tsar Peter the Great took up residence to learn the craft of shipbuilding during his extended tour of western Europe – J. A. Van Houtte, *An Economic History of the Low Countries 800–1800* (1977), pp. 174, 268; see also R. S. Charnock, *Local Etymology: a derivative dictionary of geographical names* (1859), pp. 233–234. It is only ever referred to in these documents as the home port of the ship *Crabbe.*

60 Eyemouth, Scotland.

61 Romsdal, the area around the Romsdalfjord in western Norway, where a new trading centre was established in the early seventeenth century.

62 Larvik, Norway.

63 See *396* for French wine entry.

64 Bergen, referred to in this way to distinguish it from Bergen-op-Zoom in the Netherlands.

65 These details have all been crowded into the foot of the page. See also entry *358* for a further reference to the re-exporting of the band staves to Scotland by another merchant in a different ship.

66 See Tare in the Glossary, Appendix 1 – a reference to a deduction in the recorded weight to allow for packaging or the container.

67 Unidentified.

68 Danzig (now the Polish port of Gdansk), in the Baltic.

69 From Prussia, north Germany/Poland.

70 There is some damage to the document at this point.

71 Entry *262* above.

72 This page has been badly damaged, with a repaired fold making some entries very hard to read.

73 These details are mostly illegible and have been reconstructed from the previous entry.

74 This may be a reference to Nordmore in the Romsdal district of western Norway.

75 Possibly Sunnmore, also in the district of Romsdal.

76 See entry *397* for wine, but note also that the latter entry has the shipment originating in Amsterdam.

77 For the fate of this item, along with the Norway deals mentioned below, see entry *371*.

78 Groningen, Netherlands.

79 See entry *382* for the fate of this item.

80 See *656* for the wine entry.

81 This could well refer to Setubal, which is on the Sado river estuary, south of Lisbon, one of the principal salt producing areas of Portugal – V. M. Shillington and A. B. Wallis Chapman, *The Commercial Relations of England and Portugal* (New York, 1907), pp. 158–159; C. A. Hanson, *Economy and Society in Baroque Portugal, 1668–1703* (Minneapolis, 1981), pp. 190–193. Another possibility is that it is a perverse reference to Aveiro, the settlement of Ovar being part of that district. I am grateful to the staff of the library of the Maritime Museum at Belem, Lisbon, for further help in trying to resolve this conundrum.

82 See *678* for wine details.

83 The document is again badly damaged at this point.

84 See *406* for wine details.

85 See *398* for wine details.

86 Sir Henry Sidney of Little Walsingham was the son of a former customer of King's Lynn. He had been knighted in May 1603. See *Bacon Papers*, vol. 3, pp. 417–418, and vol. 4, p. 375; also W. A. Shaw, *The Knights of England*, vol. 2 (1971), p. 107.

87 See *400* for wine details, entered in the name of the shipmaster and not the merchant identified here.

88 See *399* for wine details.

89 A deep fold in the document, now repaired, has made the following details very hard to read.

90 See *401* and *407* for French/Rhenish and Spanish wines respectively.

91 See *402* for wine details.

92 See *403* for wine details.

93 See *665* for wine details.

94 See *666* for wine details.

95 See entry *203*, for the honey imported by the Lynn merchant William Atkin.

96 The clerk mistakenly wrote 'from' instead of 'to' for what is clearly an export shipment.

97 See entry *229* for the corresponding details.

98 This was the 'Richard/Rittger Bittings' recorded in the Elbing customs record books for this period – A. Groth, 'Trade and Merchants from Lynn in the Baltic Ports at the End of the 16th Century and in the First Half of the 17th Century', in K. Friedland and P. Richards, eds, *Essays in Hanseatic History: the King's Lynn Symposium 1998* (Larks Press, 2005), pp. 59–60.

99 The modern port of Elblag in Poland.

100 This is the only merchant's mark to appear in all of the documents comprising this volume. Snelling was an important newcomer to Lynn, described on his admission to the freedom of the borough as being 'of Norwich' but also later a freeman of London and a member of the Skinners' Company (admitted on 21 February 1615 - I am grateful to Mrs Janet Hammond for this information, which has been confirmed in correspondence with the company). He married the daughter of Alderman Matthew Clarke, searcher of the port, and later himself joined the borough corporation. He rose to prominence very quickly becoming mayor in 1622, but died prematurely at the age of only 38 during his year of office (see Appendix 2.A).

101 The clerk may have intended to write 'the Jacobe' if this refers to the same ship, master and merchant as entry *355*.

102 Another apparent clerical error, confusing the shipmaster and the merchant, from a clerk whose attention may not have been fully focused on the job in hand. The ship's home port could also, perhaps, have been misrecorded – see entries *241, 272–3* and *364*, which suggest that the ship came from Saardam, albeit quite close to Amsterdam.

103 All of the following three entries have been bracketed together in the book, the only instance of this kind of collective accounting.

104 See entry *256*, where the goods were recorded as coming into Lynn from Bergen in Norway, in the name of a different merchant.

105 It is not at all clear to which other shipment this rather vague reference applies. There do not appear to be any inward shipments of Flemish hops by the same master/merchant a year or so earlier.

106 This may refer to material for making clay pots – see Glossary.

107 See entry *294*.

108 Possibly so named in honour of Alderman Henry Violet (see Appendix 2.A), who had named his own son Grave Violet in honour of the boy's grandfather, Thomas Grave.

109 This merchant was very reluctant to take up his freedom of the borough even when pressed by the corporation. He eventually relented and went on to become a member of the governing body – see Appendix 2.A.

110 See entry *303*.

111 See entry *200* for the associated cargo items for these wine details.

112 See *203* for the other cargo items.

113 See *209* for the other cargo items.

114 These wine details do not appear to have been associated with any other cargo items in a corresponding 'general' shipment.

115 See *213* for the other cargo items.

116 See *215* for the other cargo items, and 404 for additional wine details.

117 See *230* for the other cargo items, and 405 for additional wine details.

118 See *238* for the other cargo items.

119 Now known as Bo'ness/Borrowstounness, Scotland.

120 This shipment, and its continuation in the next entry, would appear to have no other associated 'general' cargo items.

121 See *255* for the other cargo items.

122 See *288* for the other cargo items, although that entry has the ship coming from Rotterdam.

123 See *230* for the additional general cargo item.

124 See *399* for the other cargo items.

125 See *322* for other cargo items, entered in the name of Henry Congham, and not the shipmaster.

126 See *326* for other more general cargo items, and *407* for Spanish wine.

127 See *329* for other cargo items.

128 See *330* for other cargo items.

129 See *215* for other more general cargo items, and *391* for French/Rhenish wine.

130 See *230* for general cargo items, and *392* for French/Rhenish wine.

131 See *318* for other cargo items.

132 See *326* for general cargo items, and *401* for French/Rhenish wine.

133 This location remains unidentified in any really positive way. It only occurs, in its various spellings (see Index to the Text), in connection with Scottish coal imports into Lynn, and might refer to places linked to coal workings at or about Carron or Carriden (near Bo'ness), Kincardine, Kinneil, or even Queensferry – J. U. Nef, *The Rise of the British Coal Industry* (1932), vol. 1, pp. 44, 47, 48; J. Hatcher, *The History of the British Coal Industry* (Oxford, 1993), vol. 1, pp. 97, 100. The advice from the National Archives of Scotland favours Carron, a village in Larbert parish, Stirlingshire. Carron is adjacent to the Carron Iron Works which was operational from 1760, and coal working may have been carried on there in earlier times.

134 See note 81 above.

135 See *657* for wine details.

136 Nieupoort in Flanders (Hinton, *Boston*, p. 330) rather than the English port of Newhaven, which was generally known as Meching at this time.

137 Delfshaven, Netherlands, now in effect a suburb of Rotterdam, but originally developed as a harbour for the inland city of Delft. It became particularly associated with the herring fisheries – J. A. Van Houtte, *An Economic History of the Low Countries 800–1800* (1977), p. 153.

138 See *658* for details of French wines.

139 Damage to the document makes the first two entries here very hard to read.

140 See *659* for wine details.

141 Montrose, Scotland.

142 The post entry at *440* below gives the ship's name as *James*.

143 See *660* and *679* for wine details, although entry *679* has the tradeport as Amsterdam.

144 The headings at the top of this folio are particularly hard to read and a certain amount of guesswork has been used to formulate the wording given here.

145 The first sum given for this largely illegible cargo item, '5s 4d', has been unaccountably repeated by the clerk. This has been taken to be a clerical error and the repetition has been omitted.

146 This may well be an unacknowledged post entry to *461*, all other details being repeated, with a very small amount of cargo.

147 This entry has been crowded in at the foot of the page, but should clearly be an exported cargo.

148 The number of pairs of stockings (340) has been rendered in arabic numerals in the document.

149 See *667* and *682* for wine details, although the first of these additional entries was made in the name of the merchant John Greene and not the shipmaster.

150 See *669* for wine details.

151 This sum is entered in the book in arabic numerals, whereas all the rest relating to the shipment are in roman.

152 See *670* and *683* for wine details.

153 See entry *472* above.

154 See *661* for wine details.

155 See *662* for wine details.

156 See *685*, from the book of the Collector of New Impositions, where this item is recorded as having come into the port, for the named merchant, in a different ship.

157 See *680* for wine details, and also *685* for the separate recording of the New Impositions, replicating, in total, the additional sums following the + sign here.

158 This whole entry is particularly hard to decipher.

159 This cargo item is replicated in entry *685*, for the New Impositions, but the sum given in the later entry is different. None of the other items in entry *488* which show two duty amounts are similarly repeated in the book of the Collector of New Impositions.

160 See *663* for wine details.

161 Wine details can also be found in entry *681*, but for Robert Thorey, not the merchant named here, and there is a major discrepancy in the dates given for the two entries. Thorey had used the same ship, under the same master, in April – see entries *487* and *680*.

162 See *686* for the New Imposition on the raisins, but not on the sugar.

163 This line is clearly written below the details given for stranger's custom, which presumably only applied to the items above.

164 Probably a post entry to the one before, although the fact that it occurs at the turn of page leaves some room for doubt – there may have been some clerical sloppiness in transcribing details from original notes.

165 The date is hard to read and could conceivably be the 24th of the month.

166 Fox-skins.

167 He appears as 'Robert Commistable' in the Elbing customs records – Groth, 'Trade and Merchants in the Baltic Ports', pp. 59–60.

168 Another probable post entry to no. *514*.

169 Sir George Bruce of Culross was a well-connected Scottish entrepreneur, with interests in mining, saltworks and landowning, probably knighted in 1610 (see R. A. Houston, 'Bruce, Sir George (*c.*1550–1625)', *Oxford Dictionary of National Biography*, Oxford, 2004). He was the builder of the so-called 'Culross Palace' and is commemorated in an elaborate tomb in the parish church. He also traded through Boston (see Hinton, *Boston*, pp. 84–85), and probably did not endear himself to the men of Lynn when, in 1611, he attempted to revive the Wilkes salt patent (C.T. Carr, ed., *Select Charters of Trading Companies, 1530–1707,* Selden Society, 28, 1913, p. lxxiii; *Calendar of State Papers Domestic 1611–1618*, p. 22).

170 This folio has dark markings in the top right hand corner which make the entries and other details very hard to read.

171 See *671* for wine details.

172 Possibly a reference to the lord steward's department of the royal household, although why this merchant should have such exalted contacts is far from clear. Neither is it clear why the royal household should be involved in granting privileges for Iceland fishing. The lord steward was the principal officer of the royal household below stairs and was the senior member of the board of green cloth. After 1570, with one brief exception, the office was left vacant for forty-five years with the result that his responsibilities below stairs devolved upon the next senior members of the board of green cloth, the treasurer and comptroller – for further details see *Office-Holders in Modern Britain* ('Provisional Lists 1485–1646' compiled by J.C. Sainty, June 1999) , at the IHR website, URL: http://www.history.ac.uk/office/greencloth_clerk.html#5t, accessed on 28 November 2008.

173 See *672* for wine details.

174 See *673* for wine details.

175 The duplication of the word 'master' occurs as the clerk moved to a new line. See *674* for the wine details associated with the shipment.

176 The first name of the shipmaster was presumably Elisha or something similar. There is no likelihood of the 'master' being female.

177 See entry *522*, where 15 weys of salt were allowed duty free, the 10 for this entry and a further 5 for the subsequent entry, *529*.

178 See *687* for the further record of the New Imposition.

179 See *688* for the New Imposition.

180 See *689* for the New Impositions on the wainscots and sturgeon, although the total duty amount given there does not match the ones specified in this entry.

181 See *689* again for the New Impositions on these items.

182 See *690* for the New Imposition.

183 See *690* for the New Imposition.

184 Medemblik, Netherlands.

185 See *691* for some of the New Impositions on this merchant's cargo – the cinnamon and nutmeg are mentioned specifically and the rest simply collated as 'other petty grocery.' However the sums of money involved do not appear to be easily reconciled with additional amounts given in this initial entry.

186 Bolsward, Netherlands.

187 See *692* for the New Impositions on this merchant's cloth items. The sums given here do correspond to the total given in the later book.

188 See entries *563* and *565*.

189 This may be a post entry to the previous one and was so obvious that the clerk did not bother to indicate is as such.

190 Another likely post entry.

191 Another possible post entry.

192 A probable post entry to *583*, clearly inserted later.

193 Probable post entry to *585*.

194 See *675* for the wine details.

195 See *693* for separate recording of the New Imposition.

196 See *694* for the New Imposition.

197 See *694* for the New Imposition, these details and those in the previous shipment being consolidated into the same entry in the separate book. The merlins in entry *596* were not taxed separately.

198 See *676* for the wine details.

199 See *695* for the New Imposition, with the additional implication that a fother (see Glossary) was the same as a ton.

200 Possibly Limekilns on the Firth of Forth, where there were saltpans in the early-seventeenth century – C. A. Whatley, *The Scottish Salt Industry 1570–1850* (Aberdeen, 1987), pp. 12, 39

201 More probably a phonetic rendering of Inverkeithing, on the Firth of Forth, than a perverse reference to Aberdeen. I am grateful to my former colleague Tom Carslaw for this helpful suggestion, which seems to be confirmed in Whatley (note 200 above).

202 Unaccountably, the clerk has here omitted the details of the tradeport, and at the change of line after the master's name gone straight into the merchant and cargo details.

203 See *664* for wine details.

204 Cadiz.

205 And see entry *645*.

206 And see entry *642*.

207 See entry *638*.

208 See entry *638*.

209 See *677* for wine details.

210 Herrings cured at sea.

211 See *312* for other cargo items.

212 See *411* for other cargo items.

213 See *417* for other cargo items.

214 See *423* for other cargo items.

215 See *445* for other cargo items.

216 See *478* for other cargo items.

217 See *485* for other cargo items, and also *685* for the New Imposition on the brown paper.

218 See *492* for other cargo items.

219 See *627* for other cargo items.

220 See *333* for other cargo items.

221 See *334* for other cargo items.

222 See *471* for other cargo items, which were entered in the name of the shipmaster, Jacob Bonis, and not the merchant John Greene. See also *682* for an additional wine entry.

223 This is likely to be an unspecified post entry.

224 See *472* for other cargo items.

225 See *475* for other cargo items, and *683* for a further wine entry.

226 See *522* for other cargo items.

227 See *523* and *670* for other cargo items.

228 See *524* for other cargo items.

229 See *525* for other cargo items.

230 See *592* for other cargo items.

231 See *597* for other cargo items.

232 See *652* for other cargo items.

233 All of the numbers in this summary are rendered in arabic numerals in the document.

234 See *314* for other cargo items.

235 See *445* for other cargo items, but that entry has the shipment coming from Rotterdam.

236 See *487* for other cargo items, and *685* for New Impositions.

237 See *498* and *499* for more general cargo items brought into the port in this ship but in the names of other merchants and at a much earlier date. It is not clear whether the wine represents a wholly different shipment or a part of the overall cargo entered for 2 June.

238 See *471* and *667* for other cargo items, although the latter (another wine entry) is in the name of the merchant John Greene and not Bonis/Bomis.

239 See *475* for other cargo items.

240 See *525* and *674* for other cargo items.

241 All of the sums of money shown in the right hand columns in this book have been endorsed as 'p[ai]d'.

242 See *487* for the other cargo items entered in the name of this merchant, and *680* for wine.

243 See *488* for the whole cargo, although a number of the items listed there with apparently additional duty amounts are not given in this entry.

244 This item, in the name of Robert Hayes, is not listed in the corresponding entries *487–489* for the ship *Paradise* of Amsterdam, but does appear in entry *485* as coming into Lynn in the *Barbara* of Lynn, of which Hayes was the master. See also *662* for the same merchant's wine entry, also in the *Barbara* of Lynn.

245 See *499* for other cargo details, but the sugar mentioned there is not listed in this entry.

246 A further figure is given in the margin, possibly 3s 4d, but it is not at all clear.

247 See *538* for the fuller entry.

248 See *540* for all of the cargo items.

249 See *541* for the whole cargo, although the additional duties recorded there for the wainscots and sturgeon do not add up to the total given here.

250 See *542* for other cargo items.

251 See *549* for other cargo items.

252 See *550* for other cargo items.

253 See *554* for the full cargo, including a number of items charged an additional duty that are not listed here.

254 See *557* for the full list of cargo items.

255 See *593*, with a slightly different date.

256 See *594*, where apparently the six merlins were not included in the additional duty.

257 See *595* for the corresponding entry.

258 See *599*, from which it is clear that this entry relates to an export shipment, thereby explaining why it appears to be out of chronological order.

259 Indicating formal receipt by the exchequer – *Ex'* probably meant *Examinatur* (cf. Hinton, *Boston*, pp.

xix-xx). The money collected was paid directly to the government and not to the farmers.

260 Throughout this book the clerk usually wrote the names of the merchants responsible for cargoes immediately after giving the ships' details (ship name, home port, tonnage and master) and the tradeports, ending that part of the entry with the word 'with' before beginning the enumeration of cargo details on a new line. This practice has been replicated in the transcriptions that follow. It is also worth noting that the ships's tonnages in this document are invariably written in arabic numerals, regardless of what follows with cargo item details and duty amounts.

261 See *963* for wine details.

262 A hole in the document complicates the reading of many of the details in this and subsequent entries.

263 See *964* for wine details.

264 See *965* for wine details.

265 See *966* for wine details.

266 See *967* for the corresponding wine entry, although the cargo details there are illegible.

267 See *968* for the wine entry, but the cargo details are again illegible.

268 See *969* for wine details, which are there entered in the name of a different merchant.

269 This rather vague 'port of origin' is replicated in the corresponding export shipment (entry *922*), and could refer to a range of Norwegian localities ending in '-sund'. It is unlikely that it meant simply The Sound between Denmark and Sweden.

270 This entry can be compared to number *800*, equally hard to decipher because of damage to the document, and from the two together the name of the master/merchant might be Meane Meakes.

271 The space taken by the hole in the document suggests that the number of deals may be higher than round hundreds.

272 See *987* for the separate recording of the New Imposition. The sum appears to be the same but the quantity of brown paper slightly different.

273 See *988* for the New Imposition.

274 See *970* for wine details.

275 All written on a separate line in contravention of the usual format in this book.

276 Kopervik, Norway.

277 See 989 for the New Imposition.

278 Eckernforde, Schleswig-Holstein, now Germany; the former Danish name was Egernforde.

279 Unusually, for this book, written in the roman form Ciiij^{xx}.

280 Either Norden, north of Emden, or Nordenham, on the Weser river in Lower Saxony, on the opposite bank to Bremerhaven. See also *803* and *804*.

281 See *990* for the New Imposition.

282 See *971* for wine details, and also *991* for the separate recording of the New Imposition, although in the latter the shipmaster is named as the merchant.

283 Hindeloopen in Friesland, Netherlands.

284 See *992*, where the sturgeon is entered in the name of Thomas Slaney and not the shipmaster.

285 See *993* for the New Imposition.

286 See *775* and *777* above, where the initial entries are made quite separately in the names of Thomas Slaney and Thomas Brewster. It was unusual for a post entry to combine ownership of a cargo in this way.

287 Presumably a part of the shipment recorded in *774*.

288 A coarse fabric made from the hards of flax or hemp.

289 This might also be transcribed as 'Hern' and could refer to Hoorn in the Netherlands.

290 See *747* and note 270.

291 See *994* for separate recording of the New Imposition.

292 See *995* for separate recording of the New Imposition, but in the name of Thomas Snelling, not the shipmaster, and at the rate of 2s 8d.

293 See *996* for separate recording of the New Imposition – there the name is clearly given as Webster;

in this entry it has been heavily altered.

294 See *972* for wine details, which are entered in the name of John Mason, rather than William Doughty. The tonnage of the vessel was omitted by the customs clerk but does appear in entry *972*.

295 See *997* for separate recording of the New Imposition.

296 See *998* for separate recording of the New Imposition.

297 See *999* for separate recording of the New Imposition.

298 See *973* for additional wine details.

299 Presumably a reference to the Orkney Islands.

300 See *1000* for separate recording of the New Imposition.

301 See *1001* for separate recording of the New Imposition.

302 Along with the use of the word 'their' a clear indication that, although only one merchant has been named, others were involved with the shipment.

303 Tingvoll, Norway.

304 The number is written in arabic numerals in the document.

305 The clerk presumably meant 'salmon grilse', for young salmon.

306 See *974* for this merchant's wine items, which may also be associated with entry *976*, at a much later date and in the name of another merchant.

307 See *975* for wine details.

308 On this page the clerk has indented the entries to slightly different margins.

309 See *977* for wine details.

310 The clerk has written 'to Amsterdam' even though this is obviously an import shipment, as the associated wine details at entry *978*, and the following entry (*879*), make abundantly clear.

311 The clerk left a space before the ship's name, for some kind of qualifying word which he appears to have forgotten or mistaken, and subsequently filled the gap with three pen strokes.

312 See *979* for associated wine details.

313 There is no + sign for the second duty amount here, or in subsequent entries, because in the document the second sum is written directly under the first, as set out here, and not in a separate column alongside. As is clear from the preceding entry the first sum represented the regular subsidy of tonnage and the second the additional imposition.

314 Part of the cloth cargo given here was actually shipped to Dunkirk in another vessel on 22 October, with the approval, or connivance, of a customs official – see entry *951*.

315 This is probably a post entry to *918*.

316 See *737* and note 269.

317 A further possible post entry to *919* and *920*.

318 A further possible post entry to *918* and

319 A further post entry to *919*, *920* and *924*? The officers and their clerks would appear to have been particularly assiduous.

320 Probably meaning Riga, now the capital of Latvia.

321 Helsingor, also known as Elsinore, Denmark.

322 See *943* for a further reference to this item.

323 See *938*.

324 A further indication (see also entry *852*, with its post entry *862*) that although only one merchant is named for the shipment others were also involved, in some kind of partnership.

325 See the post entry at *954* for confirmation of the missing name.

326 See *920*.

327 This is the first indication that Nathaniel Maxey, who was to become a member of the borough corporation (see Appendix 2.A), was a customs officer. He would eventually become the searcher of the port – TNA PRO Exchequer Depositions, E134/8 Car I/Easter 2 and TNA PRO IND 1/17351, p. 394. See also *CSPD, 1619–1623*, p. 149, for Maxey's appointment in succession to Matthew Clarke.

328 It is not absolutely clear whether these words have been underlined or crossed out, but the entry would certainly appear to be a post entry to *948*.

329 The post entry at *959* gives the destination as Anstruther.

330 See *698* for other cargo items.

331 See *704* for other cargo items.

332 See *713* for other cargo item.

333 See *714* for other cargo items.

334 This entry, along with the one that follows, has been crowded in at the foot of the page and both are particularly hard to read.

335 See *725* for the associated entry.

336 See *727* for the associated entry.

337 See *729* for other cargo items, which are there entered in the name of the shipmaster.

338 See *759* for other cargo items.

339 See *774* for other cargo items and also *991* for separate recording of the New Imposition, where the shipmaster is named as merchant.

340 See *823* for other cargo items entered in the name of William Doughty and not John Mason.

341 See *836* for other cargo items.

342 See *859* for other cargo items.

343 See *870* for other cargo items.

344 These wine details may be associated with entry *859*, although the dates are very far apart and a quite different merchant is involved here. No other shipment appears to be linked to this particular wine entry.

345 See *874* for other cargo items.

346 See *878* for other cargo items.

347 See *887* for other cargo items.

348 A reference to either Mebø in Norway (William, *Maritime Trade*, pp.101–102) or Marienburg in the Baltic (Hinton, *Boston*, p. li).

349 See *1002* for the separate recording of the New Imposition.

350 All sums in this book, as for E190/434/2, have again been endorsed as 'paid'.

351 See *756*, where the quantity of brown paper appears to be slightly different.

352 See *758*.

353 See *764*.

354 See *772*.

355 See *774*, where the vinegar is entered in the name of John Percival and not Nicholas Tubbin, who was the shipmaster.

356 See *778*, where the sturgeon is entered in the name of the shipmaster and not the merchant identified here.

357 See *779*.

358 See *805*.

359 See *807*, which makes clear that this item was also landed from the *Red Lion* of Enkhuizen. However it is there entered in the name of the shipmaster, an alien, at the rate of 3s 4d, rather than the 2s 8d apparently charged to Thomas Snelling here.

360 See *817*, where there were apparently only ten gerfalcons.

361 See *824*.

362 See *827*.

363 See *835*.

364 See *840*.

365 See *847*.

366 For *Examinatur*, after presentation of the book to the exchequer – see note 259.

367 See *985*.

368 'This book containing eight leaves, of which the first and second are partly written and the rest are blank, this aforesaid collector handed over upon his oath' - part of the formal exchequer acquittance of the official; before the introduction of the great farm all of the port books would have been similarly endorsed.

APPENDIX 1

GLOSSARY

The main sources used in the compilation of this glossary, in addition to the *Oxford English Dictionary* and *Wightman's Arithmetical Tables*, have been:

R. D. Connor, *The Weights and Measures of England* (London, 1987)

N. Cox and K. Dannehl, eds, *Dictionary of Traded Goods and Commodities 1550–1820* (University of Wolverhampton, 2007), accessed via British History Online at URL: http://www.british-history.ac.uk/source.aspx?pubid=739 on 28 November 2008.

H. Hall and F. J. Nicholas, eds, 'The Noumbre of Weyghtes', 'Geometry upon Waightes and Measures calid the Art Statike', and 'Calendars and Tables' in *Select Tracts and Table Books Relating to English Weights and Measures, 1100–1742* (Camden Society, 3rd Series, xli, 1929)

R. W. K. Hinton, ed., *The Port Books of Boston, 1601–1640* (Lincoln Record Society, 50, 1956)

P. McGrath, ed., *Merchants and Merchandise in Seventeenth-Century Bristol* (Bristol Record Society, 19, 1955)

T. S. Willan, ed., *A Tudor Book of Rates* (Manchester, 1962)

D. Yaxley, *A Researcher's Glossary of words found in historical documents of East Anglia* (Larks Press, Guist, Norfolk, 2003)

Zupko, R. E. *British weights and measures: a history from antiquity to the seventeenth century* (Madison [WI] and London, 1977)

The editor is also very grateful to Christopher Kemp for permission to use his ongoing 'Selective Glossary' of legal, trade and other unusual terms, which is still a 'work in progress' even though it is already very comprehensive.

Aam (aume) A Dutch and German liquid measure, used in England for Rhenish wine; a cask, varying in different continental cities from 37 to 41 gallons. In some English sources said to be either 30 gallons or 40 gallons.

Bag A measure of quantity for produce, varying according to the nature of the commodity. Used in these documents for hops (where a bag might equal from 1½ to more than 2 hundredweight), currants, gherkins, sugar, figs and feathers.

Bale A large bundle or package of merchandise, done up in canvas or other wrapping. Used in these documents for madder and paper.

Balk, baulk A roughly squared beam of timber; sometimes used technically to designate Baltic timber, which was roughly dressed before shipment.

Band/bond (of pitch and tar) A reference to the consistency or viscosity of the commodity so described – great bond or small bond in the case of pitch and tar.

Barrel A measure of capacity both for liquids and dry goods, varying with the commodity. The wine barrel was fixed by statute in 1423 as 231 cubic inches (3.785 litres). The measure is used in these documents for a wide variety of goods: beer, hops, herring, codfish, tar, onions, oatmeal (where it might be the equivalent of 2½ bushels), currants and broken glass. See entries 488 and 554 for samples of different values. A small barrel was often referred to as a **firkin** (see below).

Basket The quantity which fills a basket, a basketful; used as a measure of uncertain amount. Used here for pans.

Battery Metal goods, particularly of brass or copper, wrought by hammering.

Bolt A roll of woven fabric, generally of a definite length; variously 30 yards, 28 ells, or 40 feet. Entry 622 suggests that 12 bolts of canvas constituted a truss.

Bridgewater A woollen cloth named after the place of its original manufacture.

Bunch An unspecified quantity fastened together, as used for onions in these documents.

Bundle A collection of things bound or otherwise fastened together; similar to a bunch; a package, parcel. More specifically, two reams of printing or brown paper, a quantity later fixed by statute. Also used with reference to hemp.

Butlerage See **prisage** below.

Butt A cask for wine or ale, of capacity varying from 108 to 140 gallons. A measure of capacity equivalent to 2 hogsheads – usually, in ale measure 108 gallons, in wine measure 126 gallons. Also a cask for fish, fruit, etc., of a capacity varying according to the contents and locality.

C (**centum**, **hundred**) The cardinal number now equal to ten times ten, or five score. With reference to particular commodities, often used for a definite number greater than five score, especially the **great** or **long hundred**, which usually meant six score, or a metric hundred and twenty, but might also refer to the hundredweight of 112 pounds. Some kinds of fish (cod and ling, for example) were counted in a hundred equal to 124.

Cagg Specifically a portion of sturgeon sufficient to fill a keg; also used for eels. A small barrel or cask, usually of less than 10 gallons, for other goods such as gherkins or tar.

Cake A mass or concretion of any solidified or compressed substance in a flattened form, as in oil cakes (from rapeseed or linseed) or rosen.

Cambric A fine white linen, originally made in Cambrai, Flanders.

Capraven A form of prepared or semi-prepared timber intended for use as a ship's spar.

Cask A small barrel. A measure of capacity, varying according to place, time, and commodity. Used here for mace and tallow.

Cast A certain quantity of clay made into pots. With reference to birds, the number of hawks cast off at a time, usually two; hence here probably referring to two hawks.

Cerne A quantity of liquorice. Entry 602 suggests that a cerne was equal to one hundredweight.

Chalder (chaldron) A dry measure of capacity. For lime and coal it varied from 32 to 40 bushels, according to whether the measure was stroked or heaped. In the fourteeenth century the London and Newcastle chaldrons may have been the same for measuring coal, at 17 cwt, but in the sixteenth and seventeenth centuries the London chaldron stabilised at 1.3 tons, whereas the Newcastle chaldron increased to 35 cwt and eventually to 52.5 or 53 cwt. Some authorities state that the Newcastle chaldron was about 42 cwt (1.5 London chaldrons) in the seventeenth century. Entries 295, 960 and 961 refer specifically to a Lynn chalder.

Chest A large box or case in which certain commodities, such as glass, were packed for transport; hence used as a variable measure of quantity. Used here for glass and linen. See entry 554 for two examples.

Clapholt (clapboard) A small size of split oak, imported from north Germany, and used by coopers for making barrel-staves; also for wainscoting.

Coil A length of cable, rope, etc., when 'coiled' or gathered up into a number of concentric rings, either *fake* over *fake*, or in a flat disk with the *fakes* within each other, the latter being termed a Flemish coil; hence, the quantity of cable, etc., usually wound up. Used here specifically for cordage.

Coomb (coom, comb) A dry measure of capacity, generally equal to four bushels or half a quarter, although the precise weight could vary according to the density of particular grains: roughly 14 stone for oats, 16 for barley and 18 for wheat.

Crewel A thin worsted yarn, of two threads, used for tapestry and embroidery; also for making fringes, laces, vestments, hosiery, etc.

Di' (dimidium) A half.

Diaper A linen fabric woven with a small and simple pattern, formed by the different directions of the thread and consisting of lines crossing diamond-wise, with the spaces variously filled up by other small patterns. A towel, napkin, or cloth of this material.

Dogstone A variety of millstone, later (1784) specified as not more than 4 feet in diameter and between 6 and 12 inches thick. Many dogstones were imported and since suitable stones were rare, they were heavily rated. In 1582, when prices were generally lower, the last of 9 pair was rated at £6, but by 1657 the rate was £40 for the last of 3 pair.

Dol' (doleum, **ton, tun)** See **ton** below

Dornix Cloth originally made at Doornick, Flanders.

Drifatt A large vessel (cask, barrel, tub, case, box, etc.) used to hold dry things (as opposed to liquids). Used here for skins and sugar.

Durance A stout, durable cloth.

Ell A measure of length, particularly for cloth, varying in different countries. The English ell was 45 inches, the Flemish ell 27 inches, and the French ell 54 inches.

End A piece broken, cut off, or left; a fragment, remnant. Of cloth: a half-length, or half-piece. However, used here also with reference to hops.

Fagott A bundle of iron or steel rods bound together. Later (1706) equivalent to 20 pounds in weight.

Fathum A measure of length usually approximating to 6 feet. A certain quantity of wood; later, a quantity 6 feet square in section, whatever the length may be. Also applied to reeds – 6 bundles, each a foot in diameter.

Fatt A vessel of large size for liquids; a tub, a dyer's or brewer's vat, a wine cask. Also used with reference to a container for kettles and pans.

Firkin A small cask for liquids, fish, butter, etc., originally containing a quarter of a 'barrel' or half a 'kilderkin' and therefore used as a measure of capacity: half a kilderkin. The 'barrel', 'kilderkin', and 'firkin' varied in capacity according to the commodity.

Fother (fodder) Of lead, 20 hundredweight or 2240 pounds (later usually 19½ hundredweight). Entries 599 and 695 appear to confirm that a fother of lead was the equivalent of a ton.

Fox-case The skin of a fox.

Gallon An English measure of capacity based on the volume of 8 pounds of wheat and 8 pounds of wine. The imperial gallon, as established in 1824, contains 277.274 cubic inches but in earlier times the amount varied with the commodity: ale at 282 cubic inches, corn at 268.43 cu. ins. (later at 272 or 272.25, Winchester measure) and wine at 231. A gallon contains 8 pints or 4 quarts, with 2 gallons to a peck and 8 gallons to a bushel.

Goad A cloth-measure particularly used with reference to 'cotton' and equivalent to 4½ feet or 1½ yards.

Great hundred Usually of 120, although in relation to a hundredweight it meant 112 pounds.

Gross Twelve dozen or 144.

Hinderland A kind of linen cloth imported perhaps from inland Germany.

Hogshead A large cask for liquids, of a definite capacity which varied for different liquids and commodities. A liquid measure containing 63 old wine-gallons (equal to 52½ imperial gallons).

Holmes fustian A fustian made at Ulm in Germany.

Hundred See *C* above.

Hundredweight An avoirdupois weight equal to 112 pounds, probably originally to a hundred pounds, hence the name. There were 8 stones to a hundredweight and 20 hundredweight to a ton.

Hurden A coarse fabric made from the hards of flax or hemp.

Ind' (indigenus) Native-born, indigenous, English

Keg A small barrel or cask, usually of less than 10 gallons, for goods such as gherkins or tar.

Kipp The hide of a young or small beast (a calf or lamb, or cattle of small breed), as used for leather. A set or bundle of such hides, containing a definite number.

Last A commercial denomination of weight, capacity, or quantity, varying for different kinds of goods and in different localities. Originally the 'last' was probably the quantity carried at one time by the vehicle (boat, wagon, etc.) ordinarily used for the particular kind of merchandise. As a weight, often stated to be nominally equivalent to either 2 tons or 4,000 pounds; in wool weight 4368 pounds or 12 sacks. A last of gunpowder was 2,400 pounds (24 barrels), and of feathers or flax 1,700 pounds The equivalence of the last of wool with 12 sacks seems to have led to an association of the word with the number twelve. Thus a last of hides was 12 dozen (also 20 dickers of 10 hides each); of beer 12 barrels; of pitch and tar 12 (sometimes 14) barrels; of cod and herrings 12 barrels (but of red herrings and pilchards 10,000 to 13,200 fish) As a measure for grain and malt, the last was in the sixteenth century 12 quarters, but was later 10 quarters or 80 bushels. Also sometimes used as a unit in the measurement of a ship's burden, equivalent to 2 English tons.

Lawn A kind of fine linen, resembling cambric.

Li' (librum, pound) 16 ounces weight, and 14 pounds to a stone. 20 shillings in money.

Load The specific quantity of a substance which it was customary to load at one time; hence, taken as a unit of measure or weight for certain commodities The equivalence of a load varied considerably according to the locality and to the commodity. A load of wheat was usually 40 bushels, of lime 64 (in some districts 32) bushels, of timber 50 cubic feet, of hay 36 trusses (18 hundredweight). Used here with reference to timber and bark.

Loaf A moulded conical mass of sugar; a sugar-loaf.

Luke coal Coal from Liege, Spanish Netherlands (now Belgium)

M (mille, thousand) Ten hundreds

Maslin/meslen A mixture of various kinds of grain, especially rye mixed with wheat; bread made from this. Also: a mixture of grain and pulses, especially oats mixed with peas.

Mockado A mixed fabric of wool and silk, in imitation of velvet.

Mortkin The skin of dead lambs or sheep, possibly referring to animals that had died of disease or by accident.

Mount A unit of weight formerly used for plaster of Paris, equal to 30 hundredweight.

Muscadel A variety of grape originally grown chiefly in the Bordeaux and Bergerac regions of France, used to make sweet white wines.

Muscavado Raw or unrefined sugar.

Oil cake See **cake** above.

Ounce A unit of weight equal to (originally) one-twelfth of a pound in troy and apothecaries' measure, equal to 480 grains; one-sixteenth of a pound in avoirdupois measure.

Pack A bale or bundle of a single commodity (such as wool, cloth, yarn, flax, skins etc.); any of various measures of weight or quantity, definite or indefinite, used for such commodities. Used here for yarn, skins and flax.

Penistone A kind of coarse woollen cloth used for garments, linings, etc.

Piece A standard length, varying according to the material, in which cloth or other textile fabric was woven. The standard 'piece' of cloth typically measured 24 yards in length and 7 quarters in breadth, but there were formerly many exceptions according to the quality of the fabric, its value, and place of manufacture: e.g. a piece of muslin was 14 ells in length; Hampshire calico, 28 yards by 1 quarter; bagging for hops (in Worcestershire), 36 yards by 31 inches. A 'piece' of raisins, prunes or rosin generally equalled half a hundredweight. The term could also refer to a quantity of wine, brandy, or ale, varying according to the locality but generally equivalent to a butt, or to two hogsheads. Additionally used in these documents as a measure for timber.

Pigg An oblong mass of metal (specifically lead in these documents) as formed by molten metal run from a furnace and allowed to solidify.

Pipe A large container of definite capacity for storing solids or liquids, such as meat, fish, wax, oil or wine. Typically equal to two hogsheads or 126 wine gallons, but varying with the substance or the kind of wine. Sometimes identified with **butt** (above).

Plain A plainly woven, rough or hard-wearing cloth; a kind of flannel.

Pocket A sack or bag used as a measure of quantity, varying in capacity according to the commodity contained and the locality. Chiefly used for hops and wool, a pocket of wool being half a sack (in the thirteenth century a quarter), a pocket of hops about 180–200 pounds.

Post entry Items entered in the customs record separately from the main cargo, usually some time after an initial entry and probably the result of an undercalculation of the original quantity (unless a merchant was deliberately trying to deceive the officials but was somehow found out).

Pound See *li'* above.

Prisage An ancient duty levied upon imported wine, in later times correlated to and often identified with butlerage.

Puncheon Originally a large barrel or cask, especially one of definite capacity, varying for different liquids and commodities. The capacity varied from 72 gallons, for beer, to 120 for other goods. Used in these documents exclusively as a measure for prunes.

Quarter A measure of capacity for grain, coal, etc., varying greatly according to locality and the commodity measured: often equivalent to eight bushels; nine bushels for coal; one fourth of a peck. Presumably originating as the fourth part of a chaldron (32 or 36 bushels) or similar measure. Also used to mean one fourth of a pound; or one fourth of a hundredweight, either 28 pounds or 25 pounds. As a measure of length or area originally one fourth of an ell (11¼ inches), later usually one fourth of a yard (9 inches).

Ream A quantity of paper, properly 20 quires or 480 sheets, but frequently 500 or more, to allow for waste; of paper for printing, 21½ quires or 516 sheets (a printers' ream). Sometimes used to denote a large quantity of paper, without reference to the precise number of sheets.

Remnants A fragment, a small portion, a scrap, especially among drapers and clothiers where it meant the end of a piece, left over after the main portion had been used or sold.

Roll A quantity of material (especially cloth), rolled or wound up in a cylindrical form, sometimes forming a definite measure. Used in these documents in relation to skins.

Runlet A cask or vessel of varying capacity and the quantity of liquor contained in this. Large runlets appear usually to have varied between 12 and 18½ gallons, small ones between a pint or quart and 3 or 4 gallons.

Sack A large bag, usually made of coarse flax or hemp, used for the storing and conveyance of various goods, mainly hops, wool, currants, ginger and anniseed in these documents (see, for example, entry 554). Also a general name for a class of white wines imported from Spain, often with a qualifying word indicating the place of production or exportation, such as Malaga or sherry (for Jerez).

Salmon grilse A young salmon.

Sayes Light weight cloth usually made from worsted and woollen yarn.

Score Twenty

Sea-sticks Herrings cured at sea.

Shotten Of a fish, especially a herring, one that has spawned (opposite of 'full').

Slecia From Silesia?

Slipp A long and relatively thin and narrow piece or strip of some material – e.g. filings of steel or other metal. A certain quantity of yarn. A semi-liquid material, made of finely-ground clay or flint, mixed with water to about the consistency of cream, and used for making, cementing, coating, or decorating pottery or tiles; therefore also the clay suitable for making this.

Slopps Liquid or semi-liquid food of a weak or unappealing nature; refuse liquid of any kind.

Spruce From Prussia (Spruceland). In some instances it might imply 'made of spruce fir'.

Stag (variants in these documents: 'stage', 'stagers') In relation to skins and hides, raw or unseasoned.

Stammel A coarse woollen cloth or linsey-woolsey, usually dyed red; hence also the shade or red in which the cloth was usually dyed, regarded in the seventeenth century as cheaper than 'scarlet'.

Stockfish Codfish cured without salt, by splitting open and drying hard in the air. Also: croplings, an inferior kind of stockfish; and **titlings**, a small size of stockfish.

Stone A measure of weight, usually equal to 14 pounds avoirdupois (1/8 of a hundredweight, or half a 'quarter'), but varying with different commodities from 8 to 24 pounds.

Strong beer Containing a large proportion of alcohol, as opposed to small beer.

Tare The weight of the wrapping, receptacle, or conveyance containing goods, which is deducted from the gross in order to ascertain the net weight; hence, a deduction made from the gross weight to allow for this.

Tawed Made, as of white leather, by the process of tawing. Similar to tanned in reference to treated, rather than raw, skins.

Thack tiles Tiles for roofing.

Thousand See *M* above.

Thousandweight A weight of a thousand pounds, or possibly ten hundredweight.

Ticking The case or cover containing feathers, flocks, or the like, forming a mattress or pillow; also, from the sixteenth century, applied to the strong hard linen or cotton material used for making such cases.

Tierce A measure of capacity equivalent to one third of a pipe (usually 42 gallons old wine measure, but varying for different commodities); also a cask or vessel holding this quantity, usually of wine, but also of various kinds of provisions or other goods (e.g. beef, pork, salmon, coffee, honey, sugar, tallow, tobacco).

Ton (tun) A unit used in measuring the carrying capacity or burden of a ship, originally the space occupied by a tun cask of wine. A general measure of weight, comprising 20 hundredweight or 2240 lbs. 'Tons' of different amounts were also in use locally for some commodities. A cask of definite capacity, hence a measure of capacity for wine and other liquids, usually equivalent to 2 pipes or 4 hogsheads, and containing 252 old wine-gallons.

Topnet A kind of basket made of rushes, used for packing figs, raisins, etc.and the quantity of goods (about 30 pounds but could be up to 75 pounds) contained in it.

Truss A collection of things bound together, or packed in a receptacle; a bundle or pack. Used in these documents with reference to yarn, dornix, canvas, skins, paper and feathers, but with few indications of a precise quantity. See entries 920, 923, 934 and 937 for a variety of values relating to skins.

Turney From Tournai?

Velour A woollen dress-stuff with a velvet pile.

Wadmal A kind of coarse woollen cloth from Iceland.

Wattling Possibly a corruption of wadding, referring to any loose, fibrous material for use as a padding, stuffing, quilting, etc. Alternatively, it might refer to 'webbing'.

Wey (way, weigh) A standard of dry-goods weight, varying greatly with different commodities. Of cheese - 256 pounds in Suffolk, 336 pounds in Essex. Of wool - 182 pounds avoirdupois, two weys of wool making a sack and 12 sacks a last. Of salt - 40 bushels. Of coal, corn, etc., or in general use - 224 pounds or two hundredweight.

Wisp steel Steel sold in wisps or twisted bands.

Wrappers Cloth used as a protective covering for a greater quantity of the material and allowed duty free on account of the soiling that would follow from this use.

Yard A measure of length, traditionally the standard unit of English long measure equal to three feet or thirty-six inches The earlier standard was the ell of 45 inches.

KING'S LYNN MERCHANTS

A. Those whose names appear in the port books for 1610–1614 – burgesses, and <u>members of the borough corporation</u> (underlined) serving both during the years 1610–14 and subsequently. All dates are given in New Style.

Details are derived from: the *Calendar of the Freemen of Lynn 1292–1836* (Norwich, 1913), which has been checked against both the manuscript Oath Book and the Hall Books; the corporation Hall Books themselves (for membership of the governing body); the Calendar of Fine Rolls and the *Calendar of State Papers Domestic* (for customs officers' appointments); and from Mackerell, Hovell and the wills of particular individuals. Fuller references can be found in Metters, 'Rulers', vol. 1, especially (for the corporation members) pp. 409–434.

<u>Atkin, John</u>
Free as a merchant, by purchase, during the mayoral year 1584–5.
Elected to the common council 8 June 1596, in place of John Lead (the elder), deceased.
Elected alderman 29 August 1607, in place of Michael Revett, deceased.
Mayor 1607–8 and 1615–16.
Died 15 September 1617.

Atkin, Robert
Free as a merchant, by apprenticeship to John Atkin, 1594–5.

<u>Atkin, William</u>
Free as a merchant, by patrimony, son of John Atkin, 1602–3.
Elected to the common council 31 July 1612, in place of Richard Stonham, alderman.
Elected alderman 1 March 1616, in place of Humphrey Farnaby, deceased.
Mayor 1619–20.
Died 1623.

<u>Baker, Thomas</u>
Free as a merchant, by patrimony, son of George Baker, 1567–7.
Elected to the common council 15 August 1589.
Elected alderman 4 June 1596, in place of Thomas Boston, deceased.
Mayor 1598–9.
Removed from corporation, for misdemeanours and "evil behaviour", 15 August 1608; restored 9 June 1609.
Died 1626.

Bassett, John

Free as a chandler, by patrimony, son of Stephen Bassett, 1569–70.
Elected to the common council 2 September 1586.
Elected alderman 10 April 1594, in place of Peter Cartwright, removed.
Mayor 1596–7 and 1610–11.
Died 1611.

Bloy, John

Free as a merchant, by purchase, 1598–9.

Bradford, Rowland

Free as a merchant, by gratuity, on the nomination of Mr Spence, 1610–11.

Buckenham, Henry

Free by gratuity, as miller of the town corn mills, 1614–15 (disqualified from making his apprentices free without compounding with the mayor)

Bungay, Roger

Free as a merchant, by apprenticeship to Matthew Clarke, mayor, 1613–14.
Appointed controller of the port 27 February 1626.
Elected to the common council 29 July 1633, in place of Thomas Gedney, deceased.
Removed 13 May 1636, at his own request.

Buxton, Henry

Free as a merchant, by gratuity, 1598–9.

Chapman, Thomas

Free as a merchant, by apprenticeship to William Parkin alias Woolman, 1603–4.

Corney, John

Free as a merchant, by apprenticeship to John Wadeson, deceased, and Henry Violet, 1593–4.

Doughty, William

Free as a merchant, by gratuity, servant to the recorder, 1603–4.
Elected to the common council 10 March 1609, in place of John Grebby, removed.
Elected alderman 17 March 1615, in place of Thomas Sendall, deceased.
Mayor 1618–19, 1625–6, 1633–4, and 1640–1.
Member of Parliament 1624, 1628, 1640.
Removed 18 August 1645, at his own request.

Flory, Thomas

Free as a merchant, by purchase, 1612–13.

Goldsmith, Richard

Free as a merchant, by apprenticeship to George Gibson, 1596–7.

Greene, John
Free as a brewer, by purchase, 1576–7, and as a merchant, by purchase, 1585–6.
Elected to the common council 29 August 1597.
Appointed controller of the port 17 March 1614.
Removed 9 January 1618, at his own request because now resident in the country.

Greene, Joshua
Free as a merchant, by purchase, 1598–9.
Elected to the common council 30 October 1607.
Elected alderman 13 June 1623, in place of Thomas Snelling, deceased.
Mayor 1627–8 and 1637–8.
Died 1646.

Harwick, Roger
Free as a tailor, by apprenticeship to Nicholas Simpson, 1601–2.

Hayes, Robert
Free as a merchant, by purchase, 1608–9.

Lead, John
Free as a merchant, by apprenticeship to John Bassett, 1603–4.
Elected to the common council 6 July 1632, in place of Thomas Nelson, alderman.
Died 1639.

Leighton, Stephen
Free as a merchant, by apprenticeship to Thomas Leighton, 1598–9.

Lupton, Brian
Free as a merchant, by purchase, 1603–4.

March, Thomas
Free as a merchant, by apprenticeship to John Wormell, 1611–12.
Elected to the common council 9 March 1618, in place of Gregory Gurnall, alderman.
Died September 1640.

Marshall, John
Free as a merchant, by purchase, 1582–3.

Mason, John
Free as a merchant, by patrimony, son of John Mason, 1607–8.

Maxey, Nathaniel
Free as a merchant, by purchase, 1615–16.
Appointed searcher of the port 12 June 1620.
Elected to the common council 15 February 1630, in place of James Wilcock, removed.
Elected alderman 2 August 1639, in place of Thomas Miller, deceased.

Mayor 1649, in place of Thomas Slaney, deceased.
Died 1652.

Myett, Horsebrooke
Free as a merchant (Oath Book has chandler), by purchase, 1602–3

Olley, Dennis
Free as a merchant, by apprenticeship to John Atkin, 1602–3.

Parkin (*alias* Woolman), John
Free by apprenticeship to his father William Parkin *alias* Woolman, 1606–7.

Parkin (*alias* Woolman), Thomas
Free as a merchant, by apprenticeship, 1611–12.

Parkin (*alias* Woolman), William
Free as a merchant, by apprenticeship to Richard Spence, 1569–70.
Elected to the common council 12 August 1585.
Removed 14 August 1594, partly at his own request, following a dispute.
Re-elected 27 February 1604, and restored to his former place of seniority.
Died 1623

Percival, John
Free as a merchant, by apprenticeship to Thomas Boston and to Thomas Clayborn, 1607–8.
Elected to the common council 8 March 1616, in place of William Atkin, deceased.
Removed 23 August 1616, upon his refusal to take the oath.
Re-elected to the common council 9 January 1618, in place of Thomas Snelling, alderman.
Elected alderman 13 June 1623, in place of William Atkin, deceased. Mayor 1630–1 and 1638 (in place of Thomas Miller, deceased).
Member of Parliament 1640.
Died 1644.

Ravens, John
Free as a merchant, by apprenticeship to John Greene, 1602–3.

Robinson, Henry
Free as a merchant, by purchase, 1595–6.

Robson, John
Free as a merchant, by apprenticeship to John Clarke, 1599–1600.
Elected to the common council 9 March 1618, in place of Edward Hargate, alderman.
Elected alderman 11 December 1626, in place of Thomas Baker, deceased.
Died 1630.

Selly, Stephen
Free as a merchant, by apprenticeship to Thomas Clayborn, mayor, 1592–3.

Sendall (or Sandell), John
Free as a merchant, by gratuity, 1613–14.

Slaney, Thomas
Free as a merchant, by purchase, 1622–3 (having refused to take up the freedom when ordered to do so in February 1617).
Elected to the common council 27 August 1627, in place of John Robson, alderman.
Elected alderman 26 May 1637, in place of Michael Revett, deceased.
Mayor 1648–9.
Died 10 January 1649, during his mayoral year.

Snelling, Thomas
Free as a merchant, by purchase, 1610–11 (described as being 'of Norwich', but also later a freeman of London).
Elected to the common council 5 May 1615, in place of Thomas Leighton, alderman.
Elected alderman 24 October 1617, in place of John Atkin, deceased.
Mayor 1622–3.
Died 21 April 1623, during his mayoral year.

Spence, John
Free as a merchant, by apprenticeship to George Walden, 1580–1.
Elected to the common council 9 March 1587.
Elected alderman 27 October 1600, in place of Thomas Clayborn, removed.
Mayor 1603–4 and 1614–15.
Died 1618.

Taylor, John
Free as a merchant, either by apprenticeship to Thomas Grave, 1599–1600, or by apprenticeship to Thomas Boston, 1606–7, or by purchase, 1622–3.
Elected to the common council 16 August 1624, in place of John Revett, deceased.
Removed 16 April 1632, for absenteeism.

Thory, Robert
Free as a merchant, by purchase, 1613–14.

Violet, Grave
Free as a merchant, by patrimony, son of Henry Violet, 1603–4.
Never a member of the common council.
Elected alderman 4 November 1611, in place of John Bassett, deceased.
Removed 16 April 1613, for absenteeism but following numerous requests for discharge.

Violet, Henry
Free as a merchant, by purchase, 1576–7.
Elected to the common council 22 January 1579.

Removed 17 January 1582, for libelling the mayor.

Re-elected 12 August 1585.

Elected alderman 9 March 1587.

Mayor 1590–1 and 1599–1600.

Removed 14 May 1613, because now resident in the country.

Wainford, John

Free as a merchant, by purchase, 1596–7.

Wainford, Violet

Free as a merchant and mariner, by apprenticeship to John Wainford, 1603–4.

Wallis, John

Free as a merchant, by apprenticeship to John Nelson, 1590–1.

Elected to the common council 20 April 1601, in place of Michael Revett, alderman.

Elected alderman 23 October 1607, in place of George Gibson, removed.

Mayor 1609–10, 1616–17, 1623 (in place of Thomas Snelling, deceased), 1631–2.

Member of Parliament 1620, 1624.

Died 1633.

Waters, Robert

Free as a merchant, by patrimony, son of Thomas Waters, 1607–8.

Wharton, Gervase

Free as a merchant, by apprenticeship to John Spence, 1602–3.

Elected to the common council 16 June 1623, in place of Joshua Greene, alderman.

Died 9 October 1623.

Wharton, William

Free as a merchant, by purchase, 1610–11.

Elected to the common council 22 January 1624, in place of his brother Gervase, deceased.

Removed 20 November 1637, at his own request.

White, Thomas

Free as a merchant, by apprenticeship to Thomas Clayborne senior, 1581–2.

Elected to the common council 20 April 1601, in place of John Spence, alderman.

Appointed customer of the port 22 December 1605.

Died 1610.

Woolman, William (see Parkin, William above)

Wormell, Bartholomew

Free as a merchant, by apprenticeship to Bartholomew Wormell, his father, 1596–7.

Elected to the common council 22 August 1608, in place of Thomas Soome, alderman.

Elected alderman 11 December 1626, in place of John Cooke, deceased.
Mayor 1632–3.
Died February 1642.

Wormell, John

Free as a merchant, by patrimony, son of Bartholomew Wormell, 1587–8.
Elected to the common council 12 June 1607.
Elected alderman 22 August 1608, in place of Thomas Baker, removed; and re-elected 21 August 1609, in place of John Inman, removed, following the restoration of Thomas Baker.
Died 1632.

Young, John

Free as a merchant and mariner, by purchase, 1623–4.

B. Corporation members during the years 1610–14 (underlined) whose names do *not* appear in the Lynn port books, together with subsequent corporation members who were free during the years 1610–14 and who are similarly conspicuously absent from the port books

Awborne, William

Free as a merchant, by purchase, 1607–8.
Elected to the common council 16 August 1613, in place of Humphrey Farnaby, alderman.
Removed 12 May 1615, at his own request because now resident in West Lynn.

Bateman, William

Free as a merchant, by gratuity, 1613–14.
Elected to the common council 12 May 1615, in place of William Awborne, removed.
Died 1635.

Beane, John

Free as a merchant, by apprenticeship to William Gurlyn, 1603–4.
Elected to the common council 12 May 1615, in place of William Doughty, alderman.
Died 23 September 1621.

Carrow, Thomas

Free as a merchant, by apprenticeship to Simon Carrow, his father, 1596–7.
Elected to the common council 27 February 1618, in place of John Greene, removed.
Died 1632.

Clarke, John

Free as a merchant, by apprenticship to Thomas Boston, 1584–5.
Elected to the common council 21 August 1592, in place of John Mason, deceased.

Elected alderman 14 August 1598, in place of Roger Lawson, deceased.
Mayor 1606.
Removed 1 March 1616, at his own request, on account of his poverty.

Clarke, Matthew
Free as a merchant, by patrimony, son of Richard Clarke, 1588–9.
Elected to the common council 8 April 1594, in place of Thomas Leighton, alderman.
Removed 28 September 1599, following a dispute.
Appointed searcher of the port 16 January 1602.
Elected alderman 29 April 1603, in place of his father Richard Clarke, deceased.
Mayor 1605, 1613.
Member of Parliament 1614, 1620.
Died 1 May 1623.

Clarke, Thomas
Free as a vintner, by purchase, 1598–9.
Elected to the common council 17 August 1601, in place of Humphrey Farnaby.
Removed 29 November 1637, 'in respect of the fulness of his years.'

Dixe, Thomas
Free as a merchant, by purchase, son of John Dixe, 1606–7.
Elected to the common council 18 December 1618, in place of Thomas Grinnell, alderman.
Removed 22 January 1644, at his own request.

Ewer, Ralph
Free as a merchant, by purchase, 1610–11.
Elected to the common council 29 August 1611, in place of Thomas White, deceased.
Removed 13 May 1636, at his own request.

Farnaby, Humphrey
Free as a merchant, by purchase, 1592–3.
Elected to the common council 28 July 1589.
Removed 17 August 1601, following accusations of misdemeanours.
Restored 27 February 1604, and restored to his former place of seniority.
Elected alderman 28 April 1613, in place of Grave Violet, removed.
Removed 7 July 1615, at his own request because of sickness and infirmity.

Garrard, Thomas
Free as a grocer, by apprenticeship to Thomas Garrard, 1594–5.
Elected to the common council 9 January 1596, in place of Thomas Surflett, removed.
Died 1614.

Gedney, Thomas
Free as a merchant, by purchase, 1609–10.
Elected to the common council 16 April 1632, in place of Michael Revett, alderman.
Died 1633.

Gibson, Thomas
Free as a merchant, by purchase [*sic*], son of Clement Gibson, 1587–8.
Elected to the common council 29 August 1594.
Elected alderman 3 April 1601, in place of Thomas Leighton, removed.
Mayor 1602, 1612.
Removed 24 October 1617, on account of his long absence and at his own wish.

Goodrich, Adam
Free as a feltmaker, by purchase, 1601–2.
Elected to the common council 29 January 1627, in place of Bartholomew Wormell, alderman.
Removed 10 October 1644, at his own request.

Goodwin, Richard
Free as a merchant, by apprenticeship to John Inman, 1595–6.
Elected to the common council 23 August 1616, in place of John Percival, removed.
Elected alderman 16 January 1632, in place of Edward Hargate, deceased.
Died 30 March 1632.

Grinnell, Thomas
Free as a draper by purchase, but admitted to the company of merchants, 1591–2.
Elected to the common council 26 March 1610, in place of Simon Carrow, removed.
Elected alderman 4 December 1618, in place of John Spence, deceased.
Mayor 1626, 1636.
Died 1649.

Gurlyn, Thomas
Free as a merchant, by patrimony, son of William Gurlyn, 1605–6.
Elected to the common council 14 February 1614, in place of Thomas Garrard, deceased.
Elected alderman 15 March 1616, in place of John Clarke, removed.
Mayor 1621, 1634, 1642.
Member of Parliament 1625, 1626, 1640.
Died 1644.

Gurnall, Gregory
Free as a merchant, by apprenticeship to John Hall, 1596–7.
Elected to the common council 30 October 1607.

Elected alderman 9 March 1618, in place of Thomas Leighton, removed.
Mayor 1624.
Died 14 October 1632.

Hargate, Edward
Free as a merchant, by purchase, 1603–4.
Elected to the common council 30 October 1607.
Elected alderman 9 March 1618, in place of Thomas Gibson, removed.
Mayor 1623.
Died 1631.

Hawley, Thomas
Free as a merchant, by patrimony, son of Seth Hawley, 1600–1.
Elected to the common council 12 June 1607.
Removed 9 January 1618, for absenteeism.

Hoo, William
Free as a merchant, by purchase, 1582–3.
Elected to the common council 2 August 1583.
Elected alderman 28 July 1589.
Mayor 1595.
Died 1612.

Hopes, Richard
Free as a merchant, by apprenticeship to Joseph Hall, 1594–5.
Elected to the common council 23 August 1616, in place of Thomas Gurlyn, alderman.
Removed 2 August 1624, at his own request.

Leighton, Thomas
Free as a merchant, by patrimony, son of Thomas Leighton, 1581–2.
Elected to the common council 31 July 1607.
Elected alderman 18 February 1614, in place of Henry Violet, removed.
Removed 23 January 1618, at his own request.

Maye, John
Free as a merchant, by purchase, 1607–8.
Elected to the common council 15 April 1622, in place of John Beane, deceased.
Elected alderman 17 September 1630, in place of John Robson, deceased.
Mayor 1635, 1644.
Died 24 March 1657.

Miller, Thomas
Free as a merchant, by patrimony, son of Thomas Miller, 1611–12.
Elected to the common council 8 March 1616, in place of Thomas Revett, removed.

Elected alderman 13 June 1623, in place of Matthew Clarke, deceased.
Mayor 1628, 1638.
Died 11 April 1639, during his mayoral year.

Nelson, Thomas
Free as a draper, by patrimony, son and apprentice of George Nelson, 1600–1.
Elected to the common council 27 February 1618, in place of Thomas Hawley, removed.
Elected alderman 11 June 1632, in place of Richard Goodwin, deceased.
Mayor 1641.
Died 26 July 1654.

Porter, Elias
Free as a merchant, by patrimony, son of William Porter, 1612–13.
Elected to the common council 9 October 1635, in place of William Bateman, deceased.
Elected alderman 23 August 1644, in place of Thomas Gurlyn, deceased.
Mayor 1647.
Removed 22 June 1649, at his own request.

Revett, John
Free as a merchant, by apprenticeship to Michael Revett, his father, 1592–3.
Elected to the common council 22 August 1608, in place of John Wormell, alderman.
Died 1624.

Revett, Michael
Free as a merchant, by apprenticeship to Michael Revett, his father, 1598–9.
Elected to the common council 16 June 1623, in place of Thomas Miller, alderman.
Elected alderman 16 January 1632, in place of Gregory Gurnall, deceased.
Died 1636.

Revett, Thomas
Free as a merchant, by patrimony, son of Michael Revett, 1586–7.
Elected to the common council 3 April 1601, in place of Matthew Clarke, removed.
Removed 8 December 1615, having become Town Clerk on 29 September 1614.
Died 26 April 1633.

Robinson, Edward
Free as a mariner/shipmaster, by apprenticeship to John Benses, 1611–12.
Elected to the common council 16 April 1632, in place of John Taylor, removed.
Elected alderman 11 March 1642, in place of Mr Wormell, deceased.
Mayor 1645.
Removed 13 July 1655, at his own request because of age and infirmity.

Scarborough, Edward
Free as a tailor, by apprenticeship to John Kercher, 1596–7.
Elected to the common council 26 March 1610, in place of John Boston, removed.
Removed 31 March 1614, at his own request.

Sendall (or Sandell), Thomas
Free as a merchant, by apprenticeship to Christopher Gaunt, 1571–2.
Elected to the common council 9 August 1577.
Removed and disfranchised 23 October 1581 for refusing to be a churchwarden.
Restored to the freedom 22 December 1581 and re-elected to the common council 17 January 1582.
Elected alderman 29 August 1586.
Mayor 1587, 1601, 1608.
Died 1614.

Soome, Thomas
Free as a merchant, by apprenticeship to Robert Soome, deceased, 1593–4.
Elected to the common council 29 August 1607.
Elected alderman 22 August 1608, in place of Thomas Dyson, deceased.
Mayor 1611, 1620, 1629.
Died 14 February 1634.

Stonham, Richard
Free as a merchant, by purchase, 1595–6.
Elected to the common council 14 January 1600, in place of Thomas Maye (?)
Elected alderman 24 July 1612, in place of William Hoo (?).
Mayor 1617.
Died 1623.

Waters, Richard
Free as a merchant, by apprenticeship to John Kercher, 1606–7.
Elected to the common council 16 April 1632, in place of Richard Goodwin, alderman.
Died 1641.

Wilcock, James
Free as a goldsmith, by purchase, 1593–4.
Elected to the common council 5 May 1615, in place of Edward Scarborough, removed.
Removed 3 February 1629, at his own request on account of his poverty.

C. Other King's Lynn burgesses taking up their freedom of the borough *as merchants* during the decade 1604–14 but whose names do *not* appear in the overseas port books for 1610–14

Bassett, Thomas – Free by apprenticeship to Thomas Garrard, 1606–7.

Beaumont, John – Free by apprenticeship to Thomas Curry, grocer, 1611–12.

Boston, Jeremy – Free by apprenticeship to John Boston, 1613–14.

Broune, Thomas – Free by purchase, 1608–9.

Cartwright, John – Free by patrimony, 1608–9.

Casborne, Richard – Free by apprenticeship to Thomas Dyson, 1608–9.

Chamberlain, Robert – Free by apprenticeship to John Greene, 1607–8.

Champney, Cuthbert – Free by purchase (already free as a cordwainer), 1608–9.

Clarke, John – Free by apprenticeship to John Boston, 1607–8.

Clarke, Thomas – Free by patrimony, son of Thomas Clarke, 1611–12.

Collingwood, Thomas – Free by gratuity, 1607–8.

Collingwood, Thomas – Free by patrimony, son of John Collingwood, fishmonger, 1611–12.

Coltes *alias* **Glover, John** – Free by apprenticeship to Thomas Garrard, 1608–9.

Corney, Henry – Free by apprenticeship to John Corney, his father, 1610–11.

Curtise, Richard – Free by gratuity, 1607–8.

Davye, William – Attorney of the mayor and burgesses, free by gratuity, 1608–9.

Denison, Thomas – Free by apprenticeship to Bartholomew Wormell junior, 1609–10

Ditchfield, John – Free by patrimony, son of John Ditchfield, deceased, 1611–12.

Easem, William – Free by gratuity, 1609–10.

Farrer, John – Free by patrimony, son of John Farrer, baxter, 1611–12.

Fawsett *alias* **Codlyn, Francis** – Free by apprenticeship to Gregory Gurnall and Richard Hopes, linendrapers, 1610–11.

Fernely, John – Free by apprenticeship to Martyn Jenkinson, 1609–10.

Feveryeare, Edmund – Free by purchase, 1604–5.

Ford, George – Free by apprenticeship to John Greene, 1607–8.

Garratt, Richard – Free by purchase, 1604–5.

Gatward, Stephen – Free by apprenticeship to Thomas Dyson, 1604–5.

Gawsell, Robert – Town clerk, free as a merchant by gratuity, 1607–8.

Gibson, George – Free by gratuity (by purchase in the Oath Book), son of George Gibson, deceased, 1612–13.

Greene, Richard – Free by apprenticeship, son of John Greene, 1607–8.

Gybson, John – Free by purchase (already free as a cordwainer), 1608–9.

Gyll, William – Free by purchase (already free asa cordwainer), 1608–9.

Hawley, Seth – Free by purchase, son of Seth Hawley, 1605–6.

Holdbich, Edward – Free by apprenticeship to Thomas Dyson, 1608–9.

Hollyday, Thomas – Surgeon, free by gratuity and admitted to the company of merchants, 1608–9.

Hullior, Thomas – Free by apprenticeship to William Doughty, 1613–14.

Jackson, Matthew – Free by apprenticeship to John Atkin, mayor, 1607–8.

Jagges, Thomas – Free by apprenticeship to Henry Robinson, 1608–9.

Jenkynson, Martin, junior – Free by patrimony, 1609–10.

Kercher, John – Free by apprenticeship to Robert Kercher, his father, 1610–11.

Kercher, Robert – Free by patrimony, son of Robert Kercher, 1607–8.

Kilborne, William – Free by purchase, 1607–8.

Lacock, Edward – Free as a merchant by apprenticeship to Samuel Cheverly, tallowchandler, 1609–10.

Ladley, Bartholomew – Free by purchase, 1611–12.

Leman, Richard – Free by purchase, 1610–11.

Leach, William – Free by purchase, 1604–5.

Love, William – Gentleman, free by purchase, 1610–11.

Mathewe, Thomas – Free by apprenticeship to his father, Jonathan Mathewe, 1607–8.

Maye, William – Free partly by patrimony and partly by purchase [*sic*], 1607–8.

Moundeford, Richard – Gentleman, free by gratuity, 1613–14.

Nately, Thomas – Free by purchase, 1613–14.

Park, Zacharias – Free by apprenticeship to William Parkin *alias* Woolman, 1604–5.

Parkin *alias* Woolman, Henry – Free by gratuity, 1613–14.

Parkin *alias* Woolman, Robert – Free by apprenticeship to William Parkin *alias* Woolman, 1613–14.

Payne, John – Gentleman, free as a merchant by gratuity, 1605–6.

Powell, Lewes – Free by purchase (already free as a cordwainer), 1608–9.

Peake, William – Free by apprenticeship to John Boston, 1610–11.

Peapes, Robert – Free by purchase, 1606–7.

Ray, Jeremy Free by apprenticeship to John Clarke, 1613–14.

Salter, Ferdinando – Free by apprenticeship to Mr Gawsell, town clerk, 1609–10.

Salter, William – Free by purchase, 1606–7.

Saunders, Edmond – Free by apprenticeship to John Clarke, mayor, 1606–7.

Sendall (or Sandill), Henry – Free by gratuity, 1613–14.

Sendall (or Sandill), Humfrey – Free by gratuity, 1613–14.

Sendall (or Sandill), Richard – Free by gratuity, 1608–9.

Sendall (or Sandill), William – Free by gratuity, 1613–14.

Scot, Thomas – Free by patrimony, son of Thomas Scot, 1606–7.

Siseland, Richard – Free by purchase, 1611–12.

Slapp, Henry – Free by apprenticeship to John Atkin, 1609–10.

Steward, Augustine – Gentleman, free by gratuity (probably into the company of merchants), 1612–13.

Tyvie, Andrew – Free by apprenticeship to John Greene senior, 1610–11.

Walker, Edward – Free by patrimony, son of Edward Walker, 1606–7.

Walker, Peter – Free by apprenticeship to William Clarke, 1607–8.

Warren, Thomas – Sergeant at mace, free as a merchant by gratuity, 1605–6.

Wasselby, Thomas – Free by purchase, 1607–8.

Waynforth, Henry – Free by apprenticeship to Thomas Dyson, 1608–9

INDEX TO THE TEXT

Numbers refer to entries in the text and not to pages.
Ships' names have been *italicised* and home ports given as recorded.
Ports refer to both trade ports and ships' home ports, further classified and
emboldened as shown.
Alternative spellings of names and places, additional or alternative commodity
descriptions, where not specifically or separately indexed, and other additional details
have been provided (in parentheses).
The names of identifiable King's Lynn merchants (see Appendix 2.A) have been
emboldened and CAPITALISED.
[Square brackets] indicate entries where repeated information has been assumed or
illegible, or more speculative, information supplied.

McIlroy (Mackel Roye, Marchellory), Thomas 25, 100

Mace 116, 140, 229, 342, 488, 550, 604, 690, 712

Madder (crop madder) 302, 315

Maid (Mayde) of 'Mellquerne'174, *and see Hollands Maid*

Malt 1, 14, 26, 31, 51, 57, 61, 231, 823, 848, Flemish malt 768, 771

Maps 258

MARCH (Marche), **THOMAS** 248, 512, 542, 689, 700, 772, 776, 799, 803, 840, 871, 990, 1000

Marchant (Marchaunt), John 194

Margaret (Margeret, Margerett, Margert, Margreat, Margreate, Margrett), no homeport given 133, of Anstruther 702, 'of Barrowston alias Kercaudie' 536, of Kirkcaldy 81, 223, 226, 235, 250, 253, 268, 295, 300, 363, 370, 408, 490, 519, 535, 562, 571, [572], 606, 616–17, 629, 634–5, 643, 697, 717, 722, 736, 738, 782, 809, 814, 832, 834, 838, 856, 863, 866, 880, [881], 883, 886, 891, 899, 900, 906, 941, 945, 948, 953, 955, of (?)Limekilns 608–9, 615, 642, of Lynn 343, [344–5], 347

Margaret Alley (Margeret Alley, Margerett Alley) of Lynn 288, 397

Margaret Anne (Margerett Ann) of Lynn 262, 265

Margery (Margerry, Mergery) of Anstruther 16, 104, 619, 644, 902

Margery Anne (Margarly Ann) of Lynn 489

Marienburg, Germany/Poland, for 'Meabrogh deals', *see* Deals

MARSHALL, JOHN 315

Martin of Lynn 256, 259, 281, 337–9, 346, 359

Martin, George

Martinson (Martynson), Adrian 2

Mary (Marye) of Lynn 705, 753

Mary and Joseph (Mary and Josepth) of Lynn 962

Mary Anne (Marie Ann, Mary Ann) of Lynn 86, 217

Mary Katherine (Marie Katherin, Mary Catherin, Mary Katherin, Marye Katherin, Mary Keatherne), no homeport given 28, 29, 59, 67, 75, 83, 105, 139, 172, of Kirkcaldy 90, 121, 152, 201, 211, 231, 233, 237, 240, 244, 252, 266, 278, 298, 307, 342, 354, 358, 360, 366, 373, 377, 415–16, 424, 454, 482, 495, 510, 520, [521], 544, 575, 579, 610, 633, 641, 733, 744, 815, 833, 843, 864, 882, 894, 898, 917, 931, [932], 957, 959, of Lynn 193

MASON (Masone, Masson), Abdy 190, **JOHN** 720, 741, 756, 794, 818, 847–8, 961, 972, 1001

Masterton (Masterston, Mrasterton Messterton), Andrew (Andrewe) 28, 59, 67, 83, 105, 121, 139, 172, 193, 240, 244, 252, 266, 278, 298, 354, 358, 360, 366, 373, 377, 490, 519, 535–6, 571, [572], 815, 833, 843, John 85, 813

Masts 153, 281, 322, 324, 486, 737, 762

MAXEY (Maxei, Maxye), **NATHANIEL** (Nathaniell, Nathanyell) 470, 488, 518, 554, 570, 582, 604, 637, 685, 691, 712, 872, 875, 935, 942, 951, 958

Meakes, Meane 747, (?)800

Mebø, Norway, for 'Meabrogh deals', *see* Deals

Meching *see* Newhaven

Medemblik, Netherlands (Memlicke, Memliqua, Memlique), **shipment from** 552, **ships of** 828, 844, 946

Mellen (Mellin), James 152, Robert 619, 644, William 448

'Mellquerne', unidentified, **ship of** 174, 178

Merchant companies ('and company') 65, 140

Merlins 594, 596, 694, *and see* Falcons, Gerfalcons, Hawks, Tiercels

Mersire (Mersive), David 824, 944

Meslin (maslin) 149, 173, 221, 238

Messell (Mousleare, Muslare, Mussell, Musslere), Peter 622, 647, 703, 712, [713–14], 740, 965, [966]

Mewne (Meane) of Wells 477, 594, [595–6], 694, 981

Michael (Michaell) of Bo'ness 497, 532, 566

Middelburg, Netherlands (Midlbrough, Midlebrugh), **shipments from** 215, 391, 404, **shipment to** 961, **ships of** 215, 391, 404

Miles (Myles), Gabriel (Gabriell) 31, 49, Maurice (Morrice) 772

Miller, Thomas 165

Millstones 119, 316, 443, 727, 985, 989, French millstones 764, 1002, *and see* Dog stones, Quernstones

Mockado ('marocoe macadoes') 456, 458, 913

Moise, James 276

Molasses 224

Moncker, James 434, 446, 468

Money, Robert 982

Monk (Manck, Mancke), Alexander 213, 390

Montrose, Scotland (Montrosse, Mountrose, Mountross, Mountrosse, Muntrosse), **shipments from** 429, [432], 432, 701, 728, **shipments to** 463, 466–7, 469, **ships of** 429, 431, [432], 463, 466–7, 469, 901

GENERAL INDEX

Numbers in this index refer to pages for the introduction, including notes, and notes to the text only. Appendices 1 and 2, which are already arranged alphabetically, have not been included. Ships' names have been *italicised*